Laughter and Awkwardness in Late Medieval England

New Directions in Medieval Studies

Series Editors:
Helen Young (Deakin University, Australia)
Andrew Elliott (University of Lincoln, UK)
Adrienne Merritt (University of Colorado Boulder, USA)

This wide-ranging monograph series responds to emerging themes and interdisciplinary research methods in medieval scholarship, including the reception and reworking of the medieval in the post-medieval period. Particular concerns involve cataloguing the rich variety of experience of medieval people and exploring cultural transfer across different periods, places and groups. In doing so, *New Directions in Medieval Studies* seeks to contribute to the future directions and debates of medieval studies.

Published Titles
The Middle Ages in Popular Imagination, Paul Sturtevant
Medieval Literature on Display, Alexandra Sterling-Hellenbrand
Cultures of Compunction in the Medieval World, Graham Williams and Charlotte Steenbrugge (Eds.)
The Middle Ages in Modern Culture, Karl Alvestad and Paul Houghton (Eds.)
Medievalism in Finland and Russia, Reima Välimäki (Ed.)
Playing the Middle Ages, Robert Houghton (Ed.)

Upcoming Titles
Constructing Viking History, Thomas Smaberg
The Cult of Thomas Becket, Paul Webster
Medieval Radicalism, Daniel Wollenberg

Laughter and Awkwardness in Late Medieval England

Social Discomfort in the Literature of the Middle Ages

By David Watt

BLOOMSBURY ACADEMIC
LONDON • NEW YORK • OXFORD • NEW DELHI • SYDNEY

BLOOMSBURY ACADEMIC
Bloomsbury Publishing Plc
50 Bedford Square, London, WC1B 3DP, UK
1385 Broadway, New York, NY 10018, USA
29 Earlsfort Terrace, Dublin 2, Ireland

BLOOMSBURY, BLOOMSBURY ACADEMIC and the Diana logo are trademarks of
Bloomsbury Publishing Plc

First published in Great Britain 2023
Paperback edition published 2025

Copyright © David Watt 2023

David Watt has asserted his right under the Copyright, Designs and Patents Act, 1988,
to be identified as Editor of this work.

Cover image: © Series design by Tjaša Krivec
Cover image: Luttrell Psalter (1320–1340) © The British Library Board,
Add MS 42130, f.104r

Bloomsbury Publishing Plc does not have any control over, or responsibility for,
any third-party websites referred to or in this book. All internet addresses given
in this book were correct at the time of going to press. The author and publisher
regret any inconvenience caused if addresses have changed or sites have ceased
to exist, but can accept no responsibility for any such changes.

Every effort has been made to trace the copyright holders and obtain
permission to reproduce the copyright material. Please do get in touch with
any enquiries or any information relating to such material or the rights holder.
We would be pleased to rectify any omissions in subsequent editions of
this publication should they be drawn to our attention.

A catalogue record for this book is available from the British Library.

A catalog record for this book is available from the Library of Congress.

ISBN:	HB:	978-1-7883-1430-5
	PB:	978-1-3503-7502-4
	ePDF:	978-1-3501-4686-0
	eBook:	978-1-3501-4685-3

Typeset by Integra Software Services Pvt. Ltd.

To find out more about our authors and books visit www.bloomsbury.com
and sign up for our newsletters.

Contents

List of figures	vi
List of abbreviations	vii
Note on quotations	viii
Acknowledgements	ix
Introduction	1
1 When everything goes pear-shaped: Laughter and awkwardness in Augustine's *Confessions*	13
2 Elated or gassy? Between affect and emotion in the Luttrell Psalter	23
3 May this be true? The awkwardness of accepting grace in *Pearl*	37
4 Creating tension: Laughter and anger in *Cleanness*	47
5 Virtuous even if it displeases: *Patience*	59
6 The games people play: Laughter and belonging in *Sir Gawain and the Green Knight*	69
7 All shall be well: Laughter and belonging in Julian of Norwich's *Revelations of Divine Love*	87
8 Too much information? Suggestive diction in 'I have a Gentil Cock'	97
9 Does this stress make me look fat? Awkward questions in Thomas Hoccleve's *La Male Regle*	105
10 You're so vain, you probably think this Psalm is about you: Saving face in Thomas Hoccleve's *Series*	113
11 Great cause to laugh: Conversation and compassion in *The Book of Margery Kempe*	127
12 Sing with us, with a merry cheer! The awkwardness of going along with it in *Mankind*	143
13 Ever froward: Standing up for the audience in the Chester *Play of Noah's Flood*	161
14 Disappointing expectations: Laughter, awkwardness and the end of Sir Thomas Malory's *Morte Darthur*	169
Conclusion: An awkward age?	181
References	187
Index	193

Figures

1	London, British Library, MS Additional 42130, fol. 104r	31
2	London, British Library, MS Cotton Nero A.x., fol. 41r	39
3	London, British Library, MS Cotton Nero A.x., fol. 42r	45
4	New York, Morgan Library, MS 739, fol. 11r	56
5	New York, Morgan Library, MS 268, fol. 4v	57
6	London, British Library, MS Cotton Nero A.x., fol. 86v	62
7	London, British Library, MS Cotton Nero A.x., fol. 94v	70
8	London, British Library, MS Cotton Nero A.x., fol. 129r	80
9	Giotto di Bondone, *Legend of St Joachim, Meeting at the Golden Gate*	89
10	London, British Library, MS Sloane 2593, fol. 10v	99
11	Thanks for Pretending Not To See Me Funny eCard Sign	122
12	Oxford, Bodleian Library, MS Eng. Poet. E. 1, fol. 41v	149

Full credit details are provided in the captions to the images in the text.

Abbreviations

DIMEV   *DIMEV*: An Open-Access, Digital Edition of the *Index of Middle English Verse*

MED   *Middle English Dictionary.*

OED   *Oxford English Dictionary.*

Quotations

I have cited primarily from texts that are accessible in the sense that they are widely available and help support reading. There are many other excellent editions or translations available for most of these texts, and they might be more suitable for those who are conducting research or reading simply for pleasure.

I have used a **bold** typeface where I want to draw special attention to a particular word or phrase within a citation. I have generally used the cited editions for translations and glosses, but I have modified some of these for clarity or to invite readers to consider other connotations that might be associated with particular words or phrases.

There are two special characters that appear regularly throughout this book: thorn (Þ and þ) represents the sound made by 'th'; yogh (Ȝ and ȝ) usually represents the sounds made by 'y' or 'gh' but can sometimes represent the sound made by 'z'.

All citations from the Bible are from *The New Revised Standard Version* unless they are taken directly from primary sources (either manuscript or print) as indicated.

Acknowledgements

This book would not have been possible without the support I have enjoyed from a variety of people. That's probably true of all books, but it is especially true of this one. I was initially prompted to take on this topic at local colloquium, when Katelyn Dykstra introduced me to Adam Kotsko's *Awkwardness: An Essay* in such a thoughtful way that she helped me to understand why I kept using *The Office* to explain Thomas Hoccleve's work. I am grateful to her and to the other students and colleagues who have had to endure awkward conversations – or at least conversations about awkwardness – with me since then. I thank the members of The Department of English, Theatre, Film & Media at the University of Manitoba for allowing me to teach seminars on awkwardness and the students who helped me to develop a more nuanced and careful approach through their participation.

I am indebted to those colleagues at my own institution and elsewhere who have encouraged this work directly. First among these is Jenni Nuttall, who is not only a great friend but a great writer. I also want to thank Kathy Cawsey for her support of this project and for reading parts of this manuscript. Paul Jenkins, Jason Peters, Paul Dyck and Glenn Clark were early accomplices in this project, the latter two having joined me in a panel on Awkwardness several years ago at the meeting of the Canadian Society of Medievalists, an association that has always provided me with a vital intellectual community. I am especially grateful to Siobhain Bly Calkin, Brandon Alakas, Marc Cels, Ernst Gerhardt and Elizabeth Edwards for many engaging conversations.

The International Hoccleve Society has provided me with a community for many years, and I thank its members for not only listening to me talk about this book during informal conversations but also inviting me to present the chapter on the *Series* during the convivial Hoccleve at Home sessions we have held over the past several years. I can recall conversations with Elon Lang, Sebastian Langdell, Ruen-chuan Ma, Robert Meyer-Lee, Nicholas Perkins, Misty Schieberle, Sebastien Sobecki and Amanda Walling that helped me to orient myself at key moments. When I was struggling with the revision process, Rory Critten, Sonja Drimmer and Kenna Olsen all asked or answered vital questions that helped me to bring it all together.

Anna Henderson helped me to imagine this book as a viable project, and I am grateful to her and everyone else at Bloomsbury, especially Laura Reeves, Rhodri Mogford and Gabriella Cox who have provided the gentle reminders and practical support that I have needed to bring the project to the end. The anonymous readers at the proposal and review stage have provided exceptionally helpful feedback, which has strengthened this book substantially. I am grateful also to Bruna Lago-Fazolo, and Jonathon Vines who helped me to navigate the permissions process.

My aim has been to write a book that will convey my love for the texts that I am writing about as well as my sense of why they might matter to us even when –

perhaps especially when – they generate laughter and awkwardness. I have tried to write a book that will be accessible to many readers, but I have kept my children, Else and Sebastien, in mind above all. Even if they, like Hoccleve's friend, don't read the book to the end, I hope they will know that keeping them in mind has helped me in more ways than I can say. I hope this will remind us all of the fun we had watching *The Office* together. I also had my parents, my sister and her family in mind while writing this book, and I hope they won't judge me as harshly as I have judged myself for the expletives that I felt compelled to use in the name of accurate citation. Finally, I am deeply grateful to my wife, Jen, without whom this book would not have been written. This book is a testament to her capacity to watch awkward films and television series, her honesty as a reader of early drafts and her staunch support of my unusual approach. Jen, I love cake!

Introduction

'We live', according to Adam Kotsko, 'in an awkward age'.[1] Whether you agree with Kotsko's assessment or not, some of the most influential films and television series of the early twenty-first century – from the films of Judd Apatow to *The Office* and *Fleabag* – attracted audiences by making them cringe. The proliferation of awkwardness in contemporary culture has encouraged me to become more attuned to awkwardness in other ages. More specifically, it has encouraged me to imagine new ways in which audiences might have engaged with texts that have sometimes been regarded as examples of late-medieval decadence or dullness.[2] My aim in this book is not to suggest that we read these texts a-historically; instead, I hope to show that the conventions and techniques associated with some late-medieval texts might help us to understand why they might resonate with contemporary readers attuned to awkwardness.[3] It would have been difficult to make a case for the importance of laughter and awkwardness several decades ago, but changes in literary criticism have now made it acceptable to talk about the way a text makes us feel. Rita Felski argues that it is reasonable for contemporary readers and critics to acknowledge some texts seem to be able 'to traverse temporal boundaries and to generate new and unanticipated resonances, including those that cannot be predicted by its original circumstances'.[4] I cannot say for certain that any authors in late-medieval England intended to represent or generate awkwardness through their texts. I can say that these texts sometimes cause me to feel discomfort or awkwardness and that this feeling sometimes elicits laughter. I propose that the awkwardness engendered by the literature of late-medieval England is a feature rather than a flaw. Each of the following chapters will explore the way that laughter and awkwardness associated with social discomfort might invite late-medieval and contemporary audiences alike to contemplate belonging and to practise empathy and compassion.

---

[1] Adam Kotsko, *Awkwardness: An Essay* (Ropley: Zero Books, 2010), 3.
[2] The claim about decadence has long been associated with Johan Huizinga, *The Autumn of the Middle Ages*, trans. Rodney J. Payton and Ulrich Mammitzsch (Chicago: University of Chicago Press, 1996). For a more nuanced argument about dullness, see David Lawton, 'Dullness and the Fifteenth Century', *English Literary History* 54.4 (1987): 761–99.
[3] For a different approach to this period, see Robert J. Meyer-Lee, *Poets and Power from Chaucer to Wyatt* (Cambridge: Cambridge University Press, 2009) and the special issues of *Exemplaria* on *The Provocative Fifteenth Century* (Volumes 29.4 and 30.1) edited and introduced by Andrea Denny-Brown, 'The Provocative Fifteenth Century', *Exemplaria* 29.4, *The Provocative Fifteenth Century, Vol. 1* (2018): 267–79.
[4] Rita Felski, *Uses of Literature* (Oxford: Blackwell Publishing, 2008), 10.

Most of the chapters in this book pair a medieval text with a twenty-first century film or television programme that exploits the relationship between laughter and awkwardness to provoke an embodied response to social discomfort. The one exception is the first chapter, which pairs Augustine's *Confessions* with Judd Apatow's *The 40-Year-Old Virgin*. I have included the *Confessions* even though it was written roughly a millennium before the other texts under my consideration for two reasons. First, Augustine influenced many writers of the later Middle Ages, either directly or indirectly, so his use of laughter and awkwardness offers a helpful starting point for the approach I take to late medieval texts. Second, the resonance between Augustine's *Confessions* and Apatow's *The 40-Year-Old Virgin* will allow me to demonstrate what I think we can learn by pairing texts in this way. Apatow's use of laughter and awkwardness to help the audience comprehend, in a fully embodied way, the way that attempting to fit in can hinder a sense of belonging allowed me to recognize the possibility that Augustine might have been doing something similar when he recounts lying about his sexual exploits to impress his friends in the *Confessions*. The subsequent chapters explore resonances between pairs of texts that have helped me to make sense of the discomfort I have often felt while reading them or talking about them with others, especially my students. I can't promise this book will make reading medieval texts more comfortable, but I hope it might stimulate further conversations about the discomfort they sometimes create.

The resonances created by pairing late-medieval and early-twenty-first-century texts have helped me in three other ways. First, these pairings have enhanced my sense of what Chaucer calls 'solaas' [pleasure] when re-reading some late-medieval texts by raising the possibility these texts express a sense of humour that might challenge my expectations. Second, these pairings have reminded me that certain kinds of humour are an acquired taste: the things that generate laughter and awkwardness change over time, and I therefore hope this book will represent the resonances I perceive between late-medieval and early-twenty-first-century texts even when the latter texts no longer seem contemporary. Finally, these pairings have enhanced my attunement to the ways that late-medieval vernacular texts infused in Christian theology engaged with concepts like empathy, love and belonging might resonate with secular explorations of those concepts in the twenty-first century.

*

Awkwardness is a valuable concept because it prompts us to reflect on the challenge of living with others and with ourselves. Awkwardness is, in the realm of social interaction, what thingness is in the realm of objects. Bill Brown argues that 'we begin to confront the thingness of objects when they stop working for us'.[5] We often experience awkwardness when social interactions stop working for us. It is an embodied feeling, but it is also usually momentary. In this sense, awkwardness functions like 'ugly feelings', which Sianne Ngai describes as arising in moments that produce 'the inherently ambiguous

---

[5] Bill Brown, 'Thing Theory', in *Things*, ed. Bill Brown (Chicago: University of Chicago Press, 2004), 4.

affect of affective disorientation in general – what we might think of as a state of feeling vaguely "unsettled" or "confused", or, more precisely, a meta-feeling in which one feels confused about *what* one is feeling.[6] By creating a sense of disorientation or confusion during an interaction that has gone awry, awkwardness demands that we attend to the cultural norms and expectations that govern social situations and relationships. This book explores awkwardness that arises from the violation of norms based on shared expectations about situations that range from everyday conversations between friends to arguments about the nature of God. Adam Kotsko proposes that awkwardness works in three modes that are each defined by the way that norms are violated: '*Everyday awkwardness* names the violation of a relatively strong norm, *cultural awkwardness* the general malaise that accompanies a relatively weak norm, and *radical awkwardness* the panic brought on by the lack of any norm at all.'[7] Kotsko implies that these modes are not fully distinct from one another, and I will refer to them sparingly in what follows. I am more interested in the way that Kotkso's insight that awkwardness is caused by the violation of norms can help me to explain why awkwardness is often, though not always, connected to laughter.

Sometimes laughter causes awkwardness, and sometimes it is caused by awkwardness; they are intimately connected because they are both social phenomena that are associated with the violation of norms. In his introduction to the incongruity theory of humour, Noël Carroll explains that 'comic amusement emerges against a backdrop of presumed congruities or norms'.[8] He then provides an extensive and instructive list of possible sources of incongruity:

> deviations, disturbances, or problematizations of our concepts, rules, laws of logic and reasoning, stereotypes, norms of morality, of prudence, and of etiquette, contradictory points of view presented in tandem, and, in general, subversions of our commonplace expectations, including our expectations concerning standard emotional scenarios and schemas, our norms of grace, taste, and even the very forms of comedy itself.[9]

Moreover, he goes on to say, 'sex and sexual behaviour' are also 'a natural breeding ground for humour' because they, too, 'are freighted with so many norms and stereotypes'.[10] These sources of incongruity are all used to generate laughter through awkwardness in the texts that Kotsko discusses– *The Office*, the films of Judd Apatow and *Curb Your Enthusiasm* – and I will explore similar sources of incongruity in the following chapters. Laughter and awkwardness are connected in most of the texts I explore in this book, but not all of the examples I give are humorous. For example, someone's laughter creates awkwardness in Julian of Norwich's *Revelations of Divine*

---

[6] Sianne Ngai, *Ugly Feelings* (Cambridge, MA: Harvard University Press, 2005), chap. 1, Kobo.
[7] Kotsko, *Awkwardness*, 17.
[8] Noël Carroll, *Humour: A Very Short Introduction* (Oxford: Oxford University Press, 2014), chap. 1, Kobo.
[9] Ibid.
[10] Ibid.

Love while awkwardness is felt in *Sir Gawain and the Green Knight* when someone doesn't laugh. Sometimes I will focus on awkwardness alone, and sometimes just laughter, but my contention is that they are both social phenomena that reveal much about cultural norms and expectations when seen through the lens of incongruity.

The violation of the norms that Carroll describes can lead to other things besides laughter or even awkwardness. Sometimes the violation of accepted norms causes suffering while at other times it can establish a sense of empowerment. My focus in this book is primarily on what Peter McGraw and Joel Warner call benign violations of norms when they explain why some instances of incongruity generate laughter while others don't.[11] McGraw and Warner argue that a violation must be understood as benign to generate laughter: if people believe they or others are genuinely in danger, they are unlikely to find something funny; however, a violation that is too benign will likely result in indifference. The extent to which a norm is violated also matters, for people are unlikely to laugh if they cannot tell a norm has been violated or if they feel it has been violated too much. The benign violation theory provides a helpful reminder that the experience of incongruity is variable and that it will change over time as the norms of a given society change. The discomfort caused today by certain violations of norms or the laughter that they elicit in several scenes of the UK and American versions of *The Office* reveals not only the extent to which cultural norms determine our impression of which violations are benign and which are not but also that these cultural norms change over time. It will be important to keep this in mind when considering texts written several centuries ago.

The other thing that needs to be kept in mind when thinking about laughter and awkwardness is that judgements about how benign the violation of a norm is will depend on the way that the violation is experienced. This experience depends on the subject position of the person violating the norms and of the audience, as either individuals or a group, and this will likely influence how the violator's intentions are understood. Consider, for example, Hannah Gadsby's Netflix specials *Nanette* (2018) and *Douglas* (2019). In *Douglas*, Gadsby reveals that she received complaints and threats from people – mainly men – who complained that *Nanette* had violated the norms of comedy. Gadsby acknowledges that *Nanette* violates several comedic norms, and she reveals that was her intention. Gadsby asserts that she needed to violate the norms of stand-up comedy, a genre that has long been dominated by men, 'to tell my story properly'.[12] It is perhaps unsurprising that it was overwhelmingly men who were privileged by the status quo who felt threatened by this violation. She explains that the demands of comedy, and jokes in particular, had led her to seal off her story of coming out at its trauma point: 'Punchlines need trauma because punchlines need tension, and tension feeds trauma.'[13] Gadsby claims, rightly, that she's pretty good at balancing tension to get the laugh at the right time, and she generates a fair bit of tension and

---

[11] Peter McGraw and Joel Warner, *The Humor Code: A Global Search for What Makes Things Funny* (New York: Simon and Schuster, 2014), 63.

[12] *Nanette*, written by and featuring Hannah Gadsby, directed by Madeleine Parry and Jon Olb, aired 19 June 2018, https://www.netflix.com/title/80233611?s=i&trkid=13747225.

[13] *Douglas*, written by and featuring Hannah Gadsby, directed by Madeleine Parry, Aired 26 May 2020, https://www.netflix.com/title/81054700?s=i&trkid=13747225.

laughter by interrogating gender roles that have typically rewarded men for violating norms in malignant ways. Nonetheless, *Nanette*'s violation of the norms of comedy is doubly benign. First, it does not put anyone in harm's way. As she reminds men in the audience who might feel persecuted, 'this is theatre, fellas'. Second, her aim is to create connection through empathy rather than antipathy:

> The only way I can tell my truth and put tension in the room is with anger. And I am angry, and I believe I've got every right to be angry, but what I don't have a right to do is to spread anger. I don't. Because anger, much like laughter, can connect a room full of strangers like nothing else. But anger, even if it is connected to laughter, will not relieve tension because anger is a tension – it is a toxic, infectious tension – and it knows no other purpose than to spread blind hatred, and I want no part of it because I take my freedom of speech as a responsibility.[14]

By telling her story, Gadsby says, 'I don't want to unite you with laughter or anger. I just needed my story heard – my story felt and understood by individuals with minds of their own. Because like it or not your story is my story and my story is your story.'[15] Gadsby certainly elicits discomfort and awkwardness at times, but her purpose is to tell 'the story we need: connection'.[16] My contention that Gadsby's violation of norms is benign is subjective, but I do not think I hold this view simply because I happen to agree with her. Decisions about what constitutes a benign violation may be subjective, but they are not arbitrary.

To explain the basis through which I evaluate the benignity of a particular violation of norms, I would like to contrast two types of people whom Aaron James and Sara Ahmed have identified, in different circumstances, as the cause of awkwardness: the asshole and the feminist killjoy. I want to acknowledge that these figures are often gendered while also asserting their association with gender might be helpful for thinking through the source of awkwardness in any given situation. 'The asshole', Aaron James writes, explicitly acknowledging that he will use the masculine pronoun to refer to a figure who is more often than not male, 'feels entitled to allow himself special advantages as he pleases systematically, across a wide range of social interactions'.[17] We might feel awkward or even laugh when we encounter an asshole because we recognize a norm has been violated, even though 'one can't always pinpoint the norm of courtesy he has tread upon'.[18] Often, though, any awkward feelings we initially have about the encounter transform into disgust, sadness or anger as we realize that the asshole intended all along to benefit from violating a norm while expecting others to follow it. James suggests that 'the deeper problem is not deliberate exploitation but a kind of willful insensitivity: he sees no reason to address the ambiguities and uncertainties that inevitably arise when people interact'.[19] I believe that willful insensitivity is often

---

[14] Ibid.
[15] Ibid.
[16] Ibid.
[17] Aaron James, *Assholes: A Theory* (New York: Doubleday, 2012), chap 1, Kobo.
[18] Ibid.
[19] Ibid.

connected more closely to deliberate exploitation than James admits, but I value his focus on the asshole's refusal to deal with the complexity of human interaction. This is one way (among many) to distinguish the asshole from the feminist killjoy, who is attuned to the way that the ambiguities and uncertainties often arise in human interactions because she perceives that the norms governing those exchanges are often exploitative. As Sara Ahmed notes, feminists often need to be willful when pointing out how the very norms governing a situation create the conditions for deliberate exploitation as well as for willful insensitivity to that exploitation. Any individual, more often than not a woman, who draws attention to that fact is 'described as willful' insofar as 'her will does not coincide with that of others, those whose will is reified as the general or social will'.[20] In everyday interactions, the general will often takes the form of a mood or atmosphere, so the person willing to point out problems is often blamed for disrupting what appears to others to be a stable situation. 'In the thick sociality of everyday spaces', Ahmed writes, 'feminists are thus attributed as the origin of bad feeling, as the ones who ruin the atmosphere, which is how the atmosphere might be imagined (retrospectively) as shared'.[21] By standing up and speaking out, the feminist is often thought to cause awkwardness: 'To create awkwardness is to be read as being awkward. Maintaining public comfort requires that certain bodies "go along with it". To refuse to go along with it, to refuse the place in which you are placed, is to be seen as trouble, as causing discomfort for others.'[22] Many people, but especially assholes, consider feminist killjoys to be the female equivalent of the asshole and use similarly disrespectful language (or worse) to describe them. There are many reasons for this, but the most important one, from my perspective, is a fundamental misunderstanding about the role that privilege plays when we think about the impact of norms and their violation. Whereas the asshole causes awkwardness by violating norms that he expects others to follow (often with the aim of maintaining, taking advantage of or enhancing his privilege), the feminist killjoy is accused of causing awkwardness when she draws attention to the violence caused by inequitable norms (with the aim of mitigating harms caused by entrenched privilege). The assholes who threatened Hannah Gadsby because they identified her as a feminist killjoy wanted to silence her critique of the norms that sustain their privilege. She, on the other hand, was pointing out the harms caused by maintaining that privilege. While neither asshole nor killjoy is a medieval word, I think they are instructive because they have invited me to consider the causes and effects of social discomfort from the perspective of gender.

My main aim in this book is not to categorize those involved in awkward situations as assholes or feminist killjoys but to explore the ambiguities and uncertainties associated with human interaction. The terms asshole and feminist killjoy are helpful because most of the instances of awkwardness I consider take place during interactions between people or characters who fall on a continuum between these two extremes – somewhere where most people and characters probably find themselves at some point. When awkward situations remain unresolved, people blame themselves

---

[20] Sara Ahmed, *The Promise of Happiness* (Durham: Duke University Press, 2010), 64.
[21] Ibid., 65.
[22] Ibid., 68–9.

or others, often using words that connote the concepts of asshole or killjoy even when they don't use precisely that diction. Several contemporary books on awkwardness offer suggestions for dealing with both circumstances.[23] Rather than seeking to apportion blame or offer advice for navigating uncomfortable interactions, I adopt the approach Kotsko takes when he contends that 'even when personal deficits make certain individuals seem extremely awkward by nature … awkwardness remains a social phenomenon, and therefore the analysis of awkwardness should focus not on awkward individuals but on the entire social situation in which awkwardness makes itself felt'.[24] My interest here is in the way that texts depict social discomfort and convey it to their audience.

The circumstances in which the medieval texts under my consideration were written can provide some insight into why late-medieval authors and readers might have been particularly interested in awkwardness as a prevailing mood. The Hundred Years War (1337–1453), outbreaks of the Black Death (from 1348), the Papal Schism (1378–1417), the Peasants' Revolt (1381), the rise of the Wycliffite Heresy (from the 1380s on), Richard II's deposition (1399) and Henry IV's usurpation of the throne (1400), and the Wars of the Roses (1455–85) brought about hardship while also creating uncertainty and ambiguity in social interactions. People who held beliefs that contradicted those of other community members on topics such as the principles of their faith or the right way to determine a legitimate ruler undoubtedly found themselves in awkward situations that could become quite perilous indeed if they were not navigated with great care. I will occasionally connect scenes of social discomfort to specific historical events, but I am more interested in the way that the form and content of the texts under my consideration consistently convey the impression that awkwardness can be experienced as a mood or atmosphere.

While the following chapters focus primarily on the way that the form and content of late-medieval texts generate awkwardness as a mood or atmosphere that contemporary readers can feel, my aim is not to repudiate the historicist approach that dominated criticism for much of the twentieth century.[25] Rather, I follow Hans Ulrich Gumbrecht's claim that contemporary readers might gain historical insight by considering the way the text affects their senses, 'for what affects us in the act of reading involves the presence of the past in substance – not a sign of the past or its representation'.[26] While critics have often overlooked or even tried to overcome their affective responses to literature, Gumbrecht insists that it is important to consider this kind of evidence when reading for *Stimmung*, a German word that can be translated as both atmosphere and mood. 'Reading for *Stimmung*', Gumbrecht writes, 'always means paying attention to the textual dimension of the forms that envelop us and our bodies as a physical

---

[23] See, for example, Melissa Dahl, *Cringeworthy: A Theory of Awkwardness* (New York: Portfolio/Penguin, 2018) and Ty Tashiro, *Awkward: The Science of Why We're Socially Awkward and Why That's Awesome* (New York: William Morrow, 2017).
[24] Kotsko, *Awkwardness*, 7.
[25] Joseph North, *Literary Criticism: A Concise Political History* (Cambridge, MA: Harvard University Press, 2017).
[26] Ibid., 14.

reality'.[27] His argument 'is that concentrating on atmospheres and moods offers literary studies a possibility for reclaiming vitality and aesthetic immediacy that have, for the most part, gone missing'.[28] Gumbrecht contends that there is evidence for mood and atmosphere in 'the most objective phenomenal field of literary texts: in their prosody and poetic form'.[29] He goes on to argue that 'the sounds and rhythms of the words' in literary texts 'strike our bodies as they struck the spectators of that time. Therein lies an encounter – an immediacy, and an objectivity of the past-made-present – which cannot be undermined by any skepticism'.[30] Gumbrecht suggests that his approach can be enhanced by reading aloud or imagining the circumstances in which a text might have been performed, and I will regularly encourage readers of this book to do both. By so doing, my aim is not to imply that contemporary readers will all respond the same way that medieval readers did. They almost certainly won't, and this can be explained through historical, cultural and individual differences. But it's also important to note that contemporary readers do not all respond in the same way to the same texts and that readers often respond to texts differently at different times in their lives. This is important to keep in mind as we encounter texts from the past, for medieval readers also responded to texts in ways that differed from each other and changed throughout the course of their lives. These varied responses can lead to awkward situations, but they can also lead to a greater sense of connection through the process of trying to work out what others think and feel when encountering the same texts.

In addition to considering how elements of form like rhythm, sound and tone might create an awkward mood or atmosphere, this book will also explore how medieval texts can affect the senses of contemporary readers through literary elements like imagery, dialogue and plot. Drawing on recent research in neuroscience and psychology that explains how readers make meaning of sensory input whether it is coming from within the self (e.g. discomfort), from others (e.g. a facial expressions) or the environment (e.g. weather), I aim to show that it is reasonable to use the discomfort or laughter engendered in contemporary readers as evidence for the effects the description of these experiences might have had on readers in the past. This is not to say that all texts have the same effects on all readers. Lisa Feldman Barrett argues that because we inhabit diverse bodies and have a distinctive set of experiences, 'variation is the norm' when it comes to emotions.[31] Moreover, she writes, 'emotions aren't built-in, waiting to be revealed. They are *made. By us.* We don't *recognize* or *identify* emotions: we *construct* our emotional experiences, and our perceptions of others' emotions, on the spot, as needed, through a complex interplay of systems'.[32] This has profound implications not only for how we understand our own emotions but also for how we interact with others. According to Christian Keysers, our brains use the same processes to construct

---

[27] Hans Ulrich Gumbrecht, *Atmosphere, Mood, Stimmung: On a Hidden Potential of Literature*, trans. Erik Butler (Stanford: Stanford University Press, 2012), 5.
[28] Ibid., 12.
[29] Ibid.
[30] Ibid., 13.
[31] Lisa Feldman Barrett, *How Emotions are Made: The Secret Life of the Brain* (Boston: Mariner Books, 2018), 32.
[32] Ibid., 40.

our own emotional experiences and perceive those of others, which reveals we are more connected than we might think. 'While we witness the actions of others', Keysers writes, 'our own premotor cortex resonates as if it was doing the actions we observe. The mirror system builds a bridge between the minds of two people and shows us that our brains are deeply social'.[33] We engage our empathic brain whenever we encounter others, but we can improve our ability to predict and act on the emotions of others through practice. This pertains to encounters we experience through reading because, as Guillemette Bolens points out, 'the brain also simulates perceptual and motor actions when they are signified verbally'.[34] In other words, we use the same system to construct emotion when we read about perceptual and motor actions as when we encounter these stimuli with our senses. We then connect our embodied response to past experience in order to make a prediction about others' emotions. Bolens describes imagery that 'pertains to interpersonal gestures and expressive movements' as *kinesic* to distinguish it from kinesthetic and kinetic movements.[35] Together, these three authors will help me to explain why we might feel awkward in response to imagery depicting certain expressions, gestures or movements that are described when social interactions are depicted.

Awkwardness matters because the social discomfort associated with it provides opportunities both to identify instances when intentions or emotions are in conflict and to imagine how they might be aligned. As Erving Goffman notes, most everyday interactions follow norms that generally allow participants to save face in order to avoid embarrassment for all involved.[36] According to Teresa Brennan, this alignment also functions at a biological level through what she calls the transmission of affect, a phrase she uses 'to capture a process that is social in origin but biological and physical in effect'.[37] This process functions through entrainment, a neurological term to describe 'a process whereby one person's or one group's nervous and hormonal systems are brought into alignment with another's'.[38] Yet Brennan also points out that while 'transmission by which people become alike' is significant, we must also recognize that there is 'transmission in which they take up opposing positions in relation to a common affective thread'.[39] Because people are different, they do not always end up attuned with each other. Nor should they. While attunement or alignment might sound like ideals to be attained, they are not inherently good. Nonetheless, it is crucial for human beings to understand the nuanced ways in which they are connected to others because, according to Brennan, 'the ability to discern the transmission of affect may lead one to oppose the general will as an undesirable force'.[40] Gadsby recognizes this when she refuses to use anger to bring about connection. Demagogues also recognize

---

[33] Christian Keysers, *The Empathic Brain: How the Discovery of Mirror Neurons Changes our Understanding of Human Nature* (Oklahoma City, OK: Smashwords, 2011), chap. 4, Kobo.
[34] Guillemette Bolens, *The Style of Gestures: Embodiment and Cognition in Literary Narrative*, Rethinking Theory (Baltimore, MD: The Johns Hopkins University Press, 2012), 11.
[35] Ibid., 10.
[36] Erving Goffman, *Interaction Ritual: Essays on Face-to-Face Behavior* (New York: Pantheon, 1967).
[37] Teresa Brennan, *The Transmission of Affect* (Ithaca, NY: Cornell University Press, 2004), 3.
[38] Ibid., 9.
[39] Ibid.
[40] Ibid., 124.

this when they speak to crowds to create a sense of connection through proximity and anger. It can be challenging and sometimes dangerous to discern or oppose the group's will from within it. Resistance and opposition to prevailing sentiment can often lead the individual who is not aligned with others to feel awkward or be identified as awkward.

Like anger, laughter sometimes creates connection by excluding individuals and enforcing norms, but it can also create connection in other ways. The more we learn about laughter, the less surprising it is that it should serve these different functions. According to Robert Provine, 'laughter is the quintessential human social signal. Laughter is about relationships'.[41] Provine is careful about making general claims about what laughter means, and Mary Beard's work on ancient laughter provides a helpful reminder that we cannot just project our contemporary understanding of its significance onto situations in the past.[42] Nonetheless, Provine's observational approach reveals most laughter in everyday interactions (roughly 80 per cent) doesn't have anything to do with jokes or humour and that it almost disappears when people are alone. During conversation and shared laughter, Provine writes, '*The brains of speaker and audience are locked into a dual-processing mode.*'[43] Laughter is like awkwardness in that it is about social interaction, but that does not necessarily make it good or bad in its own right. It can lead young men astray, as it does in Augustine's *Confessions*; it can signify derision, as it does at some points in *Sir Gawain and the Green Knight*; and it can be used to describe what it feels like to know one belongs in heaven, as it does in Julian of Norwich's *Revelations of Divine Love*.

Ultimately, this book focuses on laughter and awkwardness because of the insight they provide into what it means to seek belonging. Many of the authors under my consideration use verbs like 'commune' or adverbs like 'together' to describe a sense of social or spiritual connection even as they depict situations in which the relationship seems to have broken down. The texts I write about all reflect some aspect of the profound desire for belonging that Brené Brown defines in the following way:

> Belonging is the innate human desire to be part of something larger than us. Because this yearning is so primal, we often try to acquire it by fitting in and by seeking approval, which are not only hollow substitutes for belonging, but often barriers to it. Because true belonging only happens when we present our authentic, imperfect selves to the world, our sense of belonging can never be greater than our level of self-acceptance.[44]

Literary scholars are usually reluctant to adopt a definition that includes the word 'innate'. There is good reason for this reluctance: many concepts that seem innate at one time or place turn out to be highly contingent when studied from another perspective. Nonetheless, contemporary neuroscientists like Christian Keysers are insistent that 'the

---

[41] Robert Provine, *Laughter: A Scientific Investigation* (London: Penguin, 2001), chap. 3, Kobo.
[42] Mary Beard, *Laughter in Ancient Rome: On Joking, Tickling, and Cracking Up* (Berkeley, CA: University of California Press, 2014).
[43] Provine, *Laughter,* chap. 3.
[44] Brené Brown, *The Gifts of Imperfection* (Center City, MN: Hazelden Press, 2010), 26.

brain is hard wired to turn us into highly social and empathic animals'[45] and that there is a desire for 'attunement' or at least 'a pleasant impression of attunement' in intimate relationships.[46] Whether the connection is biological or cultural, Brown's definition resonates with Augustine's account of conversion – turning towards God – while helping to explain why the *Confessions* and so many late-medieval texts use laughter and awkwardness to explore what belonging means, why it matters and what it costs. Most of these texts depict fitting in as a desire to align oneself with worldly interests, and therefore a kind of disorientation, while belonging is the alignment of one's intentions with God's will.

I do not think we need to adopt the Christian worldview expressed by these texts to value their representation of the relationship between fitting in and belonging. In fact, I have selected texts that seem to resonate with contemporary texts in ways that invite us to practise empathy rather than adopting a particular worldview. Whereas Keysers describes empathy as a neurological process that takes place in every interaction, Richard Sennett defines empathy from a sociological perspective as the basis for the connections that underlie cooperation. Awkward comedies like *The Office* demonstrate with exceptional clarity Sennett's assertion that 'modern society is "de-skilling" people in practicing cooperation'.[47] People can develop these skills once again, he argues, by practising empathy. 'The dialogic conversation', he writes, 'prospers through empathy, the sentiment of curiosity about who other people are in themselves'.[48] Sennett is distinguishing empathy here from 'sympathy's often instant identifications', which seems to align people who are already alike.[49] Sennett argues that 'by practicing indirection, speaking to one another in the subjunctive mood, we can experience a certain kind of sociable pleasure: being with other people, focusing on and learning about them, without forcing ourselves into the mould of being like them'.[50] This book does not aim to replicate recent studies that have shown that reading makes people more empathetic.[51] It makes the more modest argument that the late-medieval texts under my consideration provide opportunities to practise empathy – to

---

[45] Keysers, *Empathic Brain*, Chap. 6.
[46] Ibid., Chap. 9.
[47] Richard Sennett, *Together: The Rituals, Pleasures and Politics of Cooperation* (New Haven, CT: Yale University Press, 2012), 8.
[48] Ibid., 23.
[49] Ibid.
[50] Ibid.
[51] See, for example, David Comer Kidd and Emanuele Castano, 'Reading Literary Fiction Improves Theory of Mind', *Science* New Series 342.6156 (2013): 377–80; Raymond A. Mar, Keith Oatley, Jacob Hirsh, Jennifer dela Paz and Jordan B. Peterson, 'Bookworms Versus Nerds: Exposure to Fiction Versus Non-Fiction, Divergent Associations with Social Ability, and the Simulation of Fictional Social Worlds', *Journal of Research in Personality* 40 (2006): 694–712; J. Stansfield and L. Bunce, 'The Relationship between Empathy and Reading Fiction: Separate Roles for Cognitive and Affective Components', *Journal of European Psychology Students* 5.3 (2014): 9–18. Loris Vezzali, Sofia Stathi, Dino Giovannini, Dora Capozza and Elena Trifiletti, 'The Greatest Magic of Harry Potter: Reducing Prejudice: Harry Potter and Attitudes toward Stigmitized Groups', *Journal of Applied Social Psychology* 45.2 (2015): 105–21; for a critique of the premise that reading leads to empathy and a critique of the potential harms associated with this assumption, see Hannah McGregor, *A Sentimental Education* (Waterloo: Wilfred Laurier Press, 2022).

practise curiosity about others for who they are and how they behave in relationships. I hope this approach will reward those who are interested in reading texts from the past because they reveal similarities *and* differences between contemporary and medieval readers.

I have selected late-medieval texts that generate laughter and awkwardness because they invite readers to dwell in social discomfort for a while: they ask their readers to remain empathetic in the face of ambiguity, uncertainty, disorientation and discomfort in social interactions. Some of these texts generate awkwardness in sympathy with one or more characters. Augustine takes this approach, as do the four poems in Cotton Nero A.x. Other texts, mostly ones written in the fifteenth century, generate awkwardness by creating a sense of misalignment between the audience and those being represented. This is a substantial shift, and it has a parallel in the shift from irony to awkwardness that Kotsko perceives in the transition from *Seinfeld* in the late twentieth century to *Curb Your Enthusiasm* in the twenty-first (with Larry David being the connective thread between them). Although authors like Chaucer and Gower may depict awkward moments, they typically use the gap between intention and impact to generate irony rather than the kind of embodied discomfort that Thomas Hoccleve, Margery Kempe and the playwright who wrote *Mankind* seem to create. I wonder whether this shift might help explain why later readers have often had such strong visceral reactions – often, though not always, negative – to fifteenth-century texts while admiring those that came before and after. The laughter and awkwardness generated by late-medieval and early-twenty-first-century texts alike arise because social interactions are complex. Our brains and bodies can help us to recognize when we are attuned or misaligned with others, and the texts under my consideration here capitalize on that to get us to think in unsettling and humorous ways about the way we live with others and ourselves.

1

When everything goes pear-shaped: Laughter and awkwardness in Augustine's *Confessions*

I begin with Augustine's *Confessions* because my approach to studying it provides a clear example of the method I will employ in subsequent chapters. Although Augustine was writing it near the turn of the fifth century, many incidents in his spiritual autobiography resonate with secenes in both late-medieval and contemporary texts. This chapter focuses on the way that Augustine characterizes his conversion, a word that literally means 'turning towards', as a movement from awkward adolescence to spiritual maturity. He employs *kinesic* imagery to describe recognizably awkward situations as he depicts his struggle to turn away from his need to fit in with friends and towards a sense of belonging with God.

Augustine grew up in Numidia, North Africa in the late fourth century, yet many aspects of his account of his adolescence are recognizable as paradigms of awkwardness in coming-of-age stories today. For example, at one point he recounts having *the talk* with his mother, Monica, and he blames his father for precipitating this awkward conversation. As Augustine recalls, 'when at the bathhouse my father saw that I was showing signs of virility and the stirrings of adolescence, he was overjoyed to suppose that he would now be having grandchildren, and told my mother so' (II. ii [6]).[1] In retrospect, Augustine has come to understand that his father 'was drunk with the invisible wine of his perverse will directed downward to inferior things' (II.iii [6]), but this news upset his mother, who 'feared the twisted paths along which walk those who turn their backs and not their face towards you [i.e., God] (Jer. 2: 27)' (II.iii [6]). The diction Augustine uses here appears elsewhere in the *Confessions* to describe his conversion as a turn from awkwardness to grace. He calls his father's will perverse because it is turned towards worldly matters rather than spiritual ones, and the Latin adjective 'perversus' describes something or someone literally turned the wrong way or awry. This leads his mother Monica to fear that her son will also turn away from God. The imagery Augustine uses to depict the spiritual idea of conversion is notable from my perspective because it engages a *kinesic* response in the reader to emphasize its theme. According to Christian Keysers, 'while we witness the actions of others, our

---

[1] I cite from Saint Augustine, *Confessions*, trans. Henry Chadwick, Oxford World's Classics (Oxford: Oxford University Press, 1992; Reissued 2008). I cite by standard section numbers rather than page numbers to allow for readers to find the text easily in any edition.

own premotor cortex resonates as if it was doing the actions we observe.'[2] We simulate actions not only when we see them but also when we encounter words that describe those actions. Guillemette Bolens argues that 'the brain also simulates perceptual and motor actions when they are signified verbally'.[3] This does not mean we necessarily sympathize with the person whose actions we observe or read about, but it does mean that we engage the brain's empathic response in order to make sense of what we're reading in an embodied way.

The concept of an embodied response helps to explain why this scene might induce a cringe in the reader. Fearing that her husband is encouraging her fifteen-year-old son to act inappropriately, Monica confronts Augustine: 'Her concern (and in the secret of my conscience I recall the memory of her admonition delivered with vehement anxiety) was that I should not commit adultery with someone else's wife. These warnings seemed to me womanish advice which I would have blushed to take the least notice of' (II.iii[7]). When Augustine uses the word blush ('erubesco, erubescare' in Latin), the reader's brain simulates a blush, at least to some extent. The blush response is associated with a range of emotional responses, so the reader still has some work to do to understand what it would mean that Augustine might have blushed if he had paid attention to his mother's advice. As Christian Keysers notes, 'to understand the actions of other individuals, we need to map them onto our own body's motor programmes. To understand their emotions, we need to map them onto our own visceral feelings.'[4] By mapping the blush onto our body's motor programme we can then construct the emotion associated with that bodily response, making meaning based on our own experience of that action and the affects and emotions associated with it. Blushing is an action often associated with feeling shame or embarrassment. When we read about a blush, we can infer that Augustine would have felt shame if he had followed his mother's advice because we can map his reaction onto what we might feel when blushing. Augustine's use of imagery is complex here, for it aligns the reader's feelings not with an emotion Augustine felt at the time but one that he implies he should have felt when he recounts the episode. The phrase 'I would have blushed' [quibus optemperare erubescerem] is in the subjunctive mood, which indicates that he would have felt ashamed as a young man only if he had met the condition of heeding his mother's advice. He did not heed Monica's advice at the time and therefore did not blush then. The reader becomes aware that Augustine is telling this story because he now feels ashamed of his lack of shame. By telling his readers that he did not follow his mother's advice in the way he does, he reveals that he is embarrassed about not recognizing his mother's wisdom sooner. I certainly know how that feels. And I suspect I am not the only one of Augustine's readers who might have blushed to recall a similar experience when reading the scene.

Throughout Book 2 of the *Confessions*, Augustine builds on this awkward recognition that he very belatedly, through the process of conversion, came to realize that much

---

[2] Christian Keysers, *The Empathic Brain: How the Discovery of Mirror Neurons Changes our Understanding of Human Nature* (Oklahoma City, OK: Smashwords, 2011), chap. 4, Kobo.

[3] Guillemette Bolens, *The Style of Gestures: Embodiment and Cognition in Literary Narrative*, Rethinking Theory (Baltimore, MD: The Johns Hopkins University Press, 2012), 11.

[4] Keysers, *Empathic Brain*, chap. 6.

of his youth was spent aligning his will with that of his peers rather than with God, whose will is often made known through Monica. Augustine's aim as a young man is to fit in with his companions. According to Brené Brown, 'fitting in is about assessing a situation and becoming who you need to be to be accepted.'[5] For Augustine, the desire to fit in led him to lie about his sexual exploits to other young men. He says that he did not recognize that God was speaking through his mother, so he

> went on my way headlong with such blindness that among my peer group I was ashamed not to be equally guilty of shameful behavior when I heard them boasting of their sexual exploits. Their pride was the more aggressive, the more debauched their acts were; they derived pleasure not merely from the lust of the act but also from the admiration it evoked. What is more worthy of censure than vice? Yet I went deeper into vice to avoid being despised, and when there was no act by admitting to which I could rival my depraved companions, I used to pretend I had done things I had not done at all, so that my innocence should not lead my companions to scorn my lack of courage, and lest my chastity be taken as a mark of inferiority.
>
> (II.iii[7])

In his recollection of youth, Augustine realizes that he was proud about things that he now considers to be shameful and felt shame about things that he would now consider a source of pride. He did so to fit in with companions he hardly knew, not because he had any particular interest in the sexual experiences he lied about having. He reveals later that he was not indifferent to sex as a young man, but the point he is making here has much more to do with his determination to avoid being seen as awkward by admitting he had not done the things his peers had done or asking himself whether it would be appropriate to boast about these things. Augustine reveals that he was so determined to fit in with his peers that he was willing to turn away from what he knew to be his mother's will as well as God's.

Judd Apatow's *40-Year-Old Virgin* includes a scene that is parallel to the one Augustine describes, albeit with a much older protagonist.[6] Having no sexual experience of his own to share, Andy (the title character played by Steve Carrell) adopts misogynist and racist scripts drawn from popular culture to boast about his nonexistent exploits to three of his work companions because he thinks it will help him to fit in. His friends initially encourage him, heightening the discomfort caused by the conversation for them and the audience through their intermingling of homoerotic and homophobic discourse. Ultimately, though, they realize something that Augustine's companions don't seem to have recognized: Andy is boasting about doing things he has not done so that his chastity will not be taken as a mark of inferiority. This leads one of Andy's companions to ask him if he is a virgin. When he admits that he is, they laugh and promise to help him change this about himself. Clearly, Andy and his companions want to feel a sense of belonging, but they fail to recognize what Brené Brown's research

---

[5] Brené Brown, *The Gifts of Imperfection* (Center City, MN: Hazelden Press, 2010), 25.
[6] *The 40-Year-Old Virgin*, directed by Judd Apatow (Burbank, CA: Universal Pictures, 2005), DVD.

shows: 'Belonging ... doesn't require us to change who we are; it requires us to be who we are.'[7] Andy goes home that night replaying his cringeworthy behaviour. He clearly regrets what he has said, though he seems less sorry about the harmful nature of his misogyny and racism than about the fact that his adoption of these scripts did not lead to a sense of belonging but of estrangement: he feels the others were laughing at him rather than with him. Ultimately, the scene reveals much more about Andy's character than the fact that he is still a virgin. It shows that he, like Augustine several centuries before him, is so desperate to fit in with his peers that he is willing to change himself to align with values he does not hold. It also shows this does not work for him.

Sex provides a powerful way of generating awkwardness in both the *Confessions* and *The 40-Year-Old Virgin* because it is so closely associated with a range of cultural norms and stereotypes. Augustine and Andy both cause and feel discomfort when talking about sex with others, and this provides insight into the difference between fitting in and belonging they experience. Augustine, moreover, uses sexual imagery in a figurative sense in order to describe the awkwardness experienced in recognizable situations and to describe the state of his soul: 'So the soul fornicates (Ps. 72.27) when it is turned away from you and seeks outside you the pure and clean intentions which are not to be found except by returning to you. In their perverted way all humanity imitates you' (II.vi[14]). Augustine's use of the word 'fornicating' [*ita fornicatur anima*] connotes sexual imagery, but his use of the word *perverse* [perverted] to describe the way that humanity imitates God would have created for readers of Latin the image of turning away. Thus Augustine suggests that his will has taken an awkward or wrongward turn by deviating from God's will. This is also the sense that the word perverse has when it is first attested in English in the fifteenth century (*MED*, s. v. 'pervers(e)'). Slightly later in the *Confessions*, Augustine reveals that the question is which part of himself is in control. He asks his soul, 'Why then are you perversely following the leading of your flesh? If you turn away from it, it has to follow you' (IV. xi[17]). For Augustine, then, the situation in which the flesh leads the soul is perverse because it puts things the wrong way around. This can be corrected if the soul turns away [*conversam*] from physical things and turns instead to God. Sara Ahmed notes that Augustine frequently describes the will 'in terms of bodily sensations as well as orientations' and that he frequently describes the will 'as a process of being affected that involves orientations toward and away from things'.[8] Augustine's *Confessions* describes how he came to realize that the process of conversion involves a reorientation of his intentions away from those whose intentions are focused on worldly values and in line with God's will. Only by being who he truly is rather than being someone who turns away from himself to fit in can Augustine achieve belonging.

Because the *Confessions* is devoted to Augustine's yearning for belonging while also insisting that his authentic self is present all along but turned away from God, it develops a robust account of his perversity – his sense of wrong wardness or awkwardness – as a young man. Perversity is connected to sex for Augustine, but it is a symptom of his misdirected attention rather than a cause. Throughout the first

---

[7] Brown, *Imperfection*, 25.
[8] Sara Ahmed, *The Promise of Happiness* (Durham: Duke University Press, 2010), 26.

books of the *Confessions* Augustine reveals that his younger self sought to align his will with others rather than God. His reluctance to convert does not arise from a love of behaviour he later comes to regard as sinful but from a desire to fit in. When famously recalling a time when he stole pears from a tree near his vineyard, he explains that he did not desire the pears for themselves, for he regarded them as 'something which I had in plenty and of much better quality' (II.iv [9]). Augustine initially thinks that he was driven by the pleasure of stealing, which 'lay in doing what was not allowed' (II. v [9]). Upon further reflection, he realizes that what he really wanted was to feel like he fit in with the gang:

> The theft itself was a nothing, and for that reason I was the more miserable. Yet had I been alone I would not have done it – I remember my state of mind to be thus at the time – alone I would never have done it. Therefore my love in that act was to be associated with the gang in whose company I did it … I would not have needed to inflame the itch of my cupidity through the excitement generated by sharing the guilt with others. But my pleasure was not in the pears; it was in the crime itself, done in association with a sinful group.
>
> (II.viii [16])

Augustine describes his desire to feel part of something larger than himself. Stealing the pears gives him the feeling that he fits in, and it also allows him to experience what Sara Ahmed describes as 'social willing', a type of alignment that can 'also be thought of in terms of movement: When two bodies move in the same way, they are willing together'.[9] In order to move together in this way, Augustine and his friends must be attuned to one another. This process is often understood, Ahmed writes, 'as active: as a process of bringing something into a harmonious or responsive relationship'.[10] The act of theft is certainly active, and Augustine seems to derive pleasure from the sense that he is attuned or in harmony with his friends. He is not awkward relative to them, but he recognizes that his alignment with them is not praiseworthy.

Here and elsewhere in the *Confessions* Augustine provides a nuanced understanding of the kind of harmony that can be experienced through friendship or attunement with others. He acknowledges that while friendship may seem praiseworthy, it is not a good itself. 'Friendship', he writes, 'can be a dangerous enemy, a seduction of the mind lying beyond the reach of investigation …. As soon as the words are spoken "Let us go and do it", one is ashamed not to be shameless' (II.ix[17]). Augustine recognizes that attunement with others may seem to be a virtuous aim, but its value depends on the ends to which it is directed. Ahmed puts this another way: 'The problem with attunement is not that it does not happen (it most certainly does) but that it can easily become not just a description of an experience but also an ideal: as if the aim is harmony, to be willing in time with others.'[11] When he brags about his sexual exploits and steals the pears, Augustine reveals that he mistook friendship, attunement and harmony as ideals when

---

[9] Ibid., 48.
[10] Ibid., 50.
[11] Ibid., 51.

he was young and that his mistake led him to act viciously. 'When attunement becomes an aim', Ahmed writes, 'those who are not in tune or who are out of tune become the obstacles; they become the "non" attuned whose clumsiness registers as the loss of possibility'.[12] When it becomes an aim in and of itself, attunement can lead to the type of perversion that Augustine describes and cause discomfort or loss for those who resist the group's collective movement. Augustine recognizes that questioning his friends' ideas about sexual behaviour or stealing the pears would have made him vulnerable to being seen as the awkward individual who just can't fit in. By the end of the *Confessions*, after his conversion turns him towards God, that is what he has become. His contends that he has successfully re-directed his will to be aligned with God's will rather than be directed by the worldly values that he adopted when he was a young man. 'That is what free will is', Teresa Brennan writes, 'the ability not to go with the flow. But it is also the means for coming to consciousness of that divine will, the living logic that interweaves. How does one align oneself with the will that interweaves?'[13] For Augustine, as for many of the writers in the following chapters, the one that interweaves is God. Augustine's conversion therefore serves as a model for Christian practice, especially for those in the awkward position of feeling misaligned with their community because they have a different understanding of what God is calling them to do.

Laughter is relevant here insofar as Augustine initially suggests that it is what prompted the group to steal the pears. He then suggests that laughter provides a way of explaining that this decision was social in nature:

> It was all done for a giggle, as if our hearts were tickled to think we were deceiving those who would not think us capable of such behaviour and would have profoundly disapproved. Why then did I derive pleasure from an act I would not have done on my own? Is it that nobody can easily laugh when alone? Certainly no one readily laughs when alone, yet sometimes laughter overcomes individuals when no one else is present if their senses or their mind perceive something utterly absurd. But alone I would not have done it, could not conceivably have done it by myself.
>
> (II.ix [17])

The translation here uses two words that may seem quite different, 'giggle' and 'laugh', but Augustine has a consistent idea in mind because the Latin words he uses, *risus* and *ridet*, derive from the same stem. In this passage, Augustine notices something that Henry Bergson remarks upon and Robert Provine has demonstrated empirically: 'Laughter loses its meaning and disappears outside of the context of the group.'[14] Provine goes on to argue that 'laughter is the quintessential human social signal. Laughter is about relationships'.[15] Augustine's discussion of laughter reveals that he

---

[12] Ibid.
[13] Teresa Brennan, *The Transmission of Affect* (Ithaca, NY: Cornell University Press, 2004), 156.
[14] Robert Provine, *Laughter: A Scientific Investigation* (London: Penguin, 2001), chap. 3, Kobo.
[15] Ibid.

also sees laughter as a key to developing relationships as well as a way of representing them.

Like friendship, laughter can be a sign of attunement, but it is not inherently good. Laughter, as both a cause and sign of social harmony, plays

> a nonlinguistic role in social bonding, solidifying friendships and pulling people into the fold. You can define 'friends' and 'group members' as those with whom you laugh. But laughter has a darker side, as when group members coordinate their laughter to jeer and exclude outsiders .... [L]aughter has long been instrumental in the casting out of misfits, sometimes with dire consequences. Throughout the ages, cripples, mental defectives and court fools have been injured and perhaps even killed in a crescendo of teasing, laughter and violence. Laughter scorns the victims and bonds and feeds the wrath of aggressors. On a more massive scale, dark laughter has sometimes accompanied the looting, killing and raping that are among the traditional fruits of war.[16]

The value of laughter depends upon how it is directed. Because it is both a cause and sign of attunement, laughter can lead to exclusion and discomfort as well as integration and pleasure. Augustine's account of laughing with friends insightfully acknowledges that it may achieve its vicious effects most powerfully when it seems to be a benign exchange between friends. As a sign of mutual attunement, laughter also serves as a subtle reminder that those who are not aligned with the will of others in a group may find themselves excluded from it. Augustine acknowledges that laughter can be a sign of scorn, for he implores God near the beginning of the *Confessions* to 'let me speak: For I am not a man who would laugh at me' (I.v[7]). Yet Augustine also acknowledges that scorn is not the only cause of laughter. He even seems to offer an early version of the incongruity theory of humour when he suggests that we may laugh alone when we perceive something absurd. Augustine recognizes that laughter has different functions at different times: one of those functions is to delineate those who are aligned with each other or with social norms and those who are not.

Augustine's account of laughing with friends demonstrates that his fifteen-year-old self was keen to fit in with his friends. His inclination to align his will with theirs and to think nothing of God makes him cringe at the memory of having stolen the pears after his conversion – after he has re-oriented himself according to God's will. 'I have no wish to give attention to it', he says when he remembers his shamelessness: 'I have no desire to contemplate it ... As an adolescent I went astray from you (Ps. 118: 76), my God, far from your unmoved stability' (II.ix[17]). Having chosen to align his will with God's, he comes to see his alignment with his adolescent friends and their worldly values as awkward and misguided.

As Augustine grew older, laughter and awkwardness continued to inform his thinking about conversion. At one point in Book 4, he recalls an episode that caused him discomfort at the time and now makes him cringe for completely different reasons.

---

[16] Ibid.

Augustine reveals that he once had a friend whom he had 'turned ... away from the true faith' and 'towards those superstitions and pernicious mythologies which were the reason for my mother's tears over me' (IV.iv.[7]). Shortly thereafter, the friend fell ill with a fever and was baptized on the brink of death. Augustine recalls that when the friend recovered,

> I attempted to joke with him, imagining that he too would laugh with me about the baptism which he had received when far away in mind and sense. But he had already learnt that he had received the sacrament. He was horrified at me as if I were an enemy, and with amazing and immediate frankness advised me that, if I wished to be his friend, I must stop saying this kind of thing to him.
>
> (IV.iv[8])

Augustine's friend refuses to share in the joke, and his rebuke makes Augustine feel 'dumbfounded and perturbed' (IV.iv[8]). Although he initially keeps his feelings to himself, Augustine plans to tell him off later, implying that his friend is to blame for causing discomfort. It is only after he embraces his friend's faith that Augustine realizes he was wrong for trying to turn his friend away – to pervert him – from his vocation. He anticipates the Reddit thread AITA (Am I the Asshole?) but differentiates himself from many of the people who post there because he recognizes the answer would be yes. While he once thought his intentions were good, he now acknowledges that he was in the wrong for wanting to rebuke his friend as a killjoy.

In his interpretation of this episode, Augustine once again employs *kinesic* imagery to describe the reorientation of body and soul. His descriptions of turning and re-turning compel the reader's brain to engage in a simulation of that movement – one that is here and elsewhere in literature, as in life, associated with awkwardness. Later in Book 4 Augustine tells God, 'Our good is life with you forever, and because we turned away from that, we became twisted. Let us now return to you that we may not be overturned' (IV.xvi[31]). Having once proclaimed the Church taught things that he now recognizes it does not, he acknowledges, 'So I was confused with shame. I was being turned around' (VI.iv[5]). Augustine invites readers to imagine the sense of disorientation he feels by having them repeatedly simulate the act of turning in a physical sense. He finally recognizes that he will only stop twisting and turning once he converts, or turns towards, God: 'I aspired to honours, money, marriage, and you laughed at me .... I should leave all these ambitions and be converted to you ... and that by conversion I should be healed' (VI.vi[9]). Only conversion can bring about the sense of belonging that he so desperately desires.

One of the most striking examples of the discomfort that Augustine develops through his use of *kinesic* imagery occurs when he recalls the moment he identifies as the death of his youth. By this point in his life, he is now sexually active. Looking back on this time, Augustine considers himself to have been 'a slave of lust' because when 'the woman with whom I habitually slept was torn away from my side because she was a hindrance to my marriage' (VI.xv[25]) he 'procured another woman, not of course as wife' (VI.xv[25]). He recalls that this experience made him even more unhappy, and he says he is kept 'from an even deeper whirlpool of erotic indulgence' only out of 'fear of death' and God's judgement (VI.xvi[26]). He reveals that he was unhappy at this stage of life because his state of mind was so contingent on his attunement with others in his social sphere: 'Without friends I could not be happy even when my mind was at the same time a flood of indulgence in physical pleasures' (VI.xvi[26]. His profound need for belonging leaves him feeling truly alone insofar as he refuses to acknowledge God's presence and doesn't always feel that he fits in. To describe his soul's profound discomfort, Augustine invites readers to visualize his visceral discomfort: 'Turned this way and that, on its back, on its side, on its stomach, all positions are uncomfortable. You alone are repose' (VI.xvi[26]). Augustine's attitude towards women in this scene is sufficient cause for discomfort, and it anticipates the gendered aspects of awkwardness I will explore in subsequent chapters, but his imagery also establishes a connection between his bodily discomfort and the reader's response to explain the lack of rest in his soul.

The remaining books in the *Confessions* recount Augustine's sense of awkwardness in response to the grace he gradually recognizes as a call to be aligned with God. He is slow to embrace the sense of belonging he desires because he recognizes that being aligned with God will prevent him from fitting in according to the world's standards. In Book 10, he confesses,

> I cannot pretend I am not pleased by praise; but I am more delighted to have declared the truth than to be praised for it. If I were given the choice of being universally admired, though mad or wholly wrong, or of being universally abused, though steadfast and utterly certain in possessing the truth, I see which I should choose.
>
> (X.xxxvii[61])

Where once he felt put out about a friend not laughing with him when he joked about baptism, he is now willing to be the one who questions the laughter. In other words, he is now ready to be perceived as the killjoy. He probably was at times. Augustine was born in 354, so the *Confessions* recounts a period between the time when the Emperor Constantine declared Christians would no longer be persecuted by the state in 313 and its adoption as the state church of the Roman Empire in 380. He was baptized in 387 by St Ambrose in Milan before returning to North Africa and becoming bishop at Hippo from 396 until his death in 430. In his role as bishop, Constantine probably instigated uncomfortable encounters as he tried to convert others in whom he recognized his younger self.

Augustine's *Confessions* insist that his conversion marked a remarkable turning point. Earlier, he recounts in Book 6, he found himself so desperate to achieve happiness through others' approval that he was willing 'to deliver a panegyric on the emperor' during which he would 'tell numerous lies and for my mendacity would win the good opinion of people who knew it to be untrue' (VI.vi.[9]). Anxious about his speech, he 'noticed a destitute beggar. Already drunk, I think, he was joking and laughing' (VI.vi[9]). Whereas Augustine and his companions 'had no goal other than to reach a carefree cheerfulness' (VI.vi[9]), their ambition seemed to keep them unhappy. He recognizes that what the beggar 'had gained with a few coins, obtained by begging, that is the cheerfulness of temporal facility, I was going about to reach by painfully twisted and roundabout ways' (VI.vi[9]). This leads him not only to wonder if what he is really seeking is happiness but to ask himself by what means it might be achieved. Later, he recognizes that the discomfort caused by his pursuit of happiness may signal his awkwardness relative to God's will. He identifies evil with being misaligned with God: 'I inquired what wickedness is; and I did not find a substance but a perversity of will twisted away from the highest substance, you O God, towards inferior things, rejecting its own inner life (Ecclus. 10:10) and swelling with external matter' (VII.xvi[22]). Through his perversity, his turning and twisting away from God, he finds himself unhappy and uncomfortable. Ultimately, he recognizes that the problem is not an external one: 'In your eyes I have become a problem to myself, and that is my sickness' (X.xxxiii[50]). The discomfort caused by the twisting and turning that Augustine describes can only be relieved through another type of turn, a conversion that will align his intentions with God's will rather than with worldly desires. He recognizes that this will make him seem awkward in the eyes of the world, but he no longer wants to feel awkward in God's sight: he may not fit in any longer, but he will have gained a profound sense of belonging.

Augustine's *Confessions* traces his development from the discomfort he felt when he was aligned with worldly values to the sense of belonging he experienced after he reoriented himself towards God's will. He opens the *Confessions* by addressing God and insisting, 'you have made us for yourself, and our heart is restless until it rests in you' (I. i[1]). The impact of the story that follows is well encapsulated by Brené Brown's definition of belonging that I cite in the introduction, for Augustine recalls how his attempts to fit in and seek approval among worldly companions actively prevent him from experiencing true belonging. It is only through his *Confessions* that he can present his authentic, imperfect self. He acknowledges this version of himself might lead to derision among some readers, so he directs his words to God rather than 'a man who would laugh at me' (I.vi[7]). Augustine might use slightly different language than Brown does about self-acceptance: he obviously rejects aspects of his pre-conversion self. But Brown and Augustine both agree that belonging cannot happen until one accepts one is worthy of love or, as Augustine and other medieval authors might put it, grace. They also acknowledge that accepting the possibility that they themselves are worthy of love and grace can be just as awkward as (if not more awkward than) accepting that others are worthy of love and grace. This is something they share with the people and characters that appear in the following chapters.

2

Elated or gassy? Between affect and emotion in the Luttrell Psalter

What word would you use to describe what you feel when you observe the woman and child on this book's cover? Why did you choose this word and reject others? Does this word describe the people, their relationship or the way the image makes you feel? Did you consider the words 'awkwardness' and 'discomfort'? If you did, it may be because both words appear on the cover. I have asked you to reflect on the word you might use to judge the cover in order to draw your attention to the connection between language and our perceptions of emotions. The universal emotion theory contends that six words represent the basic emotions that inform our experience: Happiness, Fear, Sadness, Anger, Surprise, Disgust. These emotions are so widely recognized that Disney/Pixar used them as the basis for the personification allegory in the 2015 film *Inside Out*.[1] However, the theory of constructed emotion offers a more robust scientific explanation for emotional experiences as well as a more nuanced approach to historical and cultural differences. I will therefore turn to it to explain how I understand awkwardness and why it is helpful to use this word when thinking about our perception of social discomfort in late-medieval England. My focus in this chapter is the image that appears on the cover, the story it represents and its context in the Luttrell Psalter.

I adopt the theory of constructed emotion for several reasons. First, it helps to explain why we so often find it difficult to name the emotions we are feeling or those we perceive in others. In *How Emotions Are Made*, Lisa Feldman Barrett explains that 'what we see, hear, touch, taste, and smell are largely simulations of the world, not reactions to it'.[2] Simulations are well-informed guesses about 'what's happening in the world' that draw on 'past experiences to construct a hypothesis – the simulation', which is what allows the brain to 'impose meaning on the noise' being conveyed from the senses, 'selecting what's relevant and ignoring the rest'.[3] According to Feldman Barrett, 'simulation is the default mode for all mental activity. It also holds a key to

---

[1] *Inside Out*, directed by Pete Docter (Burbank, CA: Walt Disney Pictures, 2015), DVD, represents five of the six basic emotions in the universal emotion theory as personified entities (Surprise is left out, and Happiness is renamed Joy).
[2] Lisa Feldman Barrett, *How Emotions are Made: The Secret Life of the Brain* (Boston, MA: Mariner Books, 2018), 27.
[3] Ibid.

unlocking the mystery of how the brain creates emotions'.[4] This is because the brain processes sensations both from the outside world (through the senses) and from inside our body (heartbeat, digestion, etc.) and can trigger 'automatic changes in your body that have the potential to change your feeling'.[5] The key point for Feldman Barrett is that 'you are not a passive receiver of sensory input but an active constructor of your emotions. From sensory input and past experience, your brain constructs meaning and prescribes action'.[6] Because we inhabit diverse bodies and have a distinctive set of experiences, 'variation is the norm' when it comes to emotions.[7] As I noted in this book's introduction, Feldman Barrett insists that 'emotions aren't built-in, waiting to be revealed. They are *made*. By *us*. We don't *recognize* or *identify* emotions: we *construct* our emotional experiences, and our perceptions of others' emotions, on the spot, as needed, through a complex interplay of systems'.[8] This theory suggests that naming the emotions is an important step, but it is not a matter of being right or wrong about emotional experience. Because 'we do not "recognize" or "detect" emotions in others', we need to be very careful about the way that we align the sensory input we receive from others with the emotion we construct.[9] Moreover, our feelings often resist definition, and they change over time. The construction of emotions is an iterative process that takes place when the brain makes predictions that become simulations of sensations and movement. The brain then compares the simulation to the sensory input from the world, resolving errors in cases where they do not align. Often this gets resolved so quickly that we don't even notice it is happening. But sometimes it doesn't, and we are left with the awkward uncertainty that Sianne Ngai describes as arising in moments that produce 'the inherently ambiguous affect of affective disorientation in general – what we might think of as a state of feeling vaguely "unsettled" or "confused," or, more precisely, a meta-feeling in which one feels confused about *what* one is feeling'.[10] Awkwardness is a word that helpfully describes not only how certain kinds of discomfort feel but also how uncomfortable it can feel to have the moment of uncertainty about what we or others are feeling extended to such an extent that we become aware of the lack of resolution or attunement.

According to both Feldman Barrett and Christian Keysers, we use the same cognitive systems for constructing emotions in ourselves and others. The image on this book's cover helps to explain how this process is learned and how it works. It is impossible to tell whether the child is imitating the woman or vice versa, but they do seem to share the same facial expression. This type of mirroring is common. According to Keysers, parents often imitate the facial expressions of their baby, which allows 'the infant to focus on the mimicked facial expression'.[11] This practice provides 'the right condition

---

[4] Ibid., 28.
[5] Ibid.
[6] Ibid., 31
[7] Ibid., 32.
[8] Ibid., 40.
[9] Feldman Barrett, *Emotions*, 39.
[10] Sianne Ngai, *Ugly Feelings* (Cambridge, MA: Harvard University Press, 2005), chap. 1, Kobo.
[11] Christian Keysers, *The Empathic Brain: How the Discovery of Mirror Neurons Changes Our Understanding of Human Nature* (Oklahoma City, OK: Smashwords, 2011), chap. 8, Kobo.

for a mirror system for facial expressions to develop'.[12] When the child experiences certain emotions (happiness, sadness, fear, etc.), 'the parents' facial expression not only imitates the infant's arbitrary facial expression, but will also empathically share the infant's state, be it by smiling at the baby's happiness or looking worried or even in pain if the child is crying'.[13] This process allows the child to develop 'a shared circuit for facial expressions'.[14] Keysers notes that the same process 'applies to the movement of the eyes', which 'are a social cue of enormous importance'.[15] The similarities between the eyes of woman and child in this image suggest that it captures the process of intergenerational empathy during which children learn to associate facial expressions with certain emotions in both themselves and others. As Barbara Rosenwein writes, 'no one is born knowing appropriate modes of expression, or whether to imagine emotions as internal or external, or whether to privilege or disregard an emotion. These things make up the "feeling rules" that societies impart'.[16] One way of looking at this image is to imagine that it represents the process through which feeling rules are taught.

Because sighted humans generally learn to perceive instances of emotions by looking at the facial expressions of others, you probably found it reasonable for me to ask what you felt when you looked at the woman and child. It is possible, indeed even likely, that you supplemented this information by engaging in what Keysers calls 'direct facial mimicry', copying the expression on one face or the other (or both).[17] According to Keysers, 'when we see someone wince in pain, our face contracts as if in pain. We can then deduce the emotional state of that person by sensing the configuration of our own (mimicked) facial expressions'.[18] Both Keysers and Feldman Barrett explain that this process works through simulation in a way that seems counter-intuitive at first. Normally we think that our face reflects some inward emotion, but Keysers points out that 'a substantial number of experiments show that our bodily state, including our facial expression, can influence our feelings'.[19] This means that we use our bodies to understand what others are feeling: 'To understand the actions of other individuals, we need to map them onto our own body's motor programs. To understand their emotions, we need to map them onto our own visceral feelings.'[20] When I look at the cover of this book, my inclination is to cringe or look askance. I am inclined to mimic the expressions on the faces of mother and child by moving my head one way and my eyes the other. Even if I don't actually cringe or look askance at the image, I simulate those movements in my brain. This is because, as Keysers and Bolens both argue, we often engage our empathic response even when we encounter imagery that represents facial expressions either in the visual arts or through figurative language. In the case of the book's cover, I am responding to a visual representation of these two figures

[12] Ibid.
[13] Ibid.
[14] Ibid.
[15] Ibid.
[16] Barbara Rosenwein, *Emotional Communities in the Early Middle Ages* (Ithaca, NY: Cornell University Press, 2006), 15.
[17] Keysers, *Empathic Brain*, chap. 6.
[18] Ibid.
[19] Ibid.
[20] Ibid.

whereas the examples I will share in the rest of the book focus mainly on imagery created by figurative language.

When I look at the cover, my response proceeds in two stages. My initial response is to sense discomfort, which is not an emotion but an affect. According to Feldman Barrett, affect can be described as a simpler feeling than emotion. It always has two features: the first is valence, which describes how pleasant or unpleasant you feel; the second is arousal, which describes 'how calm or agitated you feel'.[21] Elation is normally on the pleasant valence, high arousal end of the spectrum; discomfort is on the unpleasant valence side of the spectrum, and its level of arousal would depend upon the level of discomfort. While this may seem straightforward, not all affects can be easily aligned with an emotional response. For example, when Anna anticipates the party for her sister's coronation in Disney's 2013 film *Frozen*, she sings, 'Can't tell if I'm elated or gassy, but I'm somewhere in that zone'.[22] Feldman Barrett describes a similar experience. Initially surprised by what she took to be butterflies in her stomach when she was having lunch with someone whom she had not previously found attractive, she was relieved to discover that she was not infatuated with this person but sick to her stomach (mercifully for both parties, she discovered this after returning home from the meal). What both cases help me to understand about the discomfort I experience when looking at the image from the Luttrell psalter is that it can sometimes take time to align our emotional experience with our affective experience. And awkwardness is often what is felt during that moment before we experience a re-alignment between affect and emotion.

While not everyone agrees about how the relationship between affect and emotion functions, many scholars agree that language plays a significant role in their alignment. One important difference between the two, according to Feldman Barrett, is that affect 'depends on interoception', which also means that it 'is a constant current throughout your life, even when you are completely still or asleep. It does not turn on and off in response to events that you experience as emotional'.[23] Affects can therefore be understood as a series of sensations that may be ongoing while emotions are 'not reactions *to* the world' but 'your constructions *of* the world'.[24] Theresa Brennan provides a slightly different way of distinguishing between the two by defining 'feelings as sensations that have found the right match in words'.[25] The key point for the purposes of this book is that the same affect can give rise to a variety of emotions or *vice versa*, and it takes time to find the right match between words and feelings.

This claim might seem counterintuitive, so I will provide an example of the way that an affect like discomfort can give rise to happiness as an emotion before turning to Brian Massumi for an example of the way that the perception of sadness as an emotion can give rise to pleasure as an affective response. My example comes from

---

[21] Feldman Barrett, *Emotions*, 72.
[22] *Frozen*, directed by Chris Buck and Jennifer Lee (2013; Burbank, CA: Walt Disney Pictures, 2014), DVD.
[23] Feldman Barrett, *Emotions*, 72.
[24] Ibid., 104.
[25] Teresa Brennan, *The Transmission of Affect* (Ithaca, NY: Cornell University Press, 2004), 5.

running. It probably won't be a surprise to hear that I feel more discomfort when I am running quickly than when I am running more slowly. What may be more surprising is that I feel far happier when I experience a higher level of discomfort during a race than when I feel less discomfort. This is connected partly to the possibility that I will attain my goal time, but I have also learned that I feel far happier when I know I am pushing myself to the limits of my endurance than when I take it easy, regardless of the time I run. Brian Massumi shares a story about researchers who were 'taken aback by their results' in a study that found children watching images of a short film about a snowman rated the 'sad' scenes 'the *most pleasant;* the sadder the better'.[26] Massumi argues that this finding reveals that 'the event of image reception is multilevel, or at least bi-level', and, moreover, that 'both levels, intensity and qualification are immediately embodied'.[27] Understanding the distinction between affect and emotion can help us to understand both how we can use our embodied responses to understand the representation of embodied responses to gain some insight into affects and emotions experienced in the past, but it also reminds us that we can never be entirely certain about what others – in the past or the present – are feeling. And that very uncertainty can cause both discomfort and awkwardness.

While there are some cases when the words discomfort and awkward can be used interchangeably, the word awkward is often used to describe some experiences of physical or social discomfort and not others. All instances of awkwardness involve some discomfort but not all instances of discomfort are awkward, so it follows that the word awkward is the right match for the way that certain types of discomfort feel. That suggests that it may describe an emotion. This would be a problem for the theory of universal emotions, but it is not a problem for the model of constructed emotions that Feldman Barrett proposes. 'Emotion words', she writes, 'reflect the varied emotional meanings you construct from mere physical signals in the world using your emotional knowledge'.[28] They are important because they allow us to describe our predictions and share concepts with others. Nonetheless, 'you can experience and perceive an emotion even if you don't have a word for it'.[29] This is a crucial point for my study because only one of the authors under my consideration uses the word awkward. I hope to show that this does not mean they did not experience the concept we describe when we use it. What seems clear to me is that medieval authors were working with a much broader palette of emotional concepts than can be captured by the six words used by the theory of universal emotions. Feldman Barrett reveals that this kind of expanded range of concepts can be described as 'emotional granularity'.[30] She goes on to say that 'the easiest way to gain concepts is to learn new words'.[31] If they don't already exist, we can invent them. That seems to be exactly what happened with the word awkward,

---

[26] Brian Massumi, *Parables for the Virtual: Movement, Affect, Sensation* (Durham, NC: Duke University Press, 2002), 24, 23.
[27] Ibid., 24.
[28] Feldman Barrett, *Emotions*, 104.
[29] Ibid.
[30] Ibid., 181.
[31] Ibid.

which first appears in Middle English in a text written around the time that the image on the cover was made.

It might seem odd to argue that the concept of awkwardness reflects emotional granularity when it has been used to describe such a variety of actions, feelings, situations and people. I nonetheless think its range of meanings reflects attempts over time to explore how a sense of alignment or misalignment can make people feel. Both the *Oxford English Dictionary* (*OED*) and the *Middle English Dictionary* (*MED*) suggest that the word derives from the adjective 'auk', which the *OED* defines as 'Directed the other way or in the wrong direction, back-handed, from the left hand' or 'Untoward, froward, perverse, in nature or disposition'. Drawing on this definition, Adam Kotkso suggests that 'the – *ward* of *awkward* is the selfsame – *ward* as in *forward* or *backward*'.[32] Kotsko's account of awkward as a compound formed from two words is reasonable. This is one typical way that words develop, and the fact that both the *OED* and *MED* provide examples of the word 'awkward' that pre-date the word 'auk' by about forty years is likely a result of the fact that both cite only examples preserved in writing. Words and concepts often circulate in other ways before they are written down. I also rely upon written evidence regarding the concept of awkwardness in this book, though I will also attend to the ways that the concept seems to have been expressed through imagery connected to early uses of the word 'awkward'.

In its earliest usage, the word 'awkward' describes movement that is not aligned with the expectations associated with a given action or situation. The word 'awkward' in these early examples has a slightly more restricted meaning than it carries today, but we still use the word to describe a physical movement that does not align with our expectations. The *Alliterative Morte Darthur*, written around 1400, uses the word to describe the orientation of two different sword-strokes. In the first case, the emperor strikes Arthur's visor awkwardly:

The emperour thane egerly at Arthure he strykez,
Awkwarde on þe umbrere, and egerly hym hittez.
[The emperor then eagerly at Arthur he strikes,
Awkward on the visor, and eagerly him hits.][33]

The *Middle English Dictionary* definition, which indicates that this adverb can be understood to mean 'backhandedly' (*MED*, s.v. 'auk-ward'), seems entirely reasonable. The reason that 'awkward' was selected in this instance becomes clear when we consider the second example, which appears about 300 lines later. In this case, a wounded knight named Sir Priamus 'girdes at Sir Gawain as he by glentes, / And **awkward** egerly sore him smites' [charges at Sir Gawain as he steps aside / And **awkward** eagerly strikes him hard].[34] The word 'awkward' alliterates with the word

---

[32] Adam Kotsko, *Awkwardness: An Essay* (Portland, OR: Ropley Zero Books, 2010), 6.
[33] *King Arthur's Death: The Middle English* Stanzaic Morte Arthur *and* Alliterative Morte Arthure, ed. Larry D. Benson, rev. Edward E. Foster, TEAMS Middle English Texts Series (Kalamazoo, MI: Medieval Institute Publications, 1994), 2246–7.
[34] Ibid., 2562–4.

'egerly' in both lines, so the explanation for its use here may be prosaic (in the sense that it meets the demands of the metre). When using the *Alliterative Morte Arthur* as a source for his *Morte Darthur*, Sir Thomas Malory reveals that the word 'overthwarte' [crosswise or backhanded] might have been an option as well, for he uses it in place of 'awkwarde' to describe the emperor's stroke. This initially seems like a significant change, for Malory's prose often follows the *Alliterative Morte* verbatim. Yet Malory's version of the scene in which Priamus 'girdis to Sir Gawayne and **awkewarde** hym strikes' [charges to Sir Gawain and **awkwardly** him strikes] seems to confirm that he was making a decision about when to use the word.[35] The image of the backhanded stroke that the word denoted in Middle English is connected to our understanding of awkwardness today because it asks us to imagine someone moving in a way that does not seem to align with how others expect that person to move. In other words, it involves a violation of a simulation constructed by the mind that is based on perceptions of the other's momentum and knowledge of how one's own body moves. That sense of mis-alignment with the expected simulation is a vital component of awkwardness, and this is why social discomfort is often expressed and conveyed through physical manifestations of embodied awkwardness.

The early examples of the word awkward I have considered so far describe movement that seems unnatural in the sense that an arm or a leg might be bent in an unexpected way during an awkward fall. When the word 'awkward' appears in the most widely disseminated poem written in Middle English the conception of unnatural movement moves from the literal to the moral plane in its description of behaviour that violates expectations. Written around 1340, roughly the same time as the image on the cover was made, *The Pricke of Conscience* survives in over 130 manuscripts. As you might expect from the title, this poem is fundamentally interested in how human beings might align their will with God's by ensuring that they are attuned with his voice speaking to them. It may come as a surprise to learn that this text includes a section on fashion. It will come as less of a surprise to learn that the poem condemns those who are so preoccupied with being fashionable that they dress inappropriately:

> Thus usen men a new gette°   *fashion*
> And this worlde **aukewarde** they sette
> With suche **unkynde** pompe and pryde
> That they usen on every a syde.[36]

It is not entirely clear to me whether these lines are condemning men who employ new fashions because they make other people (the world) feel awkward with their pomp and pride or whether they set the wrong value on this world as opposed to the next. What is clear is that the adverb 'awkward' is being used here to describe a situation in which something is 'upside down' or 'awry' (*MED*, s.v. 'auk-ward'). Moreover, the word

---

[35] Sir Thomas Malory, *Le Morte Darthur*, ed. Stephen H. A. Shepherd, Norton Critical Edition (New York, NY: W. W. Norton & Company, 2004), 141.
[36] *Prik of Conscience*, ed. James H. Morey, TEAMS Middle English Texts Series (Kalamazoo, MI: Medieval Institute Publications, 2012), 2.591–4.

'unkynde' in Middle English can connote our sense of unkind, but it often denotes a sense of the unnatural. The men described in these lines may cause social discomfort, but they are also awkward in a spiritual sense: their actions seem 'unkynde' because their intentions are not aligned with God's will, which the poem takes to be natural. A sense of misalignment is what connects the use of the word 'awkward' in a physical sense in the *Alliterative Morte Arthur* to its use in a moral or spiritual sense in the *Pricke of Conscience*. This sense of disorientation or misalignment is what connects the awkwardness I perceive in the texts under my consideration in this book even if Malory is the only author under my consideration who uses the word.

When I use the word awkward to describe social discomfort, I am using it to describe the feeling I get when I recognize a mis-alignment or lack of attunement between people based on a (perceived) violation of some norm. The unpleasant discomfort caused by these situations sometimes leads to other kinds of feelings besides awkwardness, even Happiness, Fear, Sadness, Anger, Surprise, Disgust. This book focuses on the time it takes to match sensations with one of these words or many others. Awkward moments provide insight into not only the dynamic nature of emotions relative to affective experience but also the feelings one might have about the process of aligning or misaligning our emotions with our own sensations or the emotions of others. Sometimes the awkward feeling of misalignment is over very quickly and sometimes it extends over time; it normally anticipates a resolution into some emotional state, even if that resolution is a recognition that the state of awkwardness will be sustained. It is therefore important to consider the context in which awkward moments occur and the kinds of resolution that they might anticipate. Rather than focusing primarily on the historical context for the moments I discuss in this book (a subject that would likely take another book to explore), I will provide substantial information about the specific context in the given text. What I have in mind here is the way the awkward moment fits in the plot, setting or the material circumstances in which the texts were encountered as well as the mood and atmosphere created by that setting. As Feldman Barrett shows, this kind of context can help us to improve our accuracy when judging the emotions others are experiencing. She makes this point by sharing an image of Serena Williams that is cropped so that it only reveals her face. Whereas the cropped image makes it seem as though the emotion she is feeling is fear, the original photo's larger scope allows viewers to see her body language, creating a totally different impression. The larger image reveals that Williams is elated: she had just defeated her older sister Venus to win the 2008 US Open. You may experience a similar, though perhaps less dramatic, shift in interpretation when I invite you to reconsider the image on the cover of this book in the context of the page as a whole (Figure 1).

When seen from this perspective, the eyes of the woman and child do not seem to be moving quite so strikingly against the grain of their bodies, though neither they nor the other figures seem especially comfortable. Everyone here may seem awkward in a physical sense. The figure on the right looks particularly uncomfortable as he inclines his body towards mother and child while looking directly into the other man's eyes. These postures could be taken as conventional gestures meant to draw attention to the woman and child, but they also help to convey the prevailing mood of the miracle

Figure 1 London, British Library, MS Additional 42130, fol. 104r. © The British Library Board.

being depicted here (whether intentionally or not).³⁷ 'The Abbess Delivered by Our Lady' was, according to Ruth Wilson Tryon, 'one of the most popular of the miracles of Our Lady' (which is really saying something), and it even appears in John of Garland's *Liber metricus*.³⁸ It is sometimes given other titles, including 'The Miracle of the Unchaste Abbess' or 'A Prioress Delivered by Our Lady', which is the title that Wilson Tryon gives to the Middle English version she published from London, British Library, Add. MS 39996.³⁹ The story generally opens by describing an abbess who is disliked by the nuns in her charge because she imposes such severe penance on those who do not adhere to her order's rule very strictly.⁴⁰ When the other nuns discover that the abbess has become pregnant, having slept with her table servant in some versions or the man who kept the house's accounts in others, they gleefully report her to the bishop. The abbess prays to the Virgin Mary for forgiveness and deliverance. Mary comes to the abbess in a dream in which she instructs two angels to deliver the child and take him to a hermit who will raise him. The bishop arrives shortly thereafter to punish the abbess. He berates her publicly but then finds, upon further examination, the abbess bears no signs of pregnancy. Just as he is about to expel the other nuns for having falsely accused their abbess, she confesses the nuns had the story right and reveals the miracle Mary performed. No further penance is to be required and, in some versions of the story, the bishop even pays to educate the child, who becomes a bishop himself one day. Thus, Mary resolves a situation that is not only awkward but has the potential to cause even more awkwardness with remarkably little discomfort.

Expectations associated with gender norms either cause or exacerbate awkwardness in this story. The abbess's pregnancy is similar to the one experienced by Alison Scott (Katherine Heigl) in Judd Apatow's 2007 film *Knocked Up* in that it not only raises questions about her ability to pursue her vocation but also points to the asymmetrical consequences of an unplanned pregnancy for men and women. Neither story can resolve the situation through marriage, and for surprisingly similar reasons. While different versions of the 'The Abbess Delivered by Our Lady' link her to different lovers, most imply that he is too low in status for marriage to be suitable. Ben Stone (Seth Rogan) proposes to Alison (Katherine Hegel) in *Knocked Up*, but she refuses. Even if she had accepted, though, Ben's lack of money, job and maturity make him a poor match for a woman with a bright future. Both women therefore hide their pregnancy because they anticipate that they will not be allowed to pursue their vocation once their condition is known. Alison fears that she will not be able to continue presenting for the E! Channel show because her producers have made it clear to her that they

---

[37] This scene is identified by Michelle Brown in *The Luttrell Psalter: A Facsimile* (London: The British Library, 2006), 41.

[38] Ruth Wilson Tryon, 'Miracles of Our Lady in Middle English Verse', *PMLA* 38.2 (1923): 308–388, 369.

[39] Ibid., 349–50.

[40] This outline is based on the text found in Thomas Wright, ed., *A Selection of Latin Stories, from Manuscripts of the Thirteenth and Fourteenth Centuries: A Contribution to the History of Fiction during the Middle Ages* (London: The Percy Society, 1842), 38–40. I am grateful to Eric T. Metzler, whose dissertation, '"The Miracle of the Pregnant Abbess": Texts and Contexts of a Medieval Tale of Sexuality, Spirituality, and Authority' (Unpublished doctoral dissertation, Indiana University, 2001), directed me towards this volume.

expect her to be impossibly thin. The abbess is rightly worried that her pregnancy will make her position untenable, for it would not only be an unambiguous sign that she had broken her vow of chastity – something that is far harder to prove in the case of men – but also that she was a hypocrite.[41] The story seems to suggest that the nuns take pleasure when reporting the abbess to the bishop because her pregnancy reveals that while she punishes others severely for even the most minor transgressions she does not always apply the rules to herself. This description makes her sound a lot like the type of person Aaron James describes as an asshole. And, since the behaviour associated with assholes is more frequently associated with men rather than women, it is reasonable to ask whether the nuns in this story are particularly keen to accuse their abbess not only because she is a hypocrite but because she is transgressing expectations associated with her gender. The story invites this line of interpretation insofar as it shows that she fundamentally changes her behaviour at the end of the story when she confesses her sins to protect the nuns from being punished unfairly. Unexpectedly, the story seems to imply that being pregnant has made the abbess better at her vocation by both showing that she not only has been shown Mary's mercy but is now extending it to the nuns in her care. This ending makes it feel even more like *Knocked Up*, which includes a scene where the producers of Alison's show, surprised to find that viewers respond well to her pregnancy, propose that she will host a segment in which she speaks to pregnant celebrities. Whereas pregnancy initially creates discomfort for both women by threatening their plans to pursue their vocation, it ultimately reinforces their sense that they have been called to do the work they are doing.

It is not clear to me that 'The Abbess Delivered by Our Lady' was meant to make readers cringe in the same way that *Knocked Up* was. However, the depiction of this miracle in the Luttrell Psalter might allow us to speculate about what elements of the story made people uncomfortable. The image emphasizes the miraculous part of the story rather than the abbess or her pregnancy. It highlights Mary's intervention by having her deliver the child to another angel rather than having the two angels deliver him to a hermit. The abbess and her lack of chastity are effaced for all but those who know the story well enough to connect her desperate prayers to the Virgin with the psalm that begins at the capital M, six lines up from the bottom:

Miserere mei deus miserere mei;
Quoniam in te confidit anima mea
Et in umbra alarum tuarum sperabo;
Donec transeat iniquitas
Clamabo ad deum altissimum ....
[Have mercy on me, O God, have mercy on me:
for my soul trusteth in thee.

---

[41] For an account of the way that pregnancy offers an unequivocal sign of sinfulness, see Ruth Maro Karras, 'The Virgin and the Pregnant Abbess: Miracles and Gender in the Middle Ages', *Medieval Perspectives* 3 (1991): 112–32.

> And in the shadow of thy wings will I hope,
> until iniquity pass away.
> I will cry to God the most High ....]
>
> (Psalm 57.1-2)

The psalm text goes on to lament the various traps that have been set for the writer, but then ends with an exaltation of God for steadfast love. It is not hard to see why the makers of the Luttrell Psalter thought of 'The Abbess Delivered by Our Lady' when illuminating this text. The psalm text reflects the abbess's prayer while the winged angels resonate with the wings described in the text. The image, the story it represents and the psalm text all work together to invite readers to contemplate the need to call for mercy when experiencing profound discomfort. Readers who know the story are invited to imagine the physical, social and emotional discomfort that the abbess's pregnancy might have caused and the way it was relieved when she asked for mercy.

While some medieval people would have been reassured by the way that 'The Abbess Delivered by Our Lady' insists that God's mercy is available for those who seek it, not all would have been comforted by this story. Some parents may have wondered how merciful it was for the abbess to be separated from her child. Some mysogynist readers may have been alarmed by the fact that the abbess seems to escape serious penance for breaking her vow of chastity. Still other readers may have wondered why Mary answered this abbess's prayer rather than those of others. Neither the miracle story nor the illustration in the Luttrell Psalter resolve these questions. Instead, they invite us to defer our judgement about who is worthy of grace – to sit for a while not quite knowing what we feel. In this sense, the mood at the end of this miracle is similar to that at the end of *Knocked Up*, where the audience has a sense that the child will be loved and that Ben will never be worthy of Alison.

I would like to end this chapter by returning to the questions with which I began. What word did you use to describe what you feel when you observe the woman and child on this book's cover? Why did you choose this word and reject others? Does this word describe the people, their relationship or the way it makes you feel? I suspect your answer will vary from others I have heard. It may also have changed as you learned more about the image's context. This is because, according to the theory of constructed emotions, we use our brains and bodies to construct emotional experiences. Since we all have different past experiences and inhabit different bodies, Lisa Feldman Barrett points out, the only norm when it comes to emotions is variation. This does not mean we all have wildly different experiences all the time. Emotional experiences provide opportunities for attunement as well as misalignment. What is clear is we often know when something has gone awry even if we're not sure quite what it is. And everyone whom I have asked about this scene seems to agree something has gone awry. I initially found the image when I typed the terms 'awkward' and 'medieval' into a Google image search, but it also comes up under searches for 'medieval' and 'surprise'. My daughter suggested disgust might be a better word to describe this scene. It seemed to her that the image depicts a baby who is gassy or in need of a new diaper. That might seem like an odd thing to say about an image located in the margin of a holy book, but the Luttrell Psalter is famous for its earthy depictions of medieval life. A smelly bum would certainly provide a plausible explanation for the look on everyone's face, not to mention the direction of finger being pointed by the man on the right. Moreover, three of the other texts I will discuss in this book – Julian of Norwich's *Revelations of Divine Love, Mankind,* and *The Book of Margery Kempe* – all use images of humans needing to be changed because they have fouled themselves (as infants, adults or in old age) to convey a sense of God's love and grace. I am not saying that this is what the image depicts, but I am acknowledging that it is a possibility that is worth contemplating given what we know of the scene. By inviting a range of plausible interpretations, this image reminds us that that while we are constantly trying to work out what we and others are feeling, we may need to accept how difficult it is to know such things for certain. My daughter's interpretation of this image also draws our attention back to the child and what his plight reveals about the awkwardness of grace, something to which the child in *Pearl* also draws our attention.

3

May this be true? The awkwardness of accepting grace in *Pearl*

Pearl is the first of four Middle English poems preserved in a manuscript now widely known as either the *Pearl*-manuscript or the *Gawain*-manuscript, after its two most famous poems, or by its shelf-mark, London, British Library, MS Cotton Nero A.x. There is some debate about the dating and authorship of these four Middle English poems, though they were all written in the fourteenth century, for the manuscript in which they appear was made around 1400.[1] This suggests that whoever compiled the manuscript was interested in the connections between them, whether or not they shared an author, and that their themes remained relevant just as the fifteenth century was set to begin. In the next four chapters, I will argue that all four of the poems in MS Cotton Nero A.x. offer different perspectives on the relationship between awkwardness and grace that Augustine explores in his *Confessions* and that is represented in the Luttrell Psalter's image of 'The Abbess Delivered by Our Lady'.

Pearl is full of grace: the word itself appears regularly and the poem is one of the most stylistically sophisticated dream poems ever written in English. It consists of 1,212 alliterative lines organized into stanzas and sections linked through concatenation, the repetition of words within subsequent lines. The poem's final line is linked to the first, creating a graceful circular effect. Yet the poem also generates awkwardness. One of its most awkward moments occurs when a young girl, whom the dreamer identifies as his deceased daughter, tries to explain God's grace to her father. Although the dreamer is relieved to learn that his daughter is in heaven despite having died before reaching the age of two, he is taken aback when she tells him that she is a bride of Christ. His reaction reminds readers that although the poem is narrated from his perspective, it nonetheless reveals the limits of his understanding. *Pearl* is remarkable because it generates both laughter and sympathy as it tells the story of a dreamer who paradoxically grieves the loss of something that belongs to him and refuses to find solace in the fact that his pearl now belongs to God. My aim here is not to insist that contemporary readers should share the poem's Christian worldview nor to suggest that we should laugh at the

---

[1] For a recent account of the poems in this manuscript in their historical context, see David Coley, *Death and the Pearl Maiden: Plague, Poetry, England*, Interventions New Studies in Medieval Culture (Columbus, OH: The Ohio University Press, 2019).

dreamer's pain. Instead, I hope to show that *Pearl*'s combination of grief and humour is itself a violation of norms that provides insight into the dreamer's anxiety about his values and his sense of worthiness.

While I have long appreciated this poem's remarkable combination of grief and humour, Ricky Gervais's Netflix series *After Life* helped me to understand what the poem's awkwardness might be telling me about the dreamer's reluctance to accept grace.[2] *After Life* focuses on a man named Tony who is overcome by grief after having lost his wife Lisa to cancer. Tony's grief leads him to struggle with suicidal thoughts, to lash out at others and to seek connection with Lisa by watching a video she has made near the end of her life (in the first series) or videos of their time together (in the second). The videos reveal that Lisa accepted Tony for who he was. Moreover, the video she made before her death reveals that she has anticipated exactly what might happen to him without her, and she urges him to see in himself what she saw in him so that he can imagine himself worthy of others' love and affection. Lisa often uses humour to prepare herself and Tony for her death. Tony's response, both in the moment and in his interactions with others, often generates laughter for the audience because it is so incongruous with what he knows Lisa is asking him to do. Although Tony clearly loves and respects Lisa, he fails spectacularly to heed her advice, choosing instead (not always voluntarily, it must be said) to suffer and to inflict pain on others rather than to risk being vulnerable. Having lost his sense of belonging when Lisa died, he doesn't even try to fit in. Tony is therefore surprised by moments when he feels some connection with others, often people who have experienced loss as well. The show generates laughter and tears by foregrounding awkward incongruities, especially the juxtaposition of grief and hope.

The opening stanzas of *Pearl* likewise juxtapose grief and hope. Like many medieval dream poems, *Pearl* begins in a garden and describes a loss of some kind. The first stanza reveals that the garden is where the speaker lost his 'pryuy perle' [precious pearl] (12).[3] The speaker then says he is certain this must be the place he lost his pearl because its presence in this place would explain why the flowers and fruit are so full of life in August, when decay should have begun. At the end of the fifth stanza, though, he can no longer maintain this hopeful outlook; his 'wille' [soul] is overcome with 'wo' [sorrow], and he falls to the ground asleep. A manuscript image (Figure 2) suggests that he seems to have fallen somewhat awkwardly into a dream.

The remainder of the poem describes the dream that takes place in the garden, regularly reminding readers that the dreamer's perspective is limited. Just as Tony is guided and challenged by Lisa's video, the dreamer is guided and challenged by a young girl who questions the premise for his grief. She says, 'Sir, ȝe haf your tale mysetente, / To say your perle is al away …' [O sir, you're certainly misled/To say your pearl has

---

[2] *After Life*, directed by Ricky Gervais, featuring Ricky Gervais, Tom Basden, Tony Way, Kerry Godliman, aired 8 March 2019, https://www.netflix.com/title/80998491?s=i&trkid=13747225.

[3] All citations taken from *The Complete Works of the* Pearl *Poet*, ed. Malcolm Andrew and Ronald Waldron, with Clifford Peterson, trans. and intro. Casey Finch (Berkeley, CA: University of California Press, 1993). I offer my own translation of the passages in order to focus on the precise diction and imagery; Finch's translation more effectively conveys other aspects of poetic form.

Figure 2 London, British Library, MS Cotton Nero A.x., fol. 41r. © The British Library Board.

gone away …] (257–8). Identifying the dreamer as a jeweller, she suggests that even the loss of a pearl would not justify his loss of joy:

> Bot, jueler gente, if þou schal lose
> Þy joy for a gemme þat þe watz lef,

Me þynk þe put in a mad porpose,
And busyez þe aboute a raysoun bref.
[But, gentle jeweler, if you should lose
Your joy for a gem that was lost to you,
I think you would be set in a mad purpose,
And concerning yourself about a lack of reason.]

(265–8)

By pointing out that he is acting unreasonably because he is guided by worldly values rather than spiritual ones, the pearl-maiden embodies the role of the wise counsellor who traditionally appears in certain kinds of dreams. She also indicates that the dreamer's grief is clouding his judgement: 'Thow demez noȝt bot doel-dystresse' [You judge not but by your distress] (337), and she poses a key question: 'why dotz þou so?' [Why do you do so?] (338). Throughout their initial exchange, she attempts to show him that his sense of grief over the loss of a worldly belonging is misguided.

The young woman maintains this line even as it emerges that *she* is the pearl that the dreamer has lost, a revelation that seems like it might mitigate the allegation that the jeweler is too worldly. He has previously hinted at her identity by saying that his joy has returned now that he has found his pearl, but she confirms her identity by switching from the second-person pronoun, 'þy perle' [your pearl] to the first as she reveals she is now married to God:

Þow wost wel when þy perle con schede
I watz ful ȝong and tender of age;
Bot my Lorde þe Lombe þurȝ Hys godhede,
He toke myself to Hys maryage,
Corounde me quene in blysse to brede
In lenghe of dayez þat euer schal wage;
And sesed in alle Hys herytage
Hys lef is. I am holy Hysse.
Hys prese, Hys prys, and Hys parage
Is rote and grounde of alle my blysse.
[You know full well that when your pearl left,
I was too young and tender of age.
But my Lord, the Lamb, through His Godhead,
He took me myself in merciful marriage
Crowned me queen in bliss to create.
In length of days that ever shall last
And held in all His heritage
His love is. I am wholly his.
His company, His worth, and His lineage,
Is root and ground of all my bliss.]

(412–20)

The dreamer responds by expressing joy, exclaiming 'Blysful' [O bliss!], and then incredulity: 'may þys be trwe?' [may this be true?] (421). While the dreamer initially seems happy, he nonetheless expresses discomfort, and he reveals his awkwardness by prefacing his next question with the phrase, 'Dysplesez not if I speke errour' [Please don't get mad if I say something wrong] (422). Worried he will be thought a fool, he opens his mouth and removes all doubt. He asks if she has surpassed Mary in Christ's esteem: 'Art þou þe quene of heuenez blwe,/Þat al þys worlde schal do honour?' [Are you the queen of heaven's blue/That all this world shal do honour (423–4). The maiden responds by addressing Mary while 'knelande to grounde, folde vp hyr face' [kneeling to the ground and bowing her face] (434). Her words and gestures express deference to Mary, the origin of grace (436), but I can't help but wonder if it also expresses what my children feel when I say something stupid in front of their friends: it seems just as plausible to imagine this young woman is hiding her face in embarrassment about her father's *faux pas*. Whether the dreamer thinks this is what she is doing or not, he is certainly shaken by the pearl-maiden's reaction to what he has said.

While the dreamer is relieved to discover that his daughter belongs in heaven, he feels uncomfortable about the reward she has been given because it violates his understanding of grace. He signals his discomfort by worrying that his words might bring her grief (471), but he can't stop himself from pointing out that it seems implausible that heaven would choose 'To make þe quen þat watz so ȝonge' [To make you queen who are so young] (474). What more honour, he asks, is due to those who have endured bodily penance while living longer in the world? He then reveals the cause of his concern. He is worried she has been given too much:

> That Cortayse is to fre of dede,
> ȝyf hyt be soth þat þou conez saye.
> Þou lyfed not two ȝer in oure þede;
> Þou cowþez neuer God nauþer Pater ne Crede –
> And quen mad on þe fyrst day!
> I may not traw, so God me spede,
> Þat God wolde wryþe so wrange away.
> Of countes, damysel, par ma fay,
> Wer fayr in heuen to halde asstate,
> Oþer ellez a lady of lasse aray;
> Bot a quene! – hit is to dere a date.
> [That courtesy is too freely given
> If it is true what you have to say
> You lived not two years in our body:
> You knew neither God nor Pater Noster nor Crede –
> And queen made on the first day!
> I may not believe, God help me,
> That God would work in so wrong a way.
> A countess, damsel, by my faith,
> Were fair states in heaven to hold,
> Or else a lady of less array;
> But a queen! – It is too dear a reward!]
> (481–92)

Considering how overcome with grief the dreamer was at the beginning of the poem, it seems perverse to hear him insist that his daughter should not have been made queen on her first day in heaven because she was not yet two years old, could not pray and knew neither her Pater Noster nor her Creed. The specificity of his surprise here would be more comprehensible if we were medieval readers, for most medieval Christians were taught that knowledge of the Pater Noster and Creed was necessary, if not sufficient, for salvation after the Fourth Lateran Council (1215). In direct response to his claim that he can't believe God would work in a wrong way, she replies calmly that God 'may do noþynk bot ry3t' [may do nothing but what is right] (496). This line reveals a little of her theological sophistication, for it echoes a passage near the conclusion of Augustine's *Confessions* in which he contrasts human changeability with God's unchanging goodness: 'At an earlier time we were moved to do wrong and to forsake you. But you God, one and good, have never ceased to do good' (XIII.xxxviii [53]). Drawing on Augustine, then, the maiden reminds her father and readers that grace looks very different from his perspective than from God's.

In order to help her father and the reader to understand grace from God's perspective, she tells the parable of the tenants from Matthew 20.1-16. In this story, the lord hires workers throughout the day, from the morning until just before sunset, and he agrees in advance to pay each worker a penny. When they are paid, though, the workers hired in the morning complain, saying they 'had trauayled sore' (550) and that they deserve 'to take more' (552). They feel they deserve it because they put in more time and suffered more:

> More haf we serued, vus þynk so,
> þat suffred han þe dayez hete,
> þenn þyse þat wro3t not hourez two,
> And þou dotz hem vus to counterfete.
> [More have we served, we think,
> And suffered have in the day's heat,
> Then these that worked not two hours,
> Are you give the same to them as to us.]
>
> (553–6)

The lord reminds them they agreed to their pay at the beginning of the day, so they shouldn't expect more now. He asks whether he should be able to do what he wants with his wealth (565–6). He then goes further, suggesting the problem is that they are looking at things the wrong way: 'Oþer ellez þyn y3e to lyþer is lyfte/For I am goude and non byswykez' [Or else your eyes are lifted to sin/For I am good and not deceitful] (567–8). The maiden ends the parable by asserting that this model applies to God, adding that 'þe merci of God is much þe more' [the mercy of God is much the more] (576). The pearl-maiden's version of the parable echoes Augustine's words, suggesting that the problem lies in the orientation of the workers, who imagine heaven through a worldly model based on scarcity of rewards rather than one that accepts the plenitude of God's grace.

While the pearl-maiden's graceful telling and interpretation of the parable might have given the dreamer a chance to save face by pretending he understands or saying such spiritual matters are beyond him, he rejects the parable and its interpretation because it does not align with his understanding of scripture:

> Me þynk þy tale vnresounable;
> Goddez ryȝt is redy and euermore rert,
> Oþer holy wryt is bot a fable.
> In sauter is sayd a verce ouerte
> Þat spekez a point determinable:
> 'Þou quytez vchon as hys desserte,
> Þou hyȝe Kyng ay pertermynable.'
> [I think your tale unreasonable;
> God's righteousness is sure and always ready,
> Or Holy Writ is but a fiction.
> In the Psalter is written a verse openly
> That speaks a point that can be determined:
> 'You reward each one as he deserves,
> You high King always unchangeable!']
>
> (589–96)

The dreamer's citation of scripture suggests that the dreamer is not just an awkward individual – though he may be that. Instead, he is experiencing awkwardness in the sense that the norms he thinks apply to this situation do not actually apply. Like Tony in *After Life*, he says he is willing to be guided by the woman he has lost, but he can't quite accept the view she offers. He seems willing enough to follow the maiden's argument that God will grant grace to those who show contrition and who have never sinned:

> Þe gyltyf may contryssyoun hente
> And be þurȝ mercy to grace þryȝt;
> Bot he to gyle þat neuer glente
> As inoscente is saf and ryȝte.
> [The guilty may by contrition earn
> And be through mercy to grace brought.
> But he to guile that never turns
> Is innocent and safe and right.]
>
> (669–72)

He even accepts her repeated statements that God's grace is enough for all who seek it: 'Mercy and grace moste hem þen stere,/For þe grace of God is gret innoȝe' [Mercy and grace must them then lead/For the grace of God is great enough] (623–4). He is nonetheless unsure whether he should believe her, either because he is unwilling to accept her as an authority or because he cannot reconcile what she tells him with grace as he understands it from his reading of other scripture.

Pearl leaves both the dreamer and the reader in an awkward situation. It seems clear that the dreamer seems discomfited by his daughter's account of God's capacious capacity for grace. Like Tony in *After Life*, the dreamer struggles to accept what the women he has lost is telling him about his worth. In *Pearl*, the dreamer is happy to hear that his daughter belongs in heaven, and he eventually accepts the esteem she enjoys there. The final stanzas suggest he is far less sure about his own place. He asks the maiden to give him a glimpse of the heavenly Jerusalem: 'Bryng me to þat bygly bylde/And let me se þy blysful bor' [Bring me to that great hime/and let me see your blissful bower] (963–4). She agrees, but she warns him that he'll have to view it from a distance: 'To strech in þe strete þou hatz no vygour,/Bot þou wer clene, withouten mote' [To go in this street you have no power/Unless you were clean, without a spot] (971–2). In other words, this is a place where she belongs but he does not – at least not yet. Her warning finds its echo in Lisa telling Tony to go on living – not to attempt to join her.

The dreamer in *Pearl* hears her warning and heeds it for a time, providing readers with a detailed account of heavenly beauty that culminates in a crowd scene in which Christ makes an appearance. Then he sees his daughter, now amongst the crowd, and he can no longer restrain himself from attempting to cross the river. He describes the experience as one in which he is overcome by the heavenly atmosphere of delight that enters into his body through his eyes and ears in the way that Gumbrecht argues the world around us can affect our moods and triggering an automatic response through his simulation of the sensual input in the way that Feldman Barrett describes in her account of emotions:

> Delyt me drof in y3e and ere,
> My manez mynde to maddyng malte;
> Quen I se3 my frely, I wolde be þere,
> By3onde þe water þa3 ho were walte.
> I þo3t þat noþyng my3t me dere
> To fech me bur and take me halte,
> And to start in þe strem schulde non me stere,
> To swymme þe remnaunt, þa3 I þer swalte.
> Bot of þat munt I watz bifalt;
> When I schulde start in þe strem astraye,
> Out of þat caste I watz bycalt:
> Hit watz not at my Pryncez paye.
> [Delight poured into me through eye and ear,
> Moving my man's mind to madness.
> When I saw my lovely, I had to be there
> Beyond the water though she was set there.
> I thought that nothing might harm me
> To hold me back or obstruct me,
> And to start in the stream I should not delay,
> To swim the rest, though I should die there.
> But of that plan I was bereft;
> When I should start in the stream astray,
> I was called out of that attempt:
> It was not my Prince's pleasure.]

(1153–64)

Literally, the dreamer is trying to cross the river to reach his daughter. Yet, we should keep in mind that even as he describes heaven's delight as a kind of direct sensory input he is simulating this entire experience in his brain. This is a dream, after all, and therefore

Figure 3 London, British Library, MS Cotton Nero A.x., fol. 42r. © The British Library Board.

similar to the experience of reading about the dream, where readers also need to simulate the experience in order to imagine it. Figuratively, the imagery here suggests that he wants to cross the river between life and death. Like Tony in *After Life*, the dreamer is fixated on ending the pain caused by the loss of a woman he loves, and he is tempted to end his own life to be reunited with her. For a medieval reader, this would have been clearly misguided: suicide would preclude heavenly bliss, so there is no way that the dreamer could hope to reach his daughter by crossing the boundary between life and death by his own will. While Tony is prevented from taking his own life several times through a series of coincidences, providence is definitely what saves the dreamer from himself. He is told that his Prince's plan is not for him to join his daughter yet. The dreamer tells readers 'I watz restayed' [I was held back] (1168) and is brought abruptly out of his dream.

The final stanza in *Pearl* re-aligns the dreamer's desire for belonging with God. It opens by insisting that 'To pay þe Prince oþer sete saȝt/Hit is ful eþe to þe god Krystyin' [To pay the Prince or be reconciled/It is very easy for the good Christians] (1201-2). He uses different language for belonging when he says that he has found Christ to be a friend both day and night. He then reiterates the role the dream played in his orientation at the end of the poem through lines that seem to have inspired the illustration I cited above: 'Ouer þis hyul þis lote I laȝte,/For pyty of my perle **enclyin**' [Over this hill this message I received/having been **inclined** for pity of my pearl (1205-6). The beginning and end of this sentence provide physical imagery: the dreamer describes himself as enclyin (inclined, bowed, stooped or perhaps lying down) on a hill, just as he is depicted in the image. The rest of the line contains some language play. The words 'lote', which can mean word or message, and 'laȝte', which means catch, receive or possibly laugh, are linked through alliteration, and will be echoed throughout the other poems in the manuscript. The word 'pyty' also resonates throughout the manuscript and provides two explanations for why the dreamer found himself 'enclyin': he may be so inclined because of the sorrow he feels for the pearl or because of the mercy the pearl has for him. The poem as a whole seems to suggest it is both: his sorrow bent his body awkwardly towards the earth, but the mercy she has shared has reminded him of his desire to belong to something larger than himself, to commune with others and with God in 'þe forme of bred and wyn/þe preste vus schewez vch a daye' [the form of bread and wine/that the priest shows us each day] (1208-9). Another manuscript image (Figure 3) suggests she has to incline to his level, condescending to him in a positive rather than a negative way. Thus she invites him to look up again.

The concatenation of the final line creates a graceful effect, suggesting the poem itself is a finely wrought pearl of great price. It also points back to the sense of loss and grief – of profound despair about belonging – that opened the poem. Thus the reader is reminded once again of the awkward implications of what the dreamer calls his man's mind and we might understand as his limited, human perspective: even if he is assured about the grace offered to his daughter and to him, he will likely find himself inclined to feel loss, grief and vulnerability in his body once more. Like Tony, he may find that the hope of connection might make his sense of loss even more profound. While Augustine's *Confessions* and 'The Abbess Delivered by Our Lady' both suggest that mercy is available to those who ask, *Pearl* reminds us just how awkward it can feel to ask for grace and how difficult it is to consider oneself worthy of love.

4

Creating tension: Laughter and anger in *Cleanness*

Perhaps the dreamer in *Pearl* may have felt more comfortable if his daughter had told one of the stories in *Cleanness*, the next poem in MS Cotton Nero A.x, rather than the parable of the vineyard. These stories seem to confirm the *Pearl*-dreamer's initial view that few are worthy of grace because God regularly punishes those who fail to attain purity. One way to explain this would be to argue that most of the stories in *Cleanness* are mainly from the Old Testament while the parable in *Pearl* is from the New. However, *Cleanness* begins with the parable that follows the one that the *Pearl*-maiden shares in Matthew's Gospel. The parable of the Wedding Banquet initially seems to be aligned with the previous parable in that it suggests that grace is distributed according to God's will, but it ends like the rest of the stories in *Cleanness*, by showing the lengths to which God will go to punish those deemed to be unclean or impure. In the other stories God casts Adam and Eve out of paradise, floods the planet, destroys the cities of Sodom and Gomorrah, and brings about Belshazzar's downfall. The focus on God's anger in *Cleanness* means that it creates tension internally and with the poems that precede and follow it in MS Cotton Nero A.x. This tension has long made me uncomfortable, and I know that at least some other readers find it uncomfortable as well.

To make sense of the discomfort this poem causes me, I follow the suggestion Hannah Gadsby makes in her 2018 Netflix special *Nanette* and focus on how tension can be connected to both anger and laughter. At the end of *Nannette*, Gadsby insists that her aim was not to unite people through anger or laughter:

> I just needed my story heard – my story felt and understood by individuals with minds of their own. Because like it or not your story is my story and my story is your story. I just don't have the strength to take care of my story anymore. I don't want my story defined by anger. All I can ask is please help me take care of my story.[1]

While I don't think it is my place to speak for the two key characters I will discuss in this chapter, Sarah and Lot's wife, I accept my responsibility for taking care of their stories. I will therefore focus on two key moments in them: the moment when Sarah laughs at

---

[1] *Nanette*, written by and featuring Hannah Gadsby, directed by Madeleine Parry and Jon Olb, aired 19 June 2018, https://www.netflix.com/title/80233611?s=i&trkid=13747725.

God's declaration that she will bear a child and the moment when God punishes Lot's wife for being awkward in a literal and figurative sense. Both moments may generate laughter through incongruity, but this is not because the violation of norms they reveal is benign. In fact, these stories show just how devastating it can be when norms are violated to serve the needs of those in power. My aim here is not to make Sarah or Lot's wife into victims or cautionary tales but to share their stories so that anyone who might identify with them might feel less alone.

In its retelling of the story in Genesis about Abraham receiving God's blessing by hosting three strangers in the desert, *Cleanness* makes some subtle changes that focus on the awkward moment when Sarah laughs at God's proclamation that she will bear a child. Although Sarah's laughter seems to create awkwardness in both Genesis and *Cleanness*, her reaction is the result of an awkward situation rather than the response of an awkward individual. *Cleanness*, like Genesis, sets up the awkward situation by establishing an atmosphere that causes discomfort. Abraham is sitting 'vnder an oke grene' [under a green oak] (602) of Mamre seeking shelter from the bright beams of the sun and the 'hy3e hete' [high heat] (604) of the day.[2] Both Genesis and *Cleanness* contrast the comfort of Abraham's shelter with the uncomfortable heat that the three travellers endure. When he encounters the men, Abraham invites them to share his shade before rushing to the tent to tell Sarah to prepare 'kakes' [unleavened bread] (625) and selecting a calf for a servant to slaughter. When all is ready, he provides it to his guests as well as 'butter' (636) and 'mylke' [milk]. *Cleanness* diverges from its biblical source by adding that Abraham served 'potage and polment' [stew and soup] (638). *Cleanness* also differs from Genesis by using a simile to hint at the identity of the anonymous travellers when Abraham goes up to them 'as to God' (611) and then revealing to the audience that one of them is, in fact, Abraham's deity: 'And God as a glad gest mad god chere' [God as a glad guest made good cheer] (641). As a sign of his pleasure, God tells Abraham that he will return, 'And þenne schal Saré consayue and a sun bere' [And then shal Sarah conceive and bear a son] (649). Sarah overhears this exchange and laughs. God hears her laughter, and the situation goes from uncomfortable to awkward.

Sarah's laughter is both completely understandable and open to interpretation. Richard Kearney argues Sarah's laughter in the book of Genesis is an extension of the hospitality Abraham shows to the travellers. Inaugural moments of faith like this one, Kearney writes, 'often begin with someone replying to an uninvited visitor – Abraham under the Mamre tree, Mary, at the instant of the annunciation and Muhammed in the cave.'[3] Kearney's question about these moments is 'what happens in the decisive instant when the sacred stranger appears: do we respond with hostility or hospitality? Fear or trust? Or both?'[4] According to Kearney, Abraham's acceptance of the travellers is a moment when 'potential hostility becomes actual hospitality. Abraham chooses

---

[2] All citations taken from *The Complete Works of the* Pearl *Poet*, ed. Malcolm Andrew and Ronald Waldron, with Clifford Peterson, trans. and intro. Casey Finch (Berkeley, CA: University of California Press, 1993). I offer my own translation of the passages in order to focus on the precise diction and imagery; Finch's translation more effectively conveys other aspects of poetic form.

[3] Richard Kearney, *Anatheism: Returning to God after God*, Insurrections: Critical Studies in Religion, Politics, and Culture (New York: Columbia, 2011), 3.

[4] Ibid.

a God of love over a God of fear. This choice is, arguably, echoed in Sarah's laughter. For is not humor the acceptance of contradiction, of the impossible become possible, of the foreign finding a home within the familiar, of the Other entering the self and being reborn?'[5] Kearney's conception of laughter in this scene is consistent with the incongruity theory of humour. I would like to point out that one key level of incongruity in this scene is that Abraham's reward is predicated entirely on two aspects of Sarah's labour. First, Abraham orders her to drop everything to make bread quickly (the text does not reveal who made the stew, soup, butter and milk, but Sarah seems like a better bet than Abraham). Then, to reward Abraham for his hospitality, God decrees Sarah will bear a child even though they're very old. Whereas Mary seems to be offered a choice about whether she will become the mother of God, Sarah is not asked for her consent. It's not hard to imagine why Sarah might laugh in these circumstances, and her solitary laughter reveals that neither God nor Abraham seem aware of anything incongruous about their failure to acknowledge her labour. And why would they? The first rule of the Patriarchy is 'Don't talk about the Patriarchy'. Hannah Gadsby's violation of this norm is exactly what made some men very angry about *Nannette*.

Cleanness adds a detail about Sarah's laughter that might make it seem as though the incongruity theory of humour might be the wrong one to apply here, though I think it ultimately enhances the range of possible meanings for her laughter. *Cleanness* specifies the reason for Sarah's laughter: 'þenne þe burde byhynde þe dor **for busmar** laȝed' [then the woman behind the door laughed **for scorn**] (653). I have translated 'busmar' as 'scorn' because it reflects the tone conveyed by the other terms the MED provides in its definition: others include 'ridicule, mockery, derision, disdain', words that suggest Sarah's laughter might be explained by the superiority theory of laughter, which consists in 'finding oneself superior to others', often our former selves, which arises from feeling 'contempt for them'.[6] God seems to understand Sarah's laughter as an expression of scorn, and he behaves like a man by taking her laughter to be an attack on his virility:

> Se! so Saré laȝes,
> Not trawande þe tale þat I þe to schewed.
> Hopez ho oȝt may be harde My hondez to work?
> [Look, Sarah laughs,
> Not accepting the story I said would come true.
> Does she hold that My hands would find hard any task?]
>
> (661–3)

Put on the spot, Sarah tries to save face for everyone by denying she laughed at all: 'Þenne swenged for Saré and swer by hir trawþe / Þat for lot þat þay laused ho laȝed neuer' [Then Sarah came and swore by her troth / that she had never laughed at the things they said] (667–8). The mood becomes tense at this point in both Genesis and

---

[5] Ibid., 19.
[6] Noël Carroll, *Humour: A Very Short Introduction* (Oxford: Oxford University Press, 2014), chap. 1, Kobo.

Cleanness, but there is an extra edge in the Middle English poem because all of the other stories it tells depict God punishing those who do not fully align themselves with his will. From her perspective, Sarah seems to be experiencing what Adam Kotsko describes as radical awkwardness, a situation where 'there doesn't seem to be any norm governing a given situation at all'.[7] After all, the promise of her pregnancy has made it clear that God is not constrained by the same norms as others might be. Just as the conflict seems about to boil over – which seems appropriate given that the story began with a decision to be made between hostility and hospitality in the heat of the desert – God puts an end to the discussion:

> 'Now innoghe: hit is not so,' þenne nurned þe Dryȝtyn,
> For þou laȝed aloȝ, bot let we hit one.'
> ['Now enough: it is not so,' then declared the Lord,
> For you laughed low, but let's forget it.]
>
> (669–70)

So, it seems, God gets the last word. Sarah laughed, God says, but she laughed 'aloȝ', an adverb that may either describe softly, quietly or downward (perhaps under her breath), so she will not be punished, though your assessment of that claim will depend on your view of what it means for a very old woman to carry a child for nine months in a hot climate. God is apparently big enough to let it go, provided everyone accepts God's version of events.

This interpretation puts God in an unflattering light: as I noted in the introduction, Aaron James argues there's a word for those who violate norms while expecting others to adhere to them. However, another detail in *Cleanness* suggests that we might read the end of this conversation as a sign of grace. If God is omniscient, then God knows whether Sarah laughed low or not and what she said to herself when she laughed: 'May þou traw for tykle þat þou teme moȝtez, / And I so hyȝe out of age, and also my lorde?' [Can you believe for a moment that you might conceive / And I being so old, and also my lord?] (653–6). God therefore would have known Sarah used the second-person singular pronoun here. In Middle English, as in many languages today, the plural (you, ye, your) is used in formal situations and to address superiors while the singular (thee, thou, thine) is used to indicate informality, intimacy or a sense of hierarchy. English has retained the polite form of address for both the plural and the singular, a clear precedent for using the plural form of the third person pronoun (they, them, their) for gender neutrality today. The singular form of the second person pronoun seems formal to modern readers because it is often retained in prayer, where it is used to address God in an intimate manner. It is possible that Sarah is addressing God when she uses 'þou' in this passage. However, she does not know, as the reader does, that the stranger is God. It seems unlikely that she would use the informal 'þou' to address one who is supposed to be an honoured guest in her home, though this is also possible since she says it under her breath. Given the pronoun and the question she asks, it seems more likely that she is addressing herself: 'Can you believe for a moment you might conceive?'

---

[7] Adam Kotsko, *Awkwardness: An Essay* (Ropley: Zero Books, 2010), 7.

This reading suggests we might radically re-think what it means that Sarah '**for busmar** laȝed' [laughed **for scorn**] (653). She may have good reason to laugh at Abraham and his guest, but she would also have good reason to laugh at her own credulity. As the poem reminds readers, Abraham and Sarah tried for many years to have a child, but that 'such werk hem fayled / Fro mony a brod day byfore' [such work failed them / for many a long day before] (658–9). Having desired a child and attempted to conceive for many years, Sarah may be laughing at the hope Abraham's guest has sparked in her, and her laughter marks her incredulity about conceiving a child and the fact she remains hopeful this is a possibility. Read in this light, her laughter may still be an example of the superiority theory of laughter, but here her scorn is directed towards herself. She may not be questioning God's power but expressing her own vulnerability. She asks, like the dreamer in *Pearl*, who do you think you are to deserve God's grace? God's insistence she laughed at him might seem – and it might very well be – a typically masculine response; yet, it also gives her the opportunity to save face by reassuring Sarah that does not need to wonder whether she is worthy. God knows she has her doubts, but Abraham doesn't need to know about them.

Whereas this episode potentially offers a moving account of the re-alignment between human beings and God, the next episode in *Cleanness* turns on several less benign violations of norms. Kearney insists that the imagery of turning plays a key role in the story of Abraham and Sarah: 'As a result of [Abraham's] radical turning around, he opens himself and his wife Sarah to new life.'[8] The next story in both Genesis and *Cleanness* also focuses on images associated with turning but with much more violent and unsettling results. This story's misogyny and homophobia make me profoundly uncomfortable. Lacking Milton's ability, I will not attempt to justify the ways of God to men. I will suggest, however, that the juxtaposition of these two stories merits our attention since the awkwardness marked by Sarah's laughter goes unpunished while Lot's wife pays a severe price for a moment that is awkward in the sense that she turns ever so slightly away from the direction God wants her to go.

The two stories are connected because the travellers in the first story get up to travel towards Sodom immediately after God ends the conversation with Sarah. Abraham's 'mod', his mood or feeling, changes abruptly when God reveals that he plans to destroy the city as well as Gomorrah: 'Þenne arȝed Abraham and alle his mod chaunged, / For hope of þe harde hate þat hyȝt hatz oure' [Then Abraham grew faint and all his mood changed / For anticipation of this promise of punishment, painful and dire] (713–14). Believing the cities might be saved, Abraham then tries to align God's mood with his. Abraham reasons that it would be unfair to punish those who are righteous along with those who are sinful. God initially agrees that if Abraham can find fifty righteous men, 'I schal forgyue alle þe gylt þurȝ My grace one' [I shall forgive all their guilt through My grace alone] (731). Abraham gets God to agree to mellow his 'mode' [mood] (764) by agreeing that the same logic should hold true for forty, thirty, twenty and eventually ten men. If they can't find that many righteous men, Abraham asks, at least God should save his 'lef broþer' [beloved brother] Lot (772). Thanks to a sign from Abraham, Lot welcomes God's two travelling companions into his home. Lot's family welcomes them,

---

[8] Kearney, *Anatheism*, 20.

and his wife is asked to make bread for them just as Sarah did. Lot's wife is reluctant to follow his unsavoury command that she should make the bread 'wyth no sour ne no salt' [neither leaven nor salt] (820). Like Sarah, Lot's wife expresses scorn under her breath:

> Þis vnsaueré hyne
> Louez no salt in her sauce; ȝet hit no skyl were
> Þat oþer burne be boute, þaȝ boþe be nyse.
>   [So these unsavoury men
> Love no salt in their sauce; yet it is not right
> That others should go without because those two are fussy.]
>
> (822–4)

Lot's wife then shows her scorn more openly than Sarah, serving her guests salt even though God has forbidden it and revealing her feelings through her words: 'and also ho scelt hem in **scorne** þat wel her skyl knewen' [and also she spoke to them in scorn as her ability allowed her] (827). The poem asks why she was so 'wod' [mad] to speak in this way, for like Sarah, 'Ho wrathed oure Lord' [She angered our Lord] (827). Lot's guests don't seem to mind, though: they enjoy their meal.

The mood remains pleasant until a crowd arrives to demand that Lot hand over his guests so that they can 'lere hym of lof, as oure lyst biddeȝ' [teach them about love as our lust bids us] (843). The homophobia expressed in these lines is clear, especially since much more is left unsaid when the same demand is made Genesis: 'Bring them out to us, so that we may know them' (19.5). The passage in Genesis reveals that God is determined to punish Sodom because the outcry against it has become so great. The interpretive tradition has regularly inferred that the sexual sins of Sodom's population are what moves God to anger, but it is worth noting that both Genesis and *Cleanness* suggest that the people of Sodom might have avoided their fate if they had welcomed the strangers with hospitality rather than hostility. Whereas Abraham offers God a comfortable atmosphere, the crowd in Sodom creates a threatening one:

> What! Þay sputen and speken of so spitous fylþe,
> What! Þay ȝeȝed and ȝolped of ȝestande sorȝe,
> Þat ȝet þe wynd and þe weder and þe worlde stynkes
> Of þe brych þat vpbraydez þose broþelych wordes.
>   [What! They spewed and spoke of such spite-filled filth!
> What! They cried and boasted of festering sores,
> That yet the wind and the weather and the world stinks
> Of the wound that those wicked words brought forth.]
>
> (845–8)

Just as a poem can establish mood or atmosphere through words, so it seems a crowd's words can alter the wind, weather and world. This is a crowd where all seem to be fully entrained with each other as they whip themselves into a frenzy. Lot has no desire to fit in with these men, so he confronts them. Through a masterful play on words, he warns them that through 'your vylaynye, ȝe vylen yourseluen' [your villainy, you violate yourselves] (863). Then, alarmingly, Lot offers the men his daughters in place of his guests. The crowd's rejection of Lot's daughters is often read as further evidence of their homosexuality, but it can also be read as a rejection of Lot's radical hospitality because it reveals that their hostility is firmly directed towards the strangers in their midst: they are united in lust arising from their anger rather than their sexual desire. The idea that Lot can be read as hospitable by offering his daughters is not particularly appealing, but it does establish a parallel between Lot and Abraham, whose hospitality was also predicated on a woman obeying his command. In the end, *Cleanness* implies that the Sodomites are sodomites, but it also suggests they are being punished for their hostility to strangers, for violating norms associated with the relationship between hosts and guests.

Cleanness also implies that God's punishment of the Sodomites violates norms. In Genesis, God considers hiding his plans, 'seeing that Abraham shall become a great and mighty nation, and all the nations of the earth shall bless themselves by him' (Genesis 18.18). In both Genesis and Cleanness, God decides to go ahead anyway but has determined this is the test that will determine whether the people of Sodom live or die as a group. The next morning, Lot's guests, now identified as angels, tell Lot that he must leave immediately to avoid death. His family must not only go quickly but they must also avoid looking back: 'bifore your face lokes, / Bot bes neuer so bolde to blusch yow behinde' [look ahead of your faces, / But be never so bold as to glance behind you] (903–4). This leaves Lot in an awkward position. He literally does not know which way to turn because he is suddenly confronted with the knowledge that God can and will bring about far greater destruction than the crowd:

> 'Lord, what is best?
> If I me fele vpon fote þat I fle moȝt,
> Hov schulde I huyde me fro Hym þat hatz His hate kynned
> In þe brath of His breth þat brennez alle þinkez?
> To crepe fro my Creatour I know not wheder,
> Ne wheþer His fooschip me folȝez bifore oþer bihynde.
> [Lord, what is best?
> If I feel that I might be permitted to flee on foot,
> How might I hide myself from Him Whose wish this is
> In the violence of his breath that can burn all things!
> To creep from my Creator I know not where,
> Nor whether His enmity will fall from ahead or behind!]
>
> (914–18)

Whereas the crowd's words – their collective breath – transformed Sodom's atmosphere into one rife with destructive potential, God's breath will destroy everything. In answer to this question, one of the angels tells Lot he does not belong with the other men in Sodom: 'þou art oddely þyn one out of þis fylþe' [you are the odd one out of this filth] (923). Lot therefore decides to go to Zoar, and the angels again insist he must go 'wythouten agayn-tote' [without a backward glance] (931). As Lot, his wife and his daughters leave, Sodom and Gomorrah are destroyed by what insurance companies today might call 'An Act of God'.

Even if you don't know this story, you know enough about stories to know what is going to happen next. Someone looks back. Here is how the poet conveys that pivotal moment:

> Ferly ferde watz her flesch þat flowen ay ilyche,
> Trynande ay a hyʒe trot, þat **torne neuer dorsten.**
> Loth and þo luly-whit, his lefly two deʒter,
> Ay folʒed here face, bifore her boþe yʒen;
> Bot þe balleful burde, þat neuer bode keped,
> Blusched byhynden her bak þat bale for to herkken.
> Hit watz lusty **Lothes wyf þat ouer her lyfte schulder**
> **Ones ho bluschet to þe burʒe,** bot bod ho no lenger,
> Þat ho nas stadde a stiffe ston, a stalworth image,
> Al so salt as ani se – and so ho ʒet standez.
> Þay slypped bi and syʒe hir not þat wern hir samen-feres.
> [As they fled they were filled in their flesh with dread.
> They maintained a fast trot, **never turning to look.**
> Lot and his lily-whites, his lovely two daughters
> Always followed their face, looking ahead with both eyes;
> But the baleful woman, that never did as she was told,
> Looked behind her back that destruction for to harken.
> It was lusty **Lot's wife that over her left shoulder**
> **Once looked back to the city,** but she followed no longer
> Because she was stood as a stiff stone, a sturdy image
> And as salty as any sea – and so she yet stands
> The others slipped by and did not see her nor recognize her.]
>
> (975–85)

The turn over her left shoulder might have been described as awkward even in the fifteenth century. It is like the backhanded strokes described in the Arthurian Romances (see Chapter 2), especially since the left shoulder is the 'sinister' one in Latin. Her glance also invites some awkward questions.

The poem seems to recognize that readers might be worried that the punishment Lot's wife endures is disproportionate to her crime. *Cleanness* therefore reminds readers she was being punished for doing two things against God's will:

> For two fautes þat þe fol watz founde in mistrauþe:
> On, ho serued at þe soper salt bifore Dryʒten,
> And syþen, ho **blusched hir bihynde,** þaʒ hir forboden were …
> [For two faults was that fool found to be in mistruth
> One, she served at the supper salt before God,
> And then, she **looked behind her,** which was forbidden …
>
> (996–8)

The fact that this story appears shortly after another one about how eating fruit brings death into the world not just for Adam and Eve but every other generation may put this punishment into perspective. Yet the scene is preceded much more closely by the one in which God accuses Sarah of laughing for scorn. Is there a way to explain this apparent inconsistency?

I would like to propose the somewhat demoralizing view that the difference between these two situations lies in God's understanding of the two women's intentions. While it is not entirely clear where Sarah's scorn is directed, God seems to acknowledge that her laughter may not be voluntary. After all, Provine's research shows that people often laugh at things they do not actually find particularly funny; many people regret involuntarily laughing at inappropriate things almost immediately. Finding she has been heard, Sarah tries to downplay her response. As I suggested above, God may have judged Sarah to be laughing at her own hope. Lot's wife shows scorn more intentionally, expressing what Ahmed might call her willfullnes. She shows willfulness by baking the bread the way she wants to bake it and looking back at the city willfully. Unwilling to turn a blind eye to the violence around her, she provides an early model of the feminist killjoy. This becomes clearer when we consider how she has been described throughout the story, as having acted willfully by speaking scornfully, making God angry and feeling baleful about the loss of her home. This shifts the focus – God's and the reader's – to her rather than to her labour and the destruction she witnesses. She seems to create awkwardness by refusing to go along with God's plan willingly and cheerfully. 'To create awkwardness', according to Ahmed, 'is to be read as being awkward. Maintaining public comfort requires that certain bodies "go along with it." To refuse to go along with it, to refuse the place in which you are placed, is to be seen as trouble, as causing discomfort for others'.[9] While Lot stands up to the crowd in one scene, he is willing to 'go along with it' in the latter, as are his daughters. Lot's wife is unwilling just to go along with a plan to abandon her home while God destroys it. By looking back, she is literally awkward and she creates an awkward situation, for she bears witness to genocide.

Like so many who bear witness to those who abuse their power by violating norms, Lot's wife is silenced. Her turn represents the awkward situation that God seemed to fear when hiding it from Abraham: that this story would be remembered. God turns Lot's wife into a kind of embodied pun: she is turned into a pillar of salt because she insisted on putting it in her bread. In manuscript images, she can often be identified thanks to the animals who use her as a salt lick (Figures 4 and 5). Yet she ultimately stands as a monument to those who have been silenced because they are willing to be perceived as awkward for bearing witness to violence and destruction. God seems to take the same view of Lot's wife that Picasso had of his mistresses. As Hannah Gadsby notes, he once said, 'You destroy the woman, you destroy the past she represents.'[10] That is exactly why we need to tell stories like this even if they cause discomfort. Gadsby goes on to say, 'I will not allow my story to be destroyed. What I would have done to hear a story like mine. Not for blame, not for reputation, not for money, not for power, but to feel less alone. To feel connected. I want my story heard.'[11] This is the care we can offer to Lot's wife and the people of Sodom and the gift it might offer those who

---

[9] Sara Ahmed, *The Promise of Happiness* (Durham: Duke University Press, 2010), 68–9.
[10] Gadsby, *Nannette*.
[11] Ibid.

Figure 4 New York, Morgan Library, MS 739, fol. 11r. Photo provided by and reproduced with Permission of the Morgan Library & Museum, New York. Lot's wife appears in the lower right corner.

Cleanness 57

Figure 5 New York, Morgan Library, MS 268, fol. 4v. Photo provided by and reproduced with Permission of the Morgan Library & Museum, New York. Lot's wife appears in the lower left corner.

recognize themselves in those who are punished severely for being different or not fully aligning their intentions with the will of the powerful.

If these stories are to be read as cautionary tales, let them be cautionary for those who abuse their power. Gadsby insists, 'My story has value. To be rendered powerless does not destroy your humanity. Your resilience is your humanity. The only people who lose their humanity are those who believe they have the right to render another human being powerless. They are the weak. To yield and not break: that is incredible strength.'[12] *Cleanness* provides a great deal of information about Lot's state of mind, but very little about his wife's. Was she resilient? Did she choose to bear witness? The fact that we cannot answer these questions speaks volumes about the asymmetrical way that men and women are treated in this story and medieval literature in general. But her transformation also speaks to the fragility of those who wield power to exact vengeance or settle scores. Lot's wife is not usually portrayed as the hero of the story, but her awkward turn deserves another look because it draws attention both to her unhappiness and to what she is unhappy about: God's annihilation of her home and the people amongst whom she lived.

---

[12] Ibid.

5

Virtuous even if it displeases: *Patience*

Whereas *Cleanness* tells several biblical stories that depict God's destructive power, the next poem in MS Cotton Nero A.x tells a story about the lengths to which God will go to show mercy. Jonah, the protagonist of the eponymous biblical book and *Patience*, is profoundly awkward. One reason for this is that he cannot seem to imagine that not everything that happens in the book is about him. Structurally and emotionally, Jonah is like David Brent in the UK version of the *The Office* and Michael Scott in the American version in the sense that they are all at sea, out of their depth and reluctant to do the job they have been asked to do. Jonah's story begins when he refuses to go to Ninevah because he fears that the people will harm him when he delivers the news that God plans to destroy the city. He is willing to empathize with the Ninevites, but only to the extent that it allows him to imagine what they might think of him. Likewise, the UK and American versions of *The Office* begin by putting David and Michael in an awkward situation: both learn that employees at their paper companies will be made redundant, and they are profoundly concerned about how this will make them look. All three figures are simultaneously preoccupied with what others think of them and completely unable or unwilling to understand how others perceive them. All three are awkward individuals, to be sure, yet the discomfort they cause helps to reveal something about the way awkwardness functions more generally as a way of signalling a breakdown in the norms that apply to relationships, whether they are social or spiritual.

Patience frames its retelling of Jonah's story by praising patience as a virtue, 'þaȝ hit displese ofte' [though it displeases often] (1).[1] Although *Patience* adapts the book of Jonah from the Hebrew scriptures it follows the two preceding poems in MS Cotton Nero A.x, *Pearl* and *Cleanness*, by quoting Matthew's gospel. *Patience* explains how the eight Beatitudes can help Christians understand that each will be repaid what is due to them. The speaker then reveals that he is stuck with 'pouerté and pacyence' [poverty and patience], which 'arn nedes playferes' [are need's playmates] (45). The speaker resolves to accept his lot in life, asking what use it is to resist God's will with 'grychchyng' [grumbling] (53) if one is just going to end up **'bowed** to his bode'

---

[1] All citations taken from *The Complete Works of the Pearl Poet*, ed. Malcolm Andrew and Ronald Waldron, with Clifford Peterson, trans. and intro. Casey Finch (Berkeley: University of California Press, 1993). I offer my own translation of the passages in order to focus on the precise diction and imagery; Finch's translation more effectively conveys other aspects of poetic form.

[**bowed** to his bidding] (56). This question reminds the speaker of Jonah, who is the prime example of the individual who is awkward because he tries to turn away from God:

> Did not Jonas in Judé suche jape sumwhyle?
> To sette hym to sewrté, vnsounde he hym feches.
> [Did not Jonah in Judea carry on in this way?
> To seek his assurance, he finds unsound things.]
>
> (57–8)

God asks Jonah to go to Nineveh to tell them that God can no longer abide their malice but will seek vengeance upon them. In terms of both diction and plot, God's threat echoes the situation in *Cleanness* when God tells Abraham that he is about to destroy Sodom and Gomorrah. Whereas Abraham tries to intervene on behalf of the cities, though, Jonah wants nothing to do with this mission. His premonition of what will happen if he bends himself to God's will echoes the speaker's words twenty lines earlier.

> If I **bowe** to His bode and bryng hem þis tale,
> And I be nummen in Niniue, my nyes begynes.
> [If I **bow** to his bidding and bring them this tale,
> And I am taken in Nineveh, my trouble begins.]
>
> (75–6)

His more detailed explanation echoes *Cleanness* in several other ways. First, he worries that he, like the wedding guest in *Cleanness*, will be put in 'a prisoun' [a prison] or in 'stokkes' [stocks] (79) or that he'll be bound 'in a warlok' [fetters] and have his eyes removed from his head (80). Jonah thinks that his mission to tell the Ninevites that God has it in for them reveals that God has it in for him:

> 'Þis is a meruayl message a man for to preche
> Amonge enmyes so mony and mansed fendes,
> Bot if my gaynlych God such gref to me wolde
> For desert of sum sake þat I slayn were.
> At alle peryles,' quoþ þe prophete, 'I aproche hit no nerre.
> I wyl me sum oþer waye þat he ne wayte after.'
> ['That's a marvellous message for a man to preach
> Among so many enemies and menacing fiends,
> Unless my gracious God wills such grief to me
> That as the result of some sin he wants me killed.
> At all peril,' said the prophet, 'I will not approach it.
> I will go some other way where he won't come after me.']
>
> (85–6)

At this point, Jonah acts like David Brent in *The Office* when he is pressured to discipline his friend Chris Finch. David ostensibly calls Chris in front of the whole office to fire him for an offensive email, but his boss, Jennifer Taylor-Clarke, switches the phone to speaker and reveals that David is on the line with the speaking clock.[2] Jonah, like David, doesn't yet know what to do but he sure knows what he doesn't want to do. His dilemma also echoes Lot's. Whereas Lot concludes God will find him wherever he goes, Jonah decides that he should just 'tee into Tarce and tary þere a whyle' [go off to Tarshish and stay there a while] (87) until God forgets about him.

What Jonah finds is that God forgives but doesn't forget. Jonah catches a ship headed for Tarshish, and he is initially joyful that he has 'so derfly ascaped' [so boldly escaped] (110) God's command. However, readers are reminded, God could still see him, and God calls on the winds to churn up the sea. Desperate to save themselves and their ship, the other sailors toss everything they can overboard and then pray to their gods of different faiths. Finally, they decide God must be after someone, so they decide to cast lots to identify the culprit. Meanwhile, Jonah has fallen asleep. The poem provides a delightful description of his 'sloumbe-selepe' [slumbering sleep] by using graphic imagery of both the sleeping Jonah, 'sloberande he routes' [slobbering he snores] (185), and the way the sailors kick and yell to try to wake him. Jonah draws the last lot, and the sailors demand to know what he has done. He explains that the storm was sent after him and their only chance of survival is to cast him overboard. Seeing how powerful Jonah's God is, they become afraid and try to out-row the storm. Realizing they can't, they finally toss Jonah into the sea. Jonah thinks he will die, but that's only because he does not yet know what every reader does: he is about to be swallowed by 'a wylde walterande whal' [a wild wallowing whale] (247). After spending some time in the whale, which 'sauoured as hell' [stank like hell] (275), Jonah eventually agrees that he will do as God asks. God commands the whale to cast Jonah ashore, and 'Þe whal **wendez** at His wylle' [the whale **turns** at His will] (339), swims near the shore and casts Jonah out into the water. The imagery here contrasts the whale's immediate turn with Jonah's reluctance to bow to God's will. Only at this point does he agree to go to Nineveh, and only after he has asked God to 'lene me Þy grace' [give me Thy grace] (347). Conveniently, Jonah has already arrived at Nineveh.

Jonah preaches that Nineveh will be destroyed in forty days. Nothing will remain. It will be torn to the ground. He uses graphic imagery to describe how 'Vp-so-doun schal ȝe dumpe depe to þe abyme' [Upside down shall you be dumped deep into the abyss' (362) and that everyone will 'be swolȝed swyftly wyth þe swart erþe' [be swallowed swiftly by the dark earth] (363). This is one place where the comparison between Jonah and the managers from *The Office* needs a little bit of nuance. Neither David Brent nor Michael Scott is very good at management. They find themselves in that position because they were successful salesmen. Jonah, in contrast, *is* an effective preacher, even if he seems a little awkward in the manuscript image that depicts him in Nineveh (Figure 6). Jonah's words change the mood and atmosphere in Nineveh, for those who hear him are 'chylled at þe hert' [chilled to the heart] (368). Their hearts are so gripped

---

[2] *The Office*, season 1, episode 2, 'Downsize', written and directed by Ricky Gervais and Stephen Merchant, featuring Ricky Gervais, Lucy Davis and Oliver Chris, aired 16 July 2001, https://www.netflix.com/title/70136112?s=i&trkid=13747225.

Figure 6 London, British Library, MS Cotton Nero A.x., fol. 86v. © The British Library Board.

'for þe drede of Dryȝten' [for the dread of God] (372) that they repent immediately, putting on hairshirts and dropping dust on their heads. Jonah goes on preaching. When his words reach the king, he responds immediately: he 'radly vpros' [got up quickly] (378), rips his robe off, wallows in ash, dons a hairshirt and sackcloth, and weeps for 'alle his wrange dedes' [all his wrong deeds] (384). The king then ordains that all living things – animals, babies and people – should 'faste frely for her falce werkes' [fast freely for their false works] (390). The king says that no one can tell if God might forgive, and he believes that it is still possible for the Ninevites to change their ways:

> I wot His myȝt is so much, þaȝ He be myssepayed,
> Þat in His mylde amesyng He mercy may fynde.
> And if we leuen þe layk of oure layth synnes,
> And stylle steppen in þe styȝe He styȝtlez Hymseluen,
> He wyl **wende** of His wodschip and His wrath leue,
> And forgif vus þis gult, ȝif we Hym God leuen.
> [I know His might is so much, though he be mis-payed,
> That in his mild moderation He mercy may find.
> And if we leave the lack of our recent sins,
> And still step in the path He raises Himself,
> He will **turn** from His madness and His wrath leave,
> And forgive us this guilt, if we believe Him to be God.
>
> (399–404)

The last two lines of this passage tie together God taking 'leue' [leave] of his wrath with the promise that the Ninevites will 'leuen' [believe] in God. This hope is expressed in physical terms: the king believes that God will turn from his wrath if they re-align themselves by following the path he has established. The king's hope lies in his belief that God is mighty enough to offer mercy for those who return to him rather than to insist on punishment. While it is possible to reconcile this view of God with the one offered in *Cleanness*, the two poems initially seem to be proposing radically different ways of imagining God. This awkward juxtaposition reminds readers that these stories represent God from a human perspective rather than God's.

Jonah serves as a surrogate for exploring the difference between the way that human beings understand grace and the way it is understood by God. He is shocked when the Ninevites repent and God forgives them:

> Þenne al leued on His lawe and laften her synnes,
> Parformed alle þe penaunce þat þe prynce radde;
> And God þurȝ his godness forgef as He sayde;
> Þaȝ He oþer bihyȝt, withhelde His vengaunce.
> [Then they all believed in his law and left their sins,
> Performed all the penance that the prince advised;
> And God through his goodness forgave as He said;
> Though He promised to do otherwise, he withheld His vengeance.]
>
> (405–8)

Readers who are still upset about the wholesale destruction of Sodom and Gomorrah are probably more relieved than Jonah, who responds with sadness and anger:

> Muche sorȝe þenne satteled vpon segge Jonas;
> He wes as wroth as the wynde towarde our Lorde.
> [Much sorrow then settled upon the man Jonah;
> He was as angry as the wind towards our Lord.]
>
> (405–10)

As in *Cleanness*, the wind as an atmospheric element conveys Jonah's mood: a sense of anger blows through him and towards God just as God's wind destroyed Sodom and Gomorrah. Jonah is disoriented because he expects vengeance, but God offers mercy. Jonah is awkward, to be sure, but he is not simply an awkward individual, though he sure tries his best to be one for most of the text. Instead, he experiences the kind of awkwardness that the dreamer in *Pearl* experiences, for he finds himself in the position of trying and failing to understand divine grace in human terms. The sadness and anger he experiences also suggest his experience of awkwardness is as radical as Sarah's. For Kotsko, 'the discomfort of radical awkwardness is ... much greater than that of everyday awkwardness, because in place of seeing one's familiar ways of navigating the world flaunted, one feels deprived of them altogether'.[3] The conversion of the Ninevites and the grace God offers seem to shatter Jonah's worldview. It seems to him as if the norms by which he lived his life no longer apply.

Thinking everything in the book is about him, Jonah reminds God and the readers of *Patience* that he was initially unwilling to go to Nineveh because it never occurred to him that they might listen, repent and change their beliefs. Jonah then insists that God's grace has made him into a liar since his prophecy now won't come true. He therefore asks God to end his life. God gets him to reflect on this view by asking, 'is þis ryȝt so ronkly to wrath / For any dede þat I haf don oþer demed þe ȝet?' [Is it right so arrogantly to rage / About a deed that I have done or decided to do?] (431–2). Jonah refuses to provide a coherent answer to the question. Instead, he gets up 'joyless and janglande' [joyless and grumbling] (433) and heads out into a field outside the city. And this, for me, is where *Patience* gets really interesting: the rest of the poem is devoted to God's attempt to help Jonah get over himself by explaining how grace might look from God's perspective.

The closing scenes of *Patience* use mood and atmosphere to explore how Jonah might ultimately become more attuned to God's will. Like Abraham in *Cleanness*, Jonah finds the heat of the day uncomfortable. Whereas Abraham shelters in the shade of an oak in *Cleanness*, the plain upon which Jonah waits is barren, so he makes a bower out of grasses and ferns. Then, just as the action seems set to begin, he falls asleep. During the night, God 'of his grace ded growe of þat soyle / Þe fayrest bynde hym abof þat euuer burne wyste' [of his grace did grow out of that soil / The fairest woodbine above him that was ever known] (443–4). Jonah is so pleased by the new shelter, which cools him by preventing the heat of the sun from passing through, that he does not even seek food. God changes Jonah's mood by changing the atmosphere in which he finds himself, and readers share his experience of cooling off. It doesn't last, though, as the mood shifts again. As Jonah sleeps the next night, God sends a worm to destroy the woodbine and he

---

[3] Adam Kotsko, *Awkwardness: An Essay* (Ropley: Zero Books, 2010), 7.

'sayez vnte Zeferus þat he syfle warme / Þat þer quikken no cloude bifore þe cler sunne' [says unto Zephyrus that he should blow warm / So that no cloud should quicken in front of the clear sun] (471). Jonah wakes to find the woodbine dead and scorched by the sun and the warm Western wind. Jonah suffers in the heat, and his mood once again matches the atmosphere when, 'with hatel anger and hot' [with fierce and hot anger] (481), he has a meltdown:

> A, Þou Maker of man, what maystery Þe þynkez
> Þus Þy freke to forfare forbi alle oþer?
> With alle meschef þat Þou may, neuer Þou me sparez;
> I keuered me a cumfort þat is caȝt fro me,
> My wodbynde so wlonk þat wered my heued.
> Bot now I se Þou art sette my solace to reve;
> Why ne dyȝttez Þou me to diȝe? I dure to longe.
> [Ah, You Maker of man, what mastery do You think it is
> In this way Your man to ruin far more than any other?
> With all the mischief that You have, You never spare me;
> I covered myself in a comfort that is taken from me,
> My woodbine so rich that covered by head;
> But now I see you are set my solace to steal
> Why don't you let me die? I live too long.]
>
> (482–8)

Jonah seems to think he's the main character in what Joseph Campbell calls the hero's journey: he thinks this story has all been about his ability to prove himself, and he's tired of it. Losing the woodbine is the last straw. For the second time, Jonah asks God to let him die and to stop making his life miserable.

Instead of granting Jonah's request, God teaches him a lesson, though he adopts a much different approach than he took with Lot's wife (misogyny is the difference). God asks Jonah if it seems appropriate for him to be having a tantrum about the death of a woodbine that grew overnight and died the next night:

> Is þis ryȝtwys, þou renk, alle þy ronk noyse,
> So wroth for a wodbynde to wax so sone?
> Why art þou so waymot, wyȝe, for so lyttel?
> [Is this righteous, you creature, all your wild noise,
> So much anger about a woodbine that grew so quickly?
> Why are you so heated, man, for so little?]
>
> (490–2)

Instead of feeling calmed or falling asleep, as he usually does in such situations, Jonah turns up the heat, again telling God that he wishes he were dead:

> 'Hit is not lyttel,' quoþ þe lede, 'bot lykker to ryȝt;
> I wolde I were of þis worlde wrapped in moldez.'
> ['It is not little!' said the man, 'but more like justice;

I wish I were wrapped in the soil of this world.']

(493-4)

Jonah's claim that he no longer wants to live seems both ridiculous and recognizable. On the one hand, this seems like an extreme overreaction to the death of a plant that gave him shade for a day. On the other hand, the death of the woodbine seems to confirm for Jonah that God takes great pleasure from his suffering.

The death of the woodbine is not little for Jonah because he thinks it means God has turned against him. At this moment, when Jonah's mood is at its lowest point, God offers Jonah a much different perspective on the woodbine's purpose by revealing that its loss should help Jonah to empathize with God's concern about the Ninevites. I cite this passage at length to stress the extent to which it expands two short bible verses (Jonah 4.10-11):

> Þenne byþenk þe, mon, if þe forþynk sore,
> If I wolde help My hondework, haf þou no wonder;
> Þou art waxen so wroth for þy wodbynde,
> And trauaylede neuer to tent hit þe tyme of an howre,
> Bot at a wap hit here wax and away at anoþer,
> And ȝet lykez þe so luþer, þi lyf woldez þou tyne.
> Þenne wyte not Me for þe work, þat I hit wolde help,
> And rwe on þo redles þat remen for synne;
> Fyrst I made hem Myself of materes Myn one,
> And syþen I loked hem ful longe and hem on lode hade.
> And if I My trauayl schulde tyne of termes so longe,
> And type doun ȝonder toun when hit **turned** were,
> Þe sor of such a swete place burde synk to My hert,
> So mony molicious mon as mournez þerinne.
> [Then think about it, man, if you think it's so bad,
> If I would help my handiwork, have you no wonder;
> You are grown so angry for your woodbine,
> And worked never to tend it even the length of an hour
> But at a moment it here grew and at another it went away,
> And yet you like wickedness so much, you would lose your life
> Then don't wonder about Me that I would help what I made
> And pity those heedless men that lament for sin:
> First I made them Myself of My own matter
> And after I looked on them long as their guide.
> And if I My labour of such a long term should lose
> And throw down yonder town when it had **turned**,
> The pain of such a sweet place would sink to My heart
> For so many malicious men that had mourned therein.]

(*Patience* 495-508)

God reminds Jonah that he cares for the Ninevites because He made them. God depicts Himself as a father, from a medieval understanding of conception, insofar as they are made of his matter. But God also implicitly suggests She is a mother, for the translation of God's long 'travail' as 'labour' carried the same connotations then as it does now. As both father and mother, God is more emotionally invested in the Ninevites than Jonah can possibly be in the woodbine. The analogy reminds Jonah and the readers of *Patience* that God's creation and destruction of the woodbine *is* about Jonah, but not in the way Jonah thinks it is. The woodbine was not a reward or a punishment but an opportunity to imagine grace from God's perspective. If Jonah felt so sad about the loss of the woodbine that he wanted to die, how much more sorrow would be felt by God if it was necessary to destroy children to whom God was both Father and Mother? Their destruction would be even more heartbreaking given that they had finally turned, converted or become attuned with God's will once more and taken responsibility for their sin, growing into a mature faith.

The final lines of the poem suggest that God may not be as vengeful as people – especially, but not only, Jonah – imagine or even want God to be. In fact, the God in *Patience* seems to have learned something from his conversation with Abraham in *Cleanness*. In *Patience*, God points out that it would not have been right to destroy those in Nineveh who were not mentally capable of discerning sin: those without reason, small children, or the very old, or animals. He then asks,

> Why schulde I wrath wyth hem, syþen wyȝes wyl **torne**,
> And cum and cnawe Me for Kyng and My carpe leue?
> [Why should I be angry with them, if those people will **turn**
> And come and know Me for King and believe my word?]
>
> (518–19)

God then explains to Jonah that very few would thrive if he were 'not þole bot as þou' [not any more patient than you are] (521), and suddenly it becomes clear that God's patience towards humans – especially but not only Jonah – has been the subject of the poem. God's patience, God's willingness not to destroy the Ninevites, might seem displeasing to human beings who crave vengeance, but it is a 'nobel poynt' [noble point] (531) as the final line of the poem claims, echoing the first.

Although the first three poems in MS Cotton Nero A.x. differ substantially in tone, I think it is nonetheless possible to construct a coherent theology from them. I'm less sure this endeavour would turn out to be completely satisfying, for it seems to boil down to a reassurance that good Christians shouldn't worry because God only punishes those who are unwilling to bend their will to God's. Some people (e.g. Jonah and the Ninevites) seem to be shown much more patience than others (e.g. the people of Sodom and Gomorrah, including Lot's wife). Rather than try to insist that these poems present a coherent theological approach to grace and punishment, I would like to suggest that they all function like the woodbine by providing analogies designed to help readers imagine grace from God's perspective while reminding those same readers of an awkward truth: any human understanding of that perspective will necessarily be limited. As Augustine asks at the end of the *Confessions* when contemplating the fact that God alone is rest, 'what man can enable the human mind to understand this?'[4] Just

---

[4] Saint Augustine, *Confessions*, trans. Henry Chadwick, Oxford World's Classics (Oxford: Oxford University Press, 1992; Reissued 2008), XVIII.xxxviii[53].

as God uses the woodbine to help Jonah to understand not everything is about him, the three texts all invite us to think about grace from a different perspective partly by helping us to realize the limitations of the textual perspectives they have to offer. Just as *The Office* heightens the viewer's sense of awkwardness and intimacy with its managers by not turning the camera away when we want to look away, the first three poems of MS Cotton Nero A.x. compel readers to engage with discomfort and to realize that it might help to think about it from a different point of view. They also help us to empathize with those figures – the dreamer in *Pearl*, Sarah and Lot's wife in *Cleanness*, and Jonah in *Patience* – who suffer because their intentions are not fully aligned with God's will. This is, according to Brennan, 'what free will is: the ability not to go with the flow. But it is also the means for coming to consciousness of that divine will, the living logic that interweaves. How does one align oneself with the will that interweaves?'[5] That seems to be the question that the manuscript as a whole ultimately asks of its protagonists and readers. While Jonah does ultimately preach to the Ninevites as God asks him to do, he never seems to 'bowe to His bode' in the way that readers might expect. In a story where both a whale and a city turn almost immediately when God asks it of them, Jonah's refusal to bend to God's will offers a remarkable and recognizable reminder that free will is a necessary condition for awkwardness. His failure to understand the burden of care that God must feel as father and mother makes Jonah seem like an adolescent child who begrudges attention given to other siblings. What is both promising and troubling is how differently God reacts to Jonah and Lot's wife. Whereas God turns Lot's wife into salt for a minor transgression, God offers Jonah repeated opportunities to turn his life around even though he doesn't seem to learn anything at all. Unlike the Ninevites, Jonah's faith does not mature: he remains steadfast in his refusal to accept grace offered to others. Perhaps this is what ultimately makes him sympathetic and even hopeful: if someone like Jonah can be granted grace even though he refuses to accept his own worthiness or the worthiness of others, perhaps there's hope for everyone.

---

[5] Teresa Brennan, *The Transmission of Affect* (Ithaca, NY: Cornell University Press, 2004), 156.

6

The games people play: Laughter and belonging in *Sir Gawain and the Green Knight*

The setting and content of *Sir Gawain and the Green Knight* initially make it seem quite different to the preceding three poems in MS Cotton Nero A.x, yet this final poem offers an effective conclusion insofar as it transposes questions associated with awkwardness and grace from the spiritual realm to King Arthur's court. Like *Pearl*, *Cleanness* and *Patience*, it invites readers to recognize that the limits of human understanding make it difficult to accept grace: even the most noble knight might struggle to accept he is worthy of it. *Gawain* achieves this effect by employing mood, *kinesic* imagery, and dialogue to establish a series of awkward situations that seem designed to test the worthiness of Arthur's court even as they ingeniously violate the norms associated with social interaction in courtly society. Sir Gawain responds gracefully to a series of awkward circumstances until the moment when he is offered grace unexpectedly. Then things become very awkward indeed. I would like to explain this paradox by turning to *Fleabag*, which depicts a main character who, like Gawain, resists connecting with those around her because she has been so hurt by the games people play. Inspired in part by the structure of *Fleabag*, this chapter engages with *Gawain* in a recursive manner, turning back to key moments when they seem to offer insight into the present. To ensure that this method does not create undue disorientation, I begin with an overview of *Gawain*'s structure.

Gawain is involved in two interconnected exchange games in *Sir Gawain and the Green Knight*. The first begins in the poem's first Fitt (or part). The Green Knight challenges Arthur's court to a Christmastide game in which he will receive an uncontested axe blow now in exchange for the opportunity to strike an uncontested blow in one year's time. Shamed by the Green Knight's laughter at the awkward silence that greets this challenge, Arthur agrees to enter into a 'forward' [agreement] to play the game himself. Gawain realizes that Arthur's involvement puts the realm in jeopardy, so he steps in and slices the Green Knight's head from his body in front of everyone at the New Year's Feast. If the entirely green knight was not already violating nature's norms, he does so when he picks up his severed head and tells Gawain to meet him in one year's time at the Green Chapel (see Figure 7). The second Fitt creates a sense of atmosphere by describing Gawain's cold and lonely journey to find this mysterious location. Losing hope, he prays to Mary and finds himself at the castle Hautdesert three days before his appointment with the Green Knight. At Hautdesert, Gawain is greeted by a host named Bertilak who tells him the Chapel he seeks is nearby and invites him to stay in warmth and luxury until the day he is appointed to meet the Green Knight. Bertilak suggests they enter into a 'forward' to play a game: Bertilak will exchange what he wins while hunting for whatever Gawain wins while hanging around the castle. Fitt

Figure 7 London, British Library, MS Cotton Nero A.x., fol. 94v. © The British Library Board.

Three describes their exchange game, which gets awkward when Bertilak's wife violates the norms of hospitality by trying to seduce Gawain each day, insisting it would be ungracious of him to violate the norms of courtesy by refusing her. Gawain exchanges one kiss for a deer on day one, two kisses for a boar on day two, and three kisses for a fox on day three. On the final day, Gawain refuses a ring but accepts a girdle, which he does not hand over to his host because Bertilak's wife tells him that its wearer cannot be killed. On the appointed day, Gawain meets the Green Knight at the Green Chapel. After two false starts, the Green Knight finally connects with a blow, nicking Gawain's neck just a little. When Gawain realizes he has been spared, the Green Knight explains that the two games were connected: he is Bertilak, and the only reason he gave Gawain a nick in the neck was that he kept the girdle. Although the Green Knight offers reassuring words about the grace he has shown, Gawain is overcome with shame, and he lashes out in a particularly unchivalrous way.

When Gawain returns to the court to recount his story, he expresses his shame so openly that Arthur himself tries to comfort him. The whole court laughs and decides to adopt the garter as their symbol:

Þe kyng comfortez þe kny3t, and alle þe court als
La3en loude þerat and luflyly acorden
Þat lords and ledes þat longed to þe Table,
Vche burne of þe broþerhede, a bauderyk schulde haue,
A bende abelef hym aboute, of a bry3t grene,
And þat, for sake of þat segge, in swete to were.
[The king comforts the knight, and all the rest of the court
Laughs loudly thereat and **lovingly agrees**
That lords and nobles that belong to the Table,
Each man of the brotherhood, should have a baldrick
Wrapped all about him, of a bright green,
And wear it in honour for that man's sake.]

(2513–18)[1]

Robert Longsworth claims this laughter invites interpretation.[2] I agree, and I would like to focus on two questions. First, does Gawain laugh? I hope that he does, but I fear that he is the only one not laughing. My sense that Gawain does not laugh raises a second question that is specific to *Gawain*'s manuscript context: does Gawain's refusal to go along with it make him more like Lot or Jonah? In other words, does Gawain refuse to fit in or is he unable to experience belonging through shared laughter. I am not going to provide a definitive answer to these questions, but I am going to suggest

---

[1] All citations taken from *The Complete Works of the Pearl Poet*, ed. Malcolm Andrew and Ronald Waldron, with Clifford Peterson, trans. and intro. Casey Finch (Berkeley, CA: University of California Press, 1993). I offer my own translation of the passages in order to focus on the precise diction and imagery; Finch's translation more effectively conveys other aspects of poetic form.
[2] Robert Longsworth, 'Interpretive laughter in Sir Gawain and the Green Knight', *Philological Quarterly* 70.2 (1991): 141–7.

that MS Cotton Nero A.x invites us to ask them and to consider what might be gained by trying to understand the relationship between Gawain's sense of shame and the alienation he feels.

Gawain's penultimate stanza explains why Arthur feels obliged to comfort Gawain in the final stanza. It connects the shame Gawain feels with the grace he has been granted. The poet explains that Gawain 'þat þe grace had geten of his lyue' [through grace had been granted his life] (2480) before explaining that he encountered too many adventures on his return journey to describe. When he arrives at Arthur's court, Gawain focuses exclusively on the part of his adventure related to the exchange of blows. The bob and wheel that end this stanza shift the emphasis from the story's details to its mood:

> Þe chaunce of the chapel, þe chere of þe kny3t,
> Þe luf of þe ladi, þe lace at þe last,
> **Þe nirt in þe nek he naked hem schewed.**
> Þat he la3t for his vnleuté at þe leudes hondes
> > For blame.
> He tened quen he schulde telle;
> He groned for gref and grame.
> **Þe blod in his face con melle,**
> When he hit schulde schewe, for **shame**.
> [The encounter of the chapel, the demeanour of the knight,
> The love of the lady, and finally the garter.
> **The scar in the neck nakedly he showed**
> That he caught for his lack of faith at the knight's hands
> > For blame
> He grieved when he should tell;
> He groaned for grief and sorrow.
> **The blood in his face gathered together,**
> When he it should show, for **shame**.]
>
> (2496–504)

Both the image of Gawain's scar and his blush make me cringe. These images are linked neurologically and thematically, and their impact on the reader relies upon the way our empathic brains simulate instances of emotion.

The reason that I find the description of Gawain's scar hard to stomach can be explained through the function of motor neurons. Christian Keysers explains that most of us have experienced a scenario in which the pain of another makes us 'feel physically unwell. Our experience of viewing pain goes beyond mere understanding, and we literally *feel* the pain, in a vivid and localized fashion'.[3] To help readers experience this, Keysers gives the example of someone cutting a finger, but I find it much more evocative to imagine watching someone scrape hands and knees on the pavement. If you're not bothered by

---

[3] Christian Keysers, *The Empathic Brain: How the Discovery of Mirror Neurons Changes Our Understanding of Human Nature* (Oklahoma, OK: Smashwords, 2011), chap. 7, Kobo.

the image of Gawain's scar as I have presented it, it might help to recall the poem's vivid description of how the Green Knight made the cut that has now become a scar:

> He lyftes ly3tly his lome and let hit doun fayre
> With þe barbe of þe bitte bi þe bare nek.
> Þa3 he homered hertely, hurt hym no more
> Bot snyrt hym on þat syde, þat seuered þe hyde.
> Þe scharp schrank to þe flesche þur3 þe schyre grece,
> Þat þe schene blod ouer his schulderes schot to þe erþe.
> [He lightly lifts his weapon and let it down fair
> And with the barb it bit by the bare neck.
> Though he lunged heartily, he hurt him no more,
> But nicked him on that one side, that severed the skin.
> The blade sunk into to the flesh through the glistening fat,
> That the bright blood over his shoulders shot to the earth.]
>
> (2311-14)

Your empathic response to this event likely depends on how vividly you are able to stimulate it. I have a strong visceral response to this scene because my mind overdoes it a bit and I connect this moment to one I saw on television when I was child. I wasn't initially sure why the highlights package for the National Hockey League games that night included a clip of two players bundling into the Buffalo Sabres' goaltender Clint Malarchuk until I saw blood flowing across the ice. A skate blade had cut into in Malarchuk's neck, partially slicing his carotid artery and jugular vein. When I see the video I have a sense that my own neck has been cut and feel queasiness in my stomach. The incident also prompted a strong empathic response among those who witnessed the event in person: eleven fans fainted, two had heart attacks and three players vomited on the ice.[4] This is what I imagine as the potential outcome of a nick in Gawain's neck. And I suspect that any member of a society in which injuries caused by sharpened blades were commonplace must likewise have had a fairly strong response as they anticipated the blow and read about the initial flow of blood that the poem describes.

While I wouldn't describe my visceral response to Gawain's scar as awkward, it is related to awkwardness because it engages my empathic brain in the same way that Gawain's blush does later in the scene. As Gawain recounts his story, 'Þe blod in his face con melle ... for shame' [The blood in his face gathered together ... for shame] (2503-4). The brain often forms judgements about emotional states through 'direct facial mimicry'.[5] 'If we see someone wince in pain', Keysers writes, 'our face contracts as if in pain. We can then deduce the emotional state of that person by sensing the configuration of our own (mimicked) facial expression'.[6] Both Arthur and the audience deduce Gawain's emotional state from his blush by mimicking it through simulation,

---

[4] 'Zednik's injury brings Malarchuk's own nightmare back to surface', *ESPN.com news services*, 12 February 2008, https://www.espn.com/nhl/news/story?id=3242226.
[5] Keysers, *Empathic Brain*, chap. 6.
[6] Ibid.

whether or not they actually blush. Arthur recognizes Gawain needs comfort, even if he is not exactly sure why. What seems clear is that Gawain's mood does not align with the rest of the court's, and the audience is likely more attuned with him than with the others because the poem invites us to respond to his facial expression. However, that may change for the audience, if not for Gawain, as the court laughs at the end of the text. Laughter is one way that emotions can be shared through 'direct emotional contagion'.[7] Part of me wants to imagine that Gawain joins in, for this scene would then offer a moment in which he becomes realigned with the court. If Gawain does indeed laugh, he would likely even feel happier: one of the more counterintuitive findings of recent neurological research is that 'our bodily state, including our facial expression, can influence our feelings'.[8] If he doesn't join in the laughter, though, he likely feels even more alone at this point than when he set out on his journey to find the Green Chapel. This ending is so effective because it invites readers to judge whether Gawain experiences awkwardness or grace at this moment.

The goaltender Clint Malarchuk's life story makes me suspect that it was probably too soon for Gawain to laugh. Malarchuk miraculously returned to the ice ten days after his neck was cut on the ice, a moment in which he was so certain he was about to die he asked for a priest. He continued to play hockey for a time and then coached. He has now become an advocate for mental health issues, having been diagnosed with post-traumatic stress disorder (PTSD) two decades after his life-changing injury. According to the National Institute of Mental Health, 'Post-traumatic stress disorder is a disorder that develops in some people who have experienced a shocking, scary, or dangerous event.'[9] While fear is a natural response, it also 'triggers many split-second changes in the body to help defend against danger or to avoid it'.[10] PTSD occurs when those changes cause people to feel stress or fright even when they are no longer in danger. My aim here is not to diagnose Gawain with PTSD. He is a character in a poem written in a culture where this was not a known condition. However, our contemporary understanding of this condition might help us to understand why the poem takes what seems to be an odd turn near the end through its expression of Gawain's 'negative thoughts about [him] self or the world' and his 'distorted feelings like guilt and blame'.[11] The final stanzas of *Gawain* invite readers to ask what it will take for Gawain to live on after the experience of trauma – of being so certain was going to die that he asked for a priest.

Fleabag is likewise structured around the question of what it takes for its title character to live on after experiencing trauma. The entire first season is devoted to Fleabag's response to the death of her mother from breast cancer and her best friend and business partner, Boo, who walked into a bike lane thinking she would injure herself to make her boyfriend feel sorry for having slept with someone else. Although she does not disclose a specific diagnosis of her mental state, Fleabag exhibits the distorted sense of both guilt and blame that many people with PTSD experience. Like

[7] Ibid.
[8] Ibid.
[9] 'Post-Traumatic Stress Disorder', *National Institute of Mental Health,* May 2019, https://www.nimh.nih.gov/health/topics/post-traumatic-stress-disorder-ptsd/index.shtml.
[10] Ibid.
[11] Ibid.

Gawain, Fleabag feels ashamed about her actions, and many of her subsequent actions and stories make others (including the audience) blush with shame. She also makes others laugh, though she repeatedly rejects grace or consolation when it is extended to her. The show consistently connects her sense of shame to her sense that she is unworthy. It also suggests that until she can accept what she could or could not have done differently concerning Boo's death, she will not be able to experience a sense of belonging again. Somewhat surprisingly, given the trajectory of the first season, *Fleabag*'s second season explores the possibility that a relationship with a priest might offer Fleabag an opportunity for self-care and connection; Fleabag has a much different experience during her confession to the priest (also known as Hot Priest) than Gawain does, but the result is the same: neither they nor the audience feels entirely satisfied when it is over.[12]

Many critics have questioned the efficacy of the confession that Gawain makes to the priest on the night before he sets out for the Green Chapel. The poem suggests that Gawain confesses all his sins, 'Of þe more and þe mynne, and merci besechez, / And of absolucion he on þe segge calles' [for greater and lesser, and mercy beseeches, / And for absolution he calls on the priest] (1881–2). His confession seems to be pretty effective, for the priest 'asoyled hym surely and sette hym so clene / As domezday schulde haf ben diȝt on þe morn' [absolved him surely and made him so clene / As if judgment day should arrive in the morning] (1883–4). This seems apt since Gawain believes his day of judgement will come the next day. He tries to make the best of things by returning to the castle to sing 'comlych caroles' [comely carols] (1886) with the ladies. Those who see him say they have never seen him so merry. Yet it seems clear he hasn't confessed everything he has done or plans to do, for he retains the girdle that promises to protect him from harm. After he nicks Gawain's neck, the Green Knight explains that he withheld his stroke twice because Gawain dutifully exchanged all that he received during the first two days at Hautdesert castle. He gave a nick in the neck at the third blow because Gawain did not return the girdle he accepted on the final day. That girdle belongs to the Green Knight, whose wife made it, and it was he who directed her to woo Gawain:

> For hit is my wede þat þou werez, þat ilke wouen girdle.
> Myn owen wyf hit þe weued, I wot wel forsoþe.
> Now know I wel þy cosses and þy costs als,
> And þe wowing of my wyf. I wroȝt hit myseluen;
> I sende hir to assay þe, and sothly me þynkkez
> On þe fautlest freke þat euer on fote ȝede.
> [For it is my garment that you wear, that same woven girdle.
> My own wife wove it, I swear to you.
> Now know I well your kisses and your other acts,
> And the wooing of my wife. I wrought it myself;
> I sent her to test you, and truly I think

---

[12] *Fleabag*, season 2, episode 4, directed by Harry Bradbeer, written by Phoebe Waller Bridge, featuring Phoebe Waller-Bridge, Sian Clifford and Olivia Colman, aired, https://app.primevideo.com/detail?gti=amzn1.dv.gti.14b4ffae-8fb4-a5c4-b768-c7be263546b2&territory=CA&ref_=share_ios_season&r=web.

Of you as the most faultless man that ever walked on foot.]

(2361–3)

Furthermore, the Green Knight explains (possibly alluding to *Pearl*) that he has found Gawain is to other men, 'as perle bi þe quite pese is of prys more' [as a pearl that is more valuable than the pea] (2364). Yet he also invites readers to reconsider the efficacy of Gawain's confession when he explains that by keeping the girdle 'yow lakked a lyttel, sir, and lewté yow wonted' [you lacked a little, sir, loyalty you wanted], but he says he blames him the less for that because he did not act out of lust but because 'ȝe lufed your lyf' [you loved your life] (2368). Gawain's response reveals that he agrees with the Green Knight's assessment of his intentions but not his sense of Gawain's worth.

Gawain responds to the revelation that he loved his life with anger and shame. At one level, this seems entirely reasonable. If he learned one thing through the exchange of blows, it was that he was not as ready to give up his life as he wanted to believe he was. The Green Knight's words confirm something Gawain learns when he shrank away, or cringed, when enduring the first blow: he's not who he thought he was. As the Green Knight swings his axe, the poet focuses the reader's attention on Gawain:

> Bot Gawayn on þat giserne glyfte hym bysyde,
> As hit com glydande adoun on glode hym to schende,
> And **schranke** a lytel with þe schulderes for þe scharp yrne.
> [But Gawain caught a sidelong glance of that axe,
> As it came gliding down, shining, him to harm,
> And shrank a little with the shoulders anticipating the sharp iron.]

(2265–7)

The Green Knight berates Gawain at this point for disappointing his expectations. Gawain defends himself by insisting that he will 'stonde þee a strok and start no more / Til þyn ax haue me hitte' [stand you a stroke and start no more / Until your axe has hit me] (2286–7). According to Guillemette Bolens, 'a start is a spontaneous movement, an emotional reaction of the whole body' (156). When Gawain contracts his shoulders, she writes, his start 'blocks the chivalric mechanism he is supposed not only to activate but also to embody' (156). In other words, his body's instinctive response belies his claim that he will willingly endure this blow. Surely anyone who sees his body move in this way as the axe falls can not only empathize but also sympathize with him: most readers know what it feels like to flinch involuntarily and understand the embarrassment it might cause.

Gawain is initially embarrassed that his body's involuntary response betrayed him, but he is even more ashamed when the Green Knight reminds him that he acted voluntarily to preserve his life by taking the girdle. Gawain's embodied response – voluntary and involuntary – to the Green Knight's words is revealing:

> Þat oþer stif mon in study stod a gret whyle,
> So agreued for greme he gryed withinne;
> Alle **þe blode of his brest blende in his face**,
> Þat al he **schrank** for **schome** þat þe schalk talked.

Þe forme worde vpon folde þat þe freke **meled**:
'Corsed worth cowarddyse and couetyse boþe!
In yow is vylany and vyse, þat vertue disstryez.'
[That other strong man stood thoughtfully a great while,
So aggrieved for shame he shuddered within;
All **the blood of his breast rushed to his face**,
That he cringed for shame at what the man said.
The first words upon that field that the man spoke:
'Cursed be cowardice and covetousness both!
In you is villainy and vice, that virtue destroys.']
(2369–75)

Although Gawain stands still, shame makes him shudder internally and his involuntarily blush betrays him in the same way it does later when he tells the story to Arthur: he reveals the discomfort caused by his shame when he blushes and cringes (or shrinks). Whatever they think of his actions, readers are invited to share Gawain's discomfort as they imagine him blushing, shuddering and cringing. These *kinesic* images help (or even compel) readers simulate the emotion Gawain might be feeling. As the stanza reaches to its conclusion, Gawain accuses himself of faulty and false behaviour, but he tries to save face by pleading with the Green Knight: 'Letez me ouertake your wylle / And efte I schal be ware' [Allow me to overcome your (good)will / And ever I shall be grateful] (2387–8). Over the course of roughly a stanza, Gawain's mood has shifted: he goes from expressing anger at the Green Knight for playing games to being angry at himself for not playing them well enough.

Whether he is moved by Gawain's palpable discomfort or his words, the Green Knight anticipates Arthur's actions at the end of *Gawain* by trying to comfort Gawain. He uses laughter as a sign of his good will while he assures Gawain that his confession makes him as pure as one who had never sinned:

Thenn **loȝe** þat other leude and luflyly sayde,
'I halde hit hardily hole, þe harme þat I hade.
Þou art confessed so clene, beknowen of þy mysses,
And hatz þe penaunce apert of þe poynt of myn egge,
I halde þe polysed of þat plyȝt and pured as clene
As þou hadez neuer forfeted syþen þou watz fyrst borne.
[Then **laughed** that other man and lovingly said,
'I hold it hardily healed, the harm hat I had.
You are confessed so clean, having recognized your mistakes,
And have had your penance from the edge of my blade,
I hold you absolved of that plight and purified as cleanly
As if you had never sinned since you were first born.]
(2389–94)

John Burrow has pointed out that instances of laughter like this might actually reflect moments when the character might be smiling rather than laughing, but I think the effect is the same whether one interprets the expression one way or another. In his study of laughter in contemporary social exchanges, Robert Provine 'found that speakers laughed more than their audiences.'[13] In most instances, laughter serves as punctuation, for 'laughter by speakers almost always follows complete statements or questions.'[14] Laughter also usually accompanies innocuous statements rather than jokes. This all reveals that laughter is about relationships rather than simply about humour, so we need to reassess the assumptions we often make about it. Here, the Green Knight's laughter seems designed to reinforce his message to Gawain: you might not be who you thought you were, but it's going to be okay. The problem now is that Gawain is not ready to accept the person he has found himself to be.

When the Green Knight's laughter doesn't assuage Gawain, he tries some other tactics. He offers Gawain reconciliation, saying he and his wife 'schal yow wel acorde, / þat watz your enmy kene' [shall make an accord with you / that was your keen enemy] (2404–5). Gawain rejects the Green Knight's graceful offer, unleashing a violent diatribe against women that lasts a full stanza (2409–28). I'm not going to cite it here because attacks of this kind have been repeated enough in the Middle Ages and beyond. I do not want to apologize for Gawain's outburst, either. I do want to suggest that it may not be as gratuitous as I once thought it was. First, it seems totally out of character. It may not be surprising that Gawain holds latent misogynist views, but the text's emphasis on his manners heightens the sense of incongruity readers might experience when he expresses them so emphatically. Second, Gawain's desire to blame someone else for what has happened to him is exactly what we might expect of someone who has just had a traumatic experience. Having spent quite a bit of time expressing his distorted feelings of guilt, Gawain now shifts to distorted feelings of blame.

Perhaps the Green Knight's laughter triggers Gawain's outburst, for laughter is linked to many aspects of the games people play in *Gawain*. Arthur's court is initially characterized by noise and laughter. Ladies laugh out of enjoyment while simply playing their games: 'Ladies laʒed ful loude þoʒ þay lost haden' [The ladies laughed loudly, though some lost the game] (69–70). But the laughter and sense of camaraderie in Arthur's hall are completely cut off when the Green Knight appears, at which point everyone becomes completely silent. The situation becomes almost unbearably awkward because nobody knows how to react:

> And al stouned at his steuen and ston-stil seten
> In a swoghe sylence þurʒ þe sale riche.
> [And all were stunned at his voice and made still as stones
> In a dead silence throughout the rich room.]

(242–3)

The Green Knight heightens the tension by gesturing with his eyes and beard, intimidating the members of Arthur's court by issuing a silent challenge:

> runischly his rede yʒen he reled aboute,
> Bende his bresed broʒez, blyncande grene,

---

[13] Robert Provine, *Laughter: A Scientific Investigation* (London: Penguin, 2001), chap. 3, Kobo.
[14] Ibid.

Wayued his berde for to wayte quoso wolde ryse.
[Fiercely his red eyes he rolled about,
Arching his shaggy eyebrows, gleaming green,
Wagging his beard waiting to see who would rise.]

(304–6)

Even worse, from their perspective, his laughter at the lack of response causes the King to blush and then act out of shame (which, as Brené Brown insists, is never a good idea):

Wyth þis he laȝes so loude þat þe lorde greued;
Þe blod schot for scham into his schyre face
    And lere;
He wex as wroth as wynde;
So did alle þat þer were.
Þe kyng, as kene bi kynde,
    Þen stod þat stif mon nere ….
[With this he laughs so loud that the lord grieved
The blot shot for shame into his young face
    And fair;
He grew as angry as the wind;
So did all that were there.
The king, daring by nature,
    Then stood near that mighty man….]

(316–22)

The laughter that the Green Knight offers Gawain as a sign of reconciliation at the end of the text echoes the scornful laughter that he used to goad Arthur into a rash response at the beginning of the poem. If Gawain wants someone to blame other than himself, both the Green Knight and Arthur seem like pretty good candidates. After all, Gawain only ends up agreeing to exchange blows with the Green Knight because Arthur was unable gracefully to resolve an awkward situation caused by scornful laughter. Thus, the Green Knight's laughter causes and marks the 'forwarde' into which Gawain enters at the beginning of the poem.

A different sort of laughter marks the 'forwarde' that Gawain makes with his host at Hautdesert, who turns out to be the Green Knight in disguise. After they make their agreement, the poet reveals, 'þay laȝed vchone' [they both laughed] (1113). Laughter characterizes Gawain's visit at Hautdesert, for it is a feature of the banquets he enjoys each night during his stay. It also plays a key role in the wooing scenes that eventually lead Gawain to accept the girdle, so it is possible that he has become averse to laughter associated with women. Before spouting off a bunch of misogynistic claptrap, though, he should have kept in mind that the Green Knight just revealed to him that his wife was wooing Gawain under his instructions. (He will later claim that he was initially sent by Morgan le Fay to frighten Guinevere, though he never says the wooing was part of her plan.)

The wooing scenes that take place in Fitt Three are some of the most awkward in the poem or anywhere in late-medieval literature, and they use laughter to temper

Figure 8 London, British Library, MS Cotton Nero A.x., fol. 129r. © The British Library Board.

the mood. Whereas the Green Knight successfully engages Arthur by putting pressure on his ability to respond gracefully to derisive laughter, the host's wife puts pressure on Gawain's ability to respond gracefully to seductive or at least friendly laughter. The challenge for Gawain, who has a reputation as the most courteous knight in the world, is to resist her advances without offending her. Given what unfolds in Fitt Three, this is not nearly as easy as it sounds.

Having spent his first night in Hautdesert in lavish comfort, Gawain finds himself in a profoundly uncomfortable situation the next morning. He is lying in bed when he hears someone enter the room, close the door and move quickly towards the bed. Here is the response Gawain, most chivalrous of knights, is able to muster: 'þe burne schamed / And layde hym doun lystyly and let as he slepte' [the man blushed / And laid himself down lustily and pretended to be asleep] (1189–90). This does not seem to deter the host's wife, who approaches the bed in a scene that seems to unfold in slow motion (see Figure 8). She comes closer to the bed, casts up the curtains and sits on the side of the bed, gazing at Gawain: 'And lenged þere selly longe to loke quen he wakened' [And waited there a really long time to be there when he would wake up] (1194). Gawain does not know what to do next. He plays for time by pretending he's asleep:

> Þe lede lay lurked a ful longe quyle,
> Compast in his concience to quat þat cace myȝt
> Meue oþer amount. To meruayle hym þoȝt:
> Bot ȝet he sayde in hymself, 'More semly hit were
> To aspye with my spelle in space quat ho wolde.'
> [The man lay still a full long while,
> Thinking in his mind what the circumstances might
> Mean or amount to. To marvel he thought:
> But yet he said to himself: 'It would be more seemly
> To learn through conversation what she wants.']
>
> (1195–9)

Finally, he wakes up, turns towards the woman, and looks at her:

> Þen he wakenede and **wroth and to hir warde torned**
> And vnlouked his yȝe-lyddez and let as hym wondered
> And sayned hym, as bi his saȝe þe sauer to worthe,
>   With hande.
>   With chynne and cheke ful swete,
>   Boþe quit and red in blande,
>   Ful lufly con ho lete
>   Wyth lyppez smal **laȝande** …
> [Then he woke and **twisted and turned toward her**
> And unlocked his eye lids and acted as if surprised
> And crossed himself, as by act he might earn salvation,
>   With his hand.
>   With chin and cheek full sweet,
>   Both white and red mixed together,
>   Full lovely does she speak
>   With small **laughing** lips ….]
>
> (1200–7)

This is another moment where Burrow suggests the laughing lips might refer to a smile rather than an actual laugh, but laughter is not out of the question here, especially since it conforms to a pattern that she and her husband consistently use in conversation with Gawain and others. It seems appropriate that the scene should end with laughter, given the awkward tension here, which is marked by the same twisting and turning in bed that Augustine describes. The scene also resonates in a remarkable way with the opening scene of *Fleabag*, though the precise circumstances are a little different and the gender roles are reversed. Both *Fleabag* and *Gawain* ask the audience an awkward question: what can either say to resolve this situation gracefully? Both moments end with laughter, though the punch lines are quite different.

This exchange and the two subsequent ones are marked by the lady's laughter. They are connected in this way to the initial agreement and the Green Knight's final conversation with Gawain. The lady jokes that Gawain is a careless sleeper and that she will tie him up in bed if they can't come to some kind of agreement, 'Al **laȝande** þe lady lauced þo bourdez' [Al **laughing** the lady told those jokes] (1212). Gawain responds in kind, with light talk and even jokes of his own: 'he bourded aȝein with mony a blyþe **lauȝter**' [he joked again with lighthearted **laughter**] (1217). Then things take a bit of a turn, and the lady says again that she'll keep him captive since she's glad to have him alone to herself. And in case he's not sure what she's implying, she makes it pretty explicit:

Ȝe ar welcum to my cors,
Yowre awen won to wale,
Me behouez of fyne force
Your seruant be, and schale.
[You are welcome to my body,
Your own, won to deal with as you please,
Required by fine force, I am compelled
To be your servant, and I shall.]

(1237–40)

After some further conversation, Gawain thinks he has managed the situation well when she gives him good day 'and wyth a glent **laȝed**' [and with a glint **laughed**] (1290), but she doubles back to say that surely he must grant her a kiss out of courtesy. He complies and then finally gets out of bed.

Their encounters on the second and third day are similar. On the second day, the lady comes to the side of Gawain's bed and 'laȝes' [laughs] (1479) as she begins her seduction and they 'laȝed and laykurd longe' [laughed and amused themselves a while] (1554) before exchanging a second kiss. The lady raises the stakes on the third day, arriving in a very provocative outfit indeed:

Hir þryuen face and hir þrote þrowen al naked,
Hir brest bare before, and bihinde eke.
Ho comez withinne þe chamber dore and closes hit hir after …

[Her healthy face and her throat made all naked,
Her breast bare before, and also behind.
She comes within the chamber door and closes it after her ....]

(1740–2)

It is unclear whether or not medieval readers would have imagined her topless, but it is certainly clear that they would have imagined her less clad than she might have been when greeting her husband's guest in his chamber. She again invites comparisons with Fleabag, who is similarly under-dressed when Hot Priest arrives at her house as she's expecting someone else in Season 2, Episode 5. In Gawain, the lady is clearly having fun with the situation at this point, and she has become more forthright:

Þe lady luflych come **laȝande** swete,
Felle ouer his fayre face and fetly hym kissed.
[The lovely lady came **laughing** sweetly,
Fell over his fair face and elegantly kissed him.]

(1757–8)

As the exchanged continues, Gawain finds himself approaching the situation in which Launcelot finds Galahad in *Monty Python and the Holy Grail*.[15] Faced with a flirtatious woman, Gawain finds himself, like Galahad in Castle Anthrax, facing a peril that seems far too perilous for him to face alone:

With smoþe smylyng and smolt þay smeten into merþe,
Þat al watz blis and bonchef þat breke hem bitwene,
    And wynne.
Þay lauced words gode,
Much wele þen watz þerinne.
Gret perile bitwene hem stod,
Nif Maré of hir knyȝt mynne.
[With smooth and gentle smiling they fell into mirth,
That al was bliss and fortunate that passed between them,
    And blissful,
They exchanged good words,
Much richness then was therein.
Great peril between them stood,
Unless Mary remembers her knight.]

(1763–9)

Whether he shares the lady's mirth out of politeness or as a result of his empathic response, Mary's knight manages to use his skill in love-talking to parry the lady's advances:

---

[15] *Monty Python and the Holy Grail*, directed by Terry Gilliam and Terry Jones (1975; Burbank, CA: Sony Pictures Home Entertainment, 2001), DVD.

> With **luf-la3yng** a lyt he layd hym bysyde
> Alle þe spechez of specialté þat aprange of her mouthe.
> [With **love-laughing** a little he laid beside him
> All the suggestive speeches that sprang from her mouth.]
>
> (1777–8)

He manages to resist her advances while allowing both of them to save face until the moment where she offers him a gift. He refuses her gift of a ring as too rich, but he cannot resist the girdle, which may not seem valuable but does something special: anyone who wears it 'my3t not be slayn' [may not be slain] (1854). Who, after all, would want to give up living when life is filled with so much laughter? It is only later that he realizes what it costs him to accept it: the knowledge that he is not the man he thought he was.

Paradoxically, Gawain finds himself unwilling to accept the grace that the Green Knight offers him in their final encounter because he realizes he should not have accepted the promise that the girdle seemed to offer. He may not laugh with the rest of Arthur's court at the end of the text because he has been taken in before by laughter. He did so much work to fit in with his host and his wife by laughing with them and just going with it, but the sense of belonging he felt with them proved to be false. Can he risk being vulnerable again? Is the laughter at Arthur's court a sign of belonging or is it just as seductive as that he experiences in Hautdesert? Questions like these might be enough for anyone to put up barriers to connection, but Gawain has also been frightened in a way that is life changing: the Green Knight sliced his neck with an axe, and he has to live with the idea that he only survived because the other man chose to show him grace. The Green Knight may have had his reasons for what he did, but the whole situation seems pretty outrageous when considered more carefully. Should Gawain have been willing to give his life for Arthur? Perhaps. But for a game? Perhaps not. How can he live now, knowing what he knows about his own complicity in this exchange, not to mention Arthur's?

Both Fleabag and Gawain resist connecting with those around them because they have been hurt by the games people play. Both *Fleabag* and *Gawain* make it clear that their main characters are also people who feel compelled to play those games. While Gawain does not seem to accept his imperfection at the end *Gawain*, Fleabag does seem to acknowledge imperfection as the human condition in the final episode of Season 1. While she remains fixated on the mistakes she and others have made, she recognizes that the one constant is that people make mistakes. A pencil beside her bed reminds her of a conversation she had with Boo about an eleven-year-old boy who was put in juvenile prison for sticking rubber-ended pencils into the school hamster's bum because 'he liked it when their eyes popped out'.[16] Boo wants to know why they sent him away, since he clearly needed help; anyway, she says 'that's the very reason why they put rubbers on the end of pencils'.[17] Fleabag is surprised: 'To fuck hamsters?' 'No', Boo replies, 'because people make mistakes'.[18] The scene is uncomfortable, producing

---

[16] *Fleabag*, season 1, episode 6, directed by Tim Kirkby and Harry Bradbeer, written by Phoebe Waller Bridge, featuring Phoebe Waller-Bridge, Sian Clifford and Olivia Colman, aired 17 May 2019, 15 September 2016, https://app.primevideo.com/detail?gti=amzn1.dv.gti.14b4ffae-8fb4-a5c4-b768-c7be263546b2&territory=CA&ref_=share_ios_season&r=web.
[17] Ibid.
[18] Ibid.

laughter through several kinds of incongruity. It is also heartbreaking because Boo can no more correct the mistake that led to her death than Fleabag can erase what she did to Boo. Like Gawain, Fleabag seems right both to feel some guilt and to apportion some blame to others. Unlike Gawain, Fleabag recognizes that the rubber isn't on the pencil just to correct mistakes but because the one thing people can know about each other and themselves is that they will make mistakes. Augustine knew that, and so did Boo. The question for Fleabag throughout Season 1 is the same as it is for Gawain at the end of *Gawain*: will they seek connection again even though they know that they are almost certain to be hurt, to hurt others and to hurt themselves?

Ultimately, I think *Fleabag* helps to explain the awkward connection between laughter and loneliness in *Gawain*. While it might be tempting to say that Gawain and Fleabag are awkward individuals because they don't seem to respond in the way others want them to, that seems unhelpful. I think it is more helpful to consider how both texts use awkwardness to transform apparently unique circumstances into recognizable ones. Not everyone will find himself, herself or themselves caught in a game within a game or feeling responsible for causing the death of a friend. But most of us probably know what it feels like to be hurt and confused because mistakes have been made. And most of us also know that it can take time to feel ready to feel like we want to be consoled or to laugh again, especially if we're unwilling to forgive ourselves or others for making mistakes – for being human. It would probably help Gawain if anyone other than him were to take some responsibility for the events which led him to think he was going to die. Having said that, I'm heartened by thinking about the final scene in *Gawain* alongside *Fleabag*. The comfort Arthur offers and the laughter of the court may make Gawain feel even more alone at this particular moment, just as the comfort Fleabag seeks in sex and sardonic humour seems to isolate her. But perhaps, *Fleabag* seems to suggest, it is possible to imagine that gestures of comfort and eruptions of laughter will one day be seen again as opportunities to connect – to commune – with others in a way that is less concerned with fitting in and more with belonging. I do not think that Gawain or Fleabag need to change to make others more comfortable; instead, I think these texts ask us to consider the circumstances in which those who have experienced hurt, loss or trauma might find connection again. They also suggest that laughter offers a nuanced way to understand connection through entrainment, for it can seduce and disgust, and those moments can feel like heaven or like hell. In short, laughter and awkwardness offer Gawain, Fleabag and their audiences a way of exploring the different ways that humans might connect through rather than despite their imperfections.

7

All shall be well: Laughter and belonging in Julian of Norwich's *Revelations of Divine Love*

Like the poems of MS Cotton Nero A.x, Julian of Norwich's *Revelations of Divine Love* insists that it is hard for humans, imperfect as they are, to understand God's grace. Julian's book is the first known to be written in English by a woman, and it is a testament to the time she spent contemplating revelations she witnessed in May 1373, when she was thirty years old. Having suffered from an illness for some time and in fear of immanent death, she suddenly felt free from pain as she experienced a series of sixteen showings, beginning with a vision of blood running down from Jesus's head. Julian spent time throughout the rest of her life reflecting on and writing about her experience. She wrote one version of her *Revelations*, known as the short text, at some point in the 1380s (1382–8) and continued to revise it until completing the long text sometime in the early fifteenth century.[1] The remarkable sophistication exemplified by Julian's book demonstrates her intellectual capacity and her commitment to sharing the meaning of her revelations as fully as possible. The message of love revealed by her experience is the most important thing of all for Julian – more important than her experience of the revelation or even her own identity. When she became an anchorite in 1394 she gave up worldly things, including her given name. She took the name of the Church of St Julian in Norwich, where she lived in an anchorhold, a small room attached to the church building with a small opening that allowed Julian to hear mass and engage in limited conversations with her priest, confessor or other visitors, but not to depart. Julian's life as an anchorite was a fitting embodiment of her spiritual condition as one who was more attuned to God than the world. Whereas Gawain feels alienated among a crowd of people at the end of *Sir Gawain and the Green Knight* because he cannot accept that he is worthy of the grace he is offered, Julian is so secure that she and others are worthy of God's love that she no longer needs to be around other people to experience a profound sense of belonging. Like the author of *Gawain*, Julian uses laughter to explore that sense of belonging.

Knowing others would likely struggle to accept what Julian was telling them about the nature of God's love and the worthiness of others to receive it, she ends her book by writing, 'This boke is begonne by Goddys gyfte and his grace, but it is nott yett

---

[1] Nicholas Watson, 'The Composition of Julian of Norwich's *Revelation of Love*', *Speculum* 68 (1993): 637–83.

performyd as to my syght' (124).² Julian does not think her work will be finished until she conveys to others how God's love feels, and she invites readers to collaborate with her in order to understand her meaning. In this sense, Julian's *Revelations* has a lot in common with Hanna Gadsby's 2020 Netflix special, *Douglas*, which is designed to help the audience understand 'There is beauty in the way that I think'.³ Gadsby develops a sense of collaboration by establishing her audience's expectations at the beginning of the show. She describes the genres and topics that she will cover: observational comedy about Americans, a story about the dog park that includes some needling of the patriarchy, another story about a misdiagnosis, some hate-baiting, a funny lecture, a revelation about her autism, some gear on the anti-vax movement, one Louis C. K. joke, a story about a penguin who may or may not be inside a box and another lecture. She points out that the audience's advance knowledge of the Louis C. K. joke will enhance their pleasure when they recognize that she not only told us that is what would happen but that she predicted we would forget it was coming. The audience thus collaborates in fulfilling the expectations Gadsby sets out. Julian establishes her reader's expectations clearly at the start of her *Revelations*, employs parental and *kinesic* imagery to describe her orientation towards God and worries that one kind of laughter may deprive readers the opportunity to comprehend God's love, which she describes by invoking another kind of laughter.

Before I get into the structure of both texts, I would like to note that Gadsby also provides a helpful way of thinking about why Julian's experience of sixteen revelations might have made her feel more comfortable in an anchorhold than circulating in her society. When Gadsby explains how being on the autism spectrum feels, she uses the following simile: 'Basically it feels like being the only sober person in a room full of drunks, or the other way around. Basically, everyone is operating on a wavelength you can't quite key into.'⁴ She then provides a visual representation of her experience by showing her audience the woman in black in Figure 9. This image would adequately represent Julian's experience as well if the women were not only differentiated from others through her dress but also enclosed in one of the walls. Those who spoke with God tended to stand out, even in the Middle Ages, and this often created a great deal of awkwardness for them and others. Perhaps Julian's encounter with Margery Kempe (another woman who believed she spoke with God and someone to whom I will return in several chapters) in 1416 offered both of them an opportunity to feel on the same wavelength, but these kinds of encounters were few. Speaking with God often makes people feel isolated, largely because it could be so hard to communicate this kind of experience to others. I am not saying that Julian's experience of her revelations is the same as Gadsby's life with autism in a world that privileges neurotypical brains. I *am* saying that both Julian and Gadsby make it clear that they know how difficult it will be to convey their experience to someone who does not share it.

---

[2] All citations to Julian of Norwich come from *The Showings of Julian of Norwich*, ed. Denise N. Baker, Norton Critical Editions (New York: W. W. Norton and Company, 2004).

[3] *Douglas*, written by and featuring Hannah Gadsby, directed by Madeleine Parry, Aired 26 May 2020, https://www.netflix.com/title/81054700?s=i&trkid=13747225.

[4] Ibid.

Figure 9 Giotto di Bondone, *Legend of St Joachim, Meeting at the Golden Gate.* © Mondadori Portfolio/Getty Images.

Entombment in an anchorhold signalled to others that Julian was already dead to this world – that her bodily desires were no longer governing her intentions. Paradoxically, though, Julian consistently associates bodily suffering with spiritual transcendence and, especially, a sense of belonging with God. Prior to receiving her revelations from God, Julian prayed for three things: knowledge of God, bodily sickness and three wounds. When she was afflicted with her serious illness, Julian surrendered her will to God and sought a prolonged death so that she could experience Christ's suffering. As a result of this experience and her subsequent reflections, Julian came to distinguish between three different ways of knowing: bodily sight, ghostly (spiritual) sight and direct access. When she uses the word sight, she really seems to be inviting readers to imagine an appeal to the senses, either bodily or ghostly (spiritual). This becomes clearer when she explains that the pain she felt in her body gave her knowledge of Christ's pain. Thus she learns the spiritual value of compassion by literally suffering with Christ: the Latin prefix *con-* (often modified as *com-*) means together and *passio* means suffering. For Julian, the body can be used to gain a greater sense of attunement with God. As Jessica Barr has pointed out, the revelations themselves are not enough for Julian: they must be supplemented by other forms of knowledge – including bodily experience – to flesh out the truth of God's incarnation as Julian understands it.[5] She acknowledges that embodied experience may be inflected by gender, though not by focusing on this aspect of her own story. Instead, Julian excludes Eve from one story, an erasure that Barr claims has the effect of shifting the blame for the fall from the female body to the human body.[6] She then insists that human salvation depends on another body: Christ's. Julian seems to insist on the possibility that if Christ's wounded body is gendered, it can only be understood as a woman's body that gives birth, nourishes and cares for the corporate Christian body.

Julian also represents God's love for the world by invoking a mother's relationship with her child. One of the remarkable aspects of Julian's writing is that she is able to reconcile her orthodox understanding of the Trinity – a key concept that Nicholas Watson has noted that she employs to inform her hermeneutic concepts – with her view that God is both Mother and Father, which also how God is presented in *Patience*.[7] Julian reassures her readers that '*Alle shalle be welle, and thou shalt see it thy selfe that alle manner thyng shall be welle*' [All shall be well, and you shall see it yourself that all manner of things shall be well] (99) because she trusts God to care for His *and* Her children:

> And than shalle the blysse of oure moderheed [motherhood] in Crist be new to begynne in the joyes of our Fader Gad [God], whych new begynnyng shall last, without end new begynnyng. Thus I understode that all his blessyd chyldren whych be come out of hym by kynde shulde be brought agayne in to hym by grace.
>
> (99)

As she leads up to this revelation, she prays to Christ – not Mary – as if she is a child who has soiled itself and needs to be cleaned: 'My kynd Moder [Mother], my gracyous Moder, my deerworthy Moder, have mercy on me. I have made my selfe foule and unlyke to thee, and I may not nor canne amende it but with thyne helpe and grace' (96). Figuratively, she recognizes her need to be changed and her helplessness to do anything about it herself. While this image might not exactly appeal to the senses, it does engage them. It may evoke the scene from the Luttrell Psalter, for example. Even if it is the expectant mother who prays to Mary in 'The Abbess Delivered by Our Lady', the image's representation of the miracle emphasizes the child's vulnerability and need for care. Julian's imagery also evokes for me memories of what it smells and feels like to clean and change an infant. While it may seem strange to say, the smells associated with changing a diaper don't really trigger disgust for me – though they sometimes did – but feelings of love. During the years in which I was changing diapers, my children's needs seemed endless. Yet the obligation to clean my children when they soiled themselves as infants reminded me that my love for them was unconditional and based solely on their existence in the world. They needed to do nothing more than

---

[5] Jessica Barr, *Willing to Know God: Dreamers and Visionaries in the Later Middle Ages* (Columbus, OH: The Ohio State University Press, 2010).
[6] Ibid.
[7] Nicholas Watson, 'The Trinitarian Hermeneutic in Julian of Norwich's Revelation of Divine Love', in *Julian of Norwich: A Book of Essays*, ed. Sandra J. McEntire, 61–90 (New York: Garland, 1998).

exist for me to love them fully. This is why Julian's imagery speaks so powerfully about her sense of belonging: she believes God feels for her the same way that a mother feels for an infant who has fouled itself. Like a mother, God knows this is just the child's nature. Like a mother, God might get tired over time of cleaning up the child who fouls herself, and God might even be disgusted or annoyed by it, but that will not change the love felt for the child nor the care expressed in cleaning her. The structure of this image, coming as it does through Julian's call to God, extends its metaphor by suggesting that she imagines herself as a child who experiences the unconditional love of a mother willing to care for her most basic needs. Julian's imagery is particularly apt because it implies that she is like an infant (in Latin, one who is unable to speak) in the sense that she cannot seem to find the words that might convey her experience of God's love to others.

Julian's understanding of Christ as a mother allows her to develop her understanding of God's love in several ways. First, she recognizes that a mother's love for the child sometimes leads to situations the child cannot fully understand. She explains that Christ is very much like a mother who lets a child learn for itself while mitigating risk: 'the moder may suffer the chylde to fall some tyme and be dyssesyd [made uncomfortable] on dyverse manner for the one profyte, but she may nevyr suffer that ony manner of perell [peril] come to her chylde for love' (96). It is love that leads the mother to help the child avoid great peril and it is also love that leads the mother to let the child gain some experience of the world by having to endure some discomfort. Christ's love, for Julian, works in the same way. This is Julian's theme. It took more than fifteen years of pondering what seemed to be an embodied experience of showings for her understand them in a spiritual sense,

> And fro [from] the tyme that it was shewde [shown], I desyerde [desired] oftyn tymes to wytt [know] in what was oure Lord's menyng. And xv yere [fifteen years] after and mor I was answeryd in gostly [spiritual] understondyng, seyeng thus, 'What, woldest thou wytt thy Lordes menyng in this thyng? Wytt it wele, love was his menyng. Who shewyth it the? Love. Wherefore [Why] shewyth he it the? For love.
>
> (124)

While this seems like a simple message, Julian recognizes just how difficult, even awkward, it might be for readers to comprehend and accept that they are worthy of this kind of unconditional love.

The power of Julian's parental imagery became clearer to me when I was re-watching Hannah Gadsby's other Netflix special, *Nanette*.[8] There, Gadsby reveals that she did not come out as a lesbian to her grandmother because she was still ashamed of who she was. As she tells it, Gadsby knew she was worthy of her grandmother's acceptance, but she could not feel it in her heart. Having shared her coming-out story as part of her comedy routine, though, she began to recognize

---

[8] *Nanette*, written by and featuring Hannah Gadsby, directed by Madeleine Parry and Jon Olb, aired 19 June 2018, https://www.netflix.com/title/80233611?s=i&trkid=13747225.

that she was stuck in the moment of trauma that it created for her. Ultimately, she reveals that the best part of her coming-out story is that she is now friends with her mother. Her sense of her mother's unconditional love for her comes one day in Target after her mom abruptly told Hannah, 'I'm very proud I raised you kids without religion because, you know, I've raised five children with minds of their own.'[9] She then goes on to say something that has Hannah questioning comedy:

> She said to me, 'The thing I regret is that I raised you as if you were straight. I didn't know any different. I am so sorry. I am so sorry. I knew well before you did that your life was going to be so hard. I knew that, and I wanted more than anything in the world not to be the case. But I now know I made it worse. I made it worse because I wanted you to change because I knew the world wouldn't.'[10]

While Julian suggests that sometimes parents let their children get hurt so they can learn, Gadsby reminds us that sometimes parents hurt their children by trying to help them avoid pain. What really moves Gadsby is that her mother evolved, apologizing for the effect of her behaviour and continuing to offer her love whether or not Gadsby felt worthy of it.

Julian helps readers to get over the awkward implications of her revelation – that they are worthy of God's love – through the *kinesic* imagery of a turning body. Early in the text, she explains that the visions were granted not for her alone but to help others to pay attention to God: 'This vision was shewyd to my understanding, for our Lord wylle have the sowle **turned** truly in to the beholding of hym and generally of all his works' (21). For Julian, as for Richard Kearney, 'the drama of discernment involves an intense act of attention starting at the most basic carnal level and accompanying the movements of imagination, commitment, and humility (which includes the wisdom to learn from initial mistakes and misreadings).'[11] Thus Julian uses the image of turning to God in order to describe the spiritual practice she models throughout her book. She claims that her vision has revealed that heavenly rewards are a product of orientation towards God: 'I saw that when or what tyme that a man or woman be truly **turned** to God, for one day servys and for hys endelesse wylle, he shall have alle these three degrees of blesse' (25). Julian acknowledges that one needs to turn from something else towards God, and that it is not always possible to maintain that ideal orientation over a long period of time. As she describes her initial experiences, she indicates, 'this lastyd [lasted] but a whyle, and I was **turned** and left to my selfe in hevynes and werynes [weariness] of my life and irkenes [irksomeness] of my selfe that unneth [barely] I could have pacience [patience] to lyve' (25). Julian agrees with Augustine that it is possible to turn towards as well as away from God, and she likewise describes the experience of being turned away as sufficiently irksome to ask whether she can go on

---

[9] Ibid.
[10] Ibid.
[11] Thomas Kearney, *Anatheism: Returning to God after God*, Insurrections: Critical Studies in Religion, Politics, and Culture (New York: Columbia University Press, 2010), 47.

living, an experience we have already seen depicted in *Pearl* and *Patience*, and one we will see again later in *Mankind*.

The good news from Julian's perspective, though it may have been a difficult case to make theologically, is that God continues to pay attention even when human beings turn away. She demonstrates this through a vision full of *kinsesic* imagery. The story describes the state of the soul in bodily terms. Having turned away from the path, the person falls and finds himself in need of help:

And anon he fallyth in a slade [ditch] and takyth ful grett sorrow. And than he gronyth and monyth and wallowyth and wryeth, but he may nott ryse nor helpe hym selfe by no manner of weye.
And of all this the most myschefe that I saw hym in was feylyng of comfort, for he culde nott **turne** his face to loke uppe on his loving lorde, which was to hym full nere, in whom is full comfort.

(70)

Julian's imagery appeals to our sense of the body's physical discomfort as well as its orientation in space. The body falls, but the sorrow she describes it feeling comes across much more clearly through the rhyming verbs she uses: gronyth, monyth, wallowyth and wryeth. Engaging the empathic brain, we know what state our bodies are in when the only sounds we can make are groans and moans and the only movements we can make are wallowing and writhing. What is most alarming for her is the sense that the person she describes in her story cannot turn to see God, who is near: he has fallen awkwardly, unable to turn and he needs help to rise (cf. Ecclesiastes 4.10). She is alarmed, though, because, as she says, 'I lokyd alle aboute and beheld, and ferre ne nere ne hye ne lowe I saw to hym no helpe' (70). The person described in Julian's story finds himself in a desperate situation because nobody is around to help. The remarkable thing about Julian's theology is that this may not be an intractable problem, 'for he was **turnyd** fro the beholding of his lorde, but his wylle was kepte in God's syght' (72–3). In other words, though the man cannot turn himself bodily, God sees his will, so all may yet be well. Even if the man finds himself incapable of turning his body, he has hope if he can turn his will towards God.

Later, Julian claims this man's predicament is analogous to her struggle sharing her revelations. Before she describes the sixteenth revelation, which she takes as the conclusion and confirmation of the others, she takes time to describe the feebleness, wretchedness and blindness she felt during her illness, which relented for a time before her body was suddenly afflicted again. This made her mourn for her pain and the lack 'of comforte gostly and bodely' (102–3). Julian once again activates *kinesic* simulation in the reader by describing physical discomfort in order to help readers understand what she feels. She then goes on to describe the experience that eventually led her to understand, like Augustine, that spiritual comfort might come through confession. The scene takes on a double significance, for it both fits at the place in the book as she is telling it chronologically but it also took place initially before she wrote and revised her book. I will cite it in full to show how it is connected, then return to key aspects within it. The episode begins when a religious person, probably a priest or a monk, asks Julian how she is doing following a morning and afternoon of intense religious experience:

> Then cam a relygyous person to me and askyd me how I faryd [fared], and I seyde I had **ravyd** [raved] to day. And he **loght** [laughed] **lowde and inwardly**. And I seyde, 'the crosee [cross] that stode before my feace [face], me thought it bled faste.' And with this worde the person that I spake [spoke] to waxsed [grew] all sad [serious] and merveylyd. And anone [immediately] I was sore ashamyd and astonyd for my rechelesnesse [wretchedness]. And I thought this man takyth sadly the lest [least] worde that I myght sey [say] that sawe no more therof. And when I saw that he toke it so sadly [seriously] and with so grete reverence, I waxsyd [grew] full grettly ashamyd and wolde a bene shryvyn [confessed]. But I wolde telle it to no preste [priest], for I thought, 'How shulde a preste believe me when I, by seaying [saying] I **raved**, I shewed my selfe nott to belyve oure Lorde God?' Nott withstanding, I beleft [believed] hym truly for the tyme that I saw hym, and so was than my wylle and my menyng [purpose] ever for to do without end. But as a fole [fool] I lett it passe oute of my mynde.
>
> (103)

The awkwardness in the passage hinges on a misalignment between what Julian means when she says that she raved and how that is understood first by the man of religion and then by her. The *MED* cites this as the only instance of 'rave(n)' to indicate as 'to experience religious ecstasy; see a vision'. That describes exactly what she had been doing from morning until mid-afternoon on that day in May, but the rest of the exchange suggests this is not what the religious man thinks she has told him. The awkwardness in this passage arises from how hard it is, in the words of Vincent Gillespie, to eff the ineffable. How can words convey something beyond words – an intimate encounter with the divine that seems fully immersive?

As she does elsewhere in the book, Julian responds to this challenge by subtly appealing to embodied responses that figures within the text might create for readers. This begins when Julian establishes this scene as an exchange between two people. Whether or not Julian had this exact exchange with a religious man in May 1373, the passage seems to convey to readers the sense that this scene recounts a genuine encounter. It begins as one would expect a conversation like this to begin, but it does not continue that way. One thing I learned from living in England is that most people do not expect an answer when they open a conversation by saying 'Alright', which they sometimes inflect as a question but just as often end with a full stop. After years of getting this script wrong by answering the question earnestly, I finally learned that no response is actually necessary. An 'alright' in return is acceptable. The news that someone had been raving earlier would be very surprising, and almost certainly unwelcome. I think this script helps to explain the religious man's laughter, which seems to register his surprise that Julian provides him with what seems to be a response that requires further conversation. It is possible to read this exchange in a different way. To rave usually means 'to be or become mad; be in a frenzy, behave foolishly or irrationally' or even to be 'distraught because of love' (*MED*, s.v. 'rave(n)'). So perhaps the religious man is laughing at her because she has just said she's suffered from madness or that he finds her laughable because of her affliction. As Robert Provine writes, 'most of us have, in fact, laughed at social outliers, although', he hastens to add, 'we probably do not consciously choose to act this way'.[12] However we interpret the religious man's laughter, Julian's use of the adverbs 'loudly' and 'inwardly' suggests that she believes his laughter emerged unbidden from his body. By considering his laughter to be involuntary, Julian recognizes something that Provine and his team have only recently shown through their research: since '*most laughter is not a response to jokes or other formal attempts at humor*', we therefore need to re-evaluate 'what laughter signals, when we do it, what it means, and how we should study it'.[13] I think it seems very likely that the religious man's laughter signals his surprise at Julian's response, which he then takes quite earnestly. His laughter may not be entirely appropriate, but that is also revealing: 'Laughter is a potent signal that triggers a strong emotional reaction in those around us, especially if it's inappropriate.'[14] The religious man's laughter signals to Julian that her initial response has been taken in earnest when, from her perspective, it wasn't earnest enough.

Paradoxically, then, the religious man's seemingly inappropriate laughter is a gift because it helps Julian to realize that if she downplays her revelation or defers to masculine authority, she might prevent others from fully sharing in her experience. At this point, she reveals that she thought she saw the cross-bleeding before her. The religious man now grows serious, having regained control over himself. He takes her vision very seriously even though he hasn't seen it, and this makes Julian feel ashamed for initially having downplayed what she saw. She wants to confess, but she worries, 'How shulde a preste believe me when I, by seaying I raved, I shewed my selfe nott to belyve oure Lorde God?' (103). Julian's words here suggest that when she used the word 'raved' she was not describing her religious vision but doubting it, suggesting it was a kind of madness, frenzy or irrational behaviour on her part rather than an experience offered to her by God. And yet, she acknowledges at the end, she did behave foolishly by letting her experience pass out of her mind for a time (103). This passage reveals just how difficult it is for Julian to make sense of the revelations she has had and to share it with others. It reveals just how precise she needs to be about the language she will use so that her revelations induce belief rather than laughter. Or rather, she wants to induce the kind of belief that will lead to the laughter that signifies spiritual joy.

Julian hopes to express her revelations with enough care so that they will convey knowledge about an experience that feels like a different kind of laughter. In her fifth revelation, Julian sees laughter as an embodied sign of both scorn and belonging. When Julian has a vision of Christ scorning the fiend's lack of power, she suddenly knew that he wanted her to see this. That makes her laugh, and it makes others around her laugh, too. In fact, she believes that if all Christians could see this sight, they would laugh too:

---

[12] Robert Provine, *Laughter: A Scientific Investigation* (London: Penguin, 2001), chap. 2, Kobo.
[13] Ibid., chap. 3.
[14] Ibid., chap. 8.

> Also I saw oure Lorde scorning hys malys [malice] and nowghtyng [setting at nought] hys unmyght [un-might], and he wille that we do so. For this sight, I **laght** [laughed] myghtely. And that made them to **lagh** [laugh] that were abowte [about] me, and there **lawchyng** was a lykyng [pleasing] to me. I thought that I wolde [wished] that alle my evyn Crysten [even-Christians] had seen as I saw, then sholde all they a **lawchyd** [lauged] with me. But I saw not Cryst **laghyng** [laughing], but wele I wott [knew] that sight that he shewed me made me for to **laugh**. For I understode that we may **laugh** in comforting of oure selfe and joying in God, for the feend [fiend] is overcome.
>
> (23–4)

The image of contagious laughter spreading to all Christians is a powerful one. It appeals to the readers experience of laughing in a social setting where, according to Provine, 'the contagiousness, perseveration …, and social bonding of laughter … all work to enhance the power of the laugh experience in a communal setting'.[15] Julian transforms that powerful sense of entrainment that readers might have experienced from participating in communal laughter and reveals this is what it feels like to know God's grace. The feeling you get when laughing together with others is, Julian reveals, what it feels like to be in heaven. By contrast, then, it must feel like hell to Gawain if he indeed does not laugh at the end of *Gawain*.

Why isn't Christ laughing? Perhaps Julian is acknowledging the tradition that held Christ did not laugh, or perhaps she wants to distinguish Christ from humans. If laughter was seen, as it often was, as a particularly human attribute, then perhaps it is best to leave Christ out of it. Yet the image is striking because there is a sense in which Christ is somehow separate because he is at rest, being one with God. This provides a compelling analogy for Julian, who worked so diligently in her anchorhold to produce a text that communicates a message of love. Moreover, it does so in a way that generously acknowledges the role that each reader and the community of readers will play in ensuring the text is performed. Like Gadsby's *Douglas*, Julian's text very clearly lays out its expectations, then achieves them, providing readers at least a taste of a beautiful way of knowing through laughter. Like Gadsby, Julian worries that laughter might sometimes impede a sense of connection, as it did when the religious man laughed, so she devoted her life to carefully communicating the revelation of a love that is so joyful it feels like laughing with everyone in the community.

---

[15] Ibid., chap. 7.

8

Too much information? Suggestive diction in 'I have a Gentil Cock'

Recognizing that she and her readers would not always be aligned with each other, Julian of Norwich developed a collaborative approach to what she calls the performance of her work. Other fifteenth-century authors seem to have used this potential for misalignment between text and reader to generate laughter and awkwardness, too. This marks a subtle shift from the approach taken in the texts I have discussed so far, from Augustine's *Confessions* through to the poems of MS Cotton Nero A.x., which evoke an empathic response in the audience by representing scenes in which characters laugh or experience an awkward situation. Many authors prior to the fifteenth century acknowledge the potential for misunderstanding between texts and readers by exploiting the gap between intention and impact to generate irony. Fifteenth-century authors seem to have innovated by generating a sense of awkwardness by creating a misalignment between the text's implied intentions and its impact. For example, 'I have a gentil cok' generates awkwardness and uncomfortable laughter by using diction that seems to share too much information while leaving readers uncertain about what to make of it.

Since this poem is relatively short, I will cite it in full and invite you to reflect on its overall effect as you consider the following questions. First, who is the speaker and what is the tone? Second, what images appear and how are they organized?

I have a gentil° cook,°	*gentle (i.e., of noble birth) / cock*
Crowyt° me day:	*who crows*
He doth° me rysen erly	*makes*
My matyins° for to say.	*morning prayers (2 a.m.)*
I have a gentil cook,	
Comyn he is of gret:°	*great or noble family*
His comb° is of reed° coral,	*crest / red*
His tail is of get.°	*jet*
I have a gentil cock,	
Comen he is of kynde:°	*kin or nature*

His comb is of red coral,	
His tayl° is of inde.°	*tail / indigo*
His legges ben of asor,°	*are like asure*
So gentil and so smale;	
His spores° arn° of silver qwhit	*spurs / are / white*
Into the wortewale.	
His eynyn° arn of cristal,	*eyes*
Loken° all in aumber:	*set / amber*
And every nyght° he perchet° hym	*night / perches*
In myn° ladyis° chaumbyr.°	*My / lady's / chamber*

The speaker isn't named, nor is there any indication of his or her gender identity. While it is possible to read this as medieval fan fiction based on the woman who owns a particularly amorous rooster named Chaunticleer in Chaucer's *Nun's Priest Tale*, I think most readers assume the speaker is male because of the poem's subject matter and the preponderance of male narrators in medieval literature. The speaker is clearly very proud of the cock, defined by the *Middle English Dictionary* as 'the male of the common domestic fowl' or a 'rooster', and four of its five stanzas catalogue the bird's attributes (s.v. 'cok'). The bird's lineage, red crest and black tail are apparently so important to the owner that the second and third stanzas are devoted to conveying the same information twice. Both stanzas use the same metaphor to describe the rooster's crest, which is described as being made of red coral (though red is spelled two different ways in the manuscript). The two stanzas then use slightly different diction to describe the rooster's lineage and tail; in the second stanza, we learn that the bird comes from 'gret', suggesting his lineage is 'of high rank' (*MED*, s.v. 'gret'); in the third stanza, we learn he comes from 'kynde', which is usually translated as 'nature' but can also refer to those of gentle birth (*MED*, s.v. 'kind(e)'). His tail is described as being dark, though the exact colour is unclear insofar as the second stanza describes it as being made of jet (usually a black or dark brown colour) while the third describes it as being made of indigo (a very dark blue). The fourth stanza develops the imagery further, describing the bird's legs as azure and his spurs as silver white. The final stanza caps the poem off by describing the rooster's eyes as crystals set in amber. The final stanza reveals a little more about the cock's nocturnal activities: not only does it wake its owner early, but it also spends each night perched in 'myn ladyis chaumbyr'. Thus this twenty-line poem uses repetition and variation to convey the pride that the speaker, probably a male, has for a cock.

You might have noticed that I have been a little guarded about moving beyond the literal meaning of the poem. You would be right. I have withheld information that suggests this poem was not seen by its medieval audience in the same way that contemporary readers might see it. The one surviving medieval copy of the poem appears in 'a small, neatly written, little songbook' that can be dated to around 1450 (London, British Library MS Sloane 2593) along with a wide variety of other lyrics in English and three in Latin.[1] This manuscript provides some important contextual information about the poem. As you can see from the image I have provided (Figure 10), this poem sits between two others: 'I syng of a mayden' and 'Omnes gentes

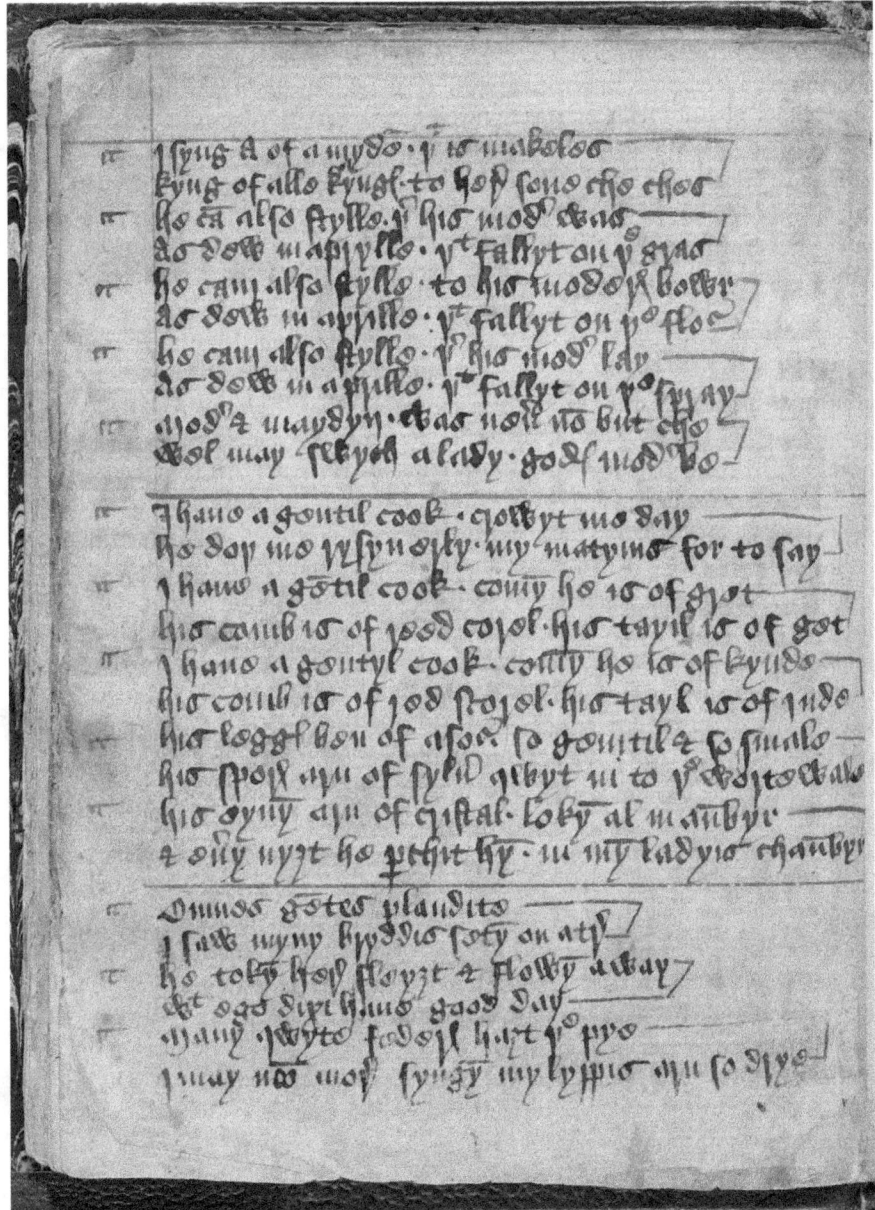

Figure 10 London, British Library, MS Sloane 2593, fol. 10v. © The British Library Board.

[1] Andrew Taylor, 'The Myth of the Minstrel Manuscript', *Speculum*, 66.1 (1991): 43–73, 61.

plaudite'. It is laid out in couplets marked by braces, with half-lines marked by means of a *punctus* (or dot) in the middle of the line. The titles that Rossell Hope Robbins provided for several of the poems in this manuscript reveal that he thought they were meant to be performed by a minstrel, probably in a public place like an inn, tavern or hall. This certainly fits with commonly held views of performance in the Middle Ages, and I will consider a performance like this in the chapter on *Mankind*. 'I have a Gentil Cock' may have been sung at some point, but those who encountered the poem in its only surviving manuscript were almost certainly devout readers. Andrew Taylor argues that MS Sloane 2593 'originated at the Benedictine monastery of Bury St. Edmunds'.[2] This context helps shed light on some of the most suggestive diction in the poem. For instance, the previous poem in the manuscript suggests that readers might interpret 'myn ladyis chaumbyr' in the poem's final stanza as a reference to the Blessed Virgin Mary. Its celebration of the Mother of God begins, 'I synge of a mayden that is makeles' [I sing of a maiden who is without compare (and/or mateless)], then goes on to praise her as a miracle of nature. Mary was important to all medieval Christians, but she was especially venerated at Bury St Edmunds, where a church dedicated to her was built on the precinct around 1125. That church would have been particularly accessible to domestic fowl when it was being rebuilt between 1425 and 1435, years that would have been in living memory at the time this manuscript was being compiled.

The monastic situation of 'I have a Gentle Cock' also suggests that this is not just any poem about a rooster. First, the cockcrow was particularly important for monks who followed the Rule of St Benedict, as they did at Bury St Edmunds. Benedictine monks, like most other monks, needed to wake in the eighth hour of the night – around 2 am in medieval England, depending on the season – to say Matins. The opening stanza reminds readers that the cock was held to be responsible for waking Monks partway through the night so they could observe their duty. This role is acknowledged in texts like the Aberdeen Bestiary, which asserts that 'at the cockcrow the devout of mind rise eagerly to pray, able once again to read the office'.[3] While the Monks at Bury St Edmund's may not have known this particular bestiary, its exploration of the rooster's significance reveals a second reason why cocks might have been held by monks to have a certain importance. After conveying the received belief that the rooster's ability to tell time reveals its intelligence, the Bestiary compares them to preachers: 'The Cock gets its understanding, says Gregory, so that it can first dispel the night-time hours, then at last utter the cry that awakes, in the same way that a holy preacher first considers the circumstances of his congregation, and only then develops a preaching style suitable for instructing them.'[4] Furthermore, the Bestiary asserts, good preachers behave like cocks while bad ones do not, for 'they have learned how to seek the good of souls, yet they apply their minds entirely to those things which relate to the pleasures of the flesh'.[5] In other words, those who know how to care for souls but devote their attention to bodily pleasure deserve special scorn.

---

[2] Ibid., 52.
[3] https://www.abdn.ac.uk/bestiary/ms24/f39r.
[4] Ibid.
[5] Ibid.

Would those responsible for the creation, compilation and circulation of 'I have a Gentil Cock' at Bury St Edmunds – the poem's author, scribe and readers – deserve praise or scorn in the eyes of the Bestiary's author? While I have claimed so far this poem may be read devoutly, you may have noticed that it is hard to read much of the poem, or to think about it for very long, without sensing that it is not about a rooster at all. Is this the author's intention, or does the fault lie with readers who, in the words of the Bestiary, 'apply their minds entirely to those things which relate to the pleasures of the flesh'? One reason that it is awkward to talk about this poem is it is difficult to tell whether or not the author would have realized that it seems to spend five stanzas describing a man's anatomy. Although the poem seems sexually suggestive from beginning to end – *especially* at the beginning and end – it is possible that fifteenth-century readers would not have recognized the sexual connotations that modern readers tend to see. The *Middle English Dictionary* and the *Oxford English Dictionary* have very few medieval examples where the word 'cok' is associated with the word penis. Both occur in compounds: 'pil-cok' and 'fide-cok'. The problem with relying on these sources in this case (I rely on them extensively throughout the book, so I don't want to impugn their authority) is that sexual innuendo from the past can be hard to identify. The *OED*'s entry on the use of the word cock in slang preserves a circumlocutory note that explains that this sometimes has to do with ideas that previous generations had about what was words are acceptable: '*N.E.D.* (1891) remarks: "The current name among the people, but *pudoris causa* [=for reasons of modesty], not admissible in polite speech or literature; in scientific language the Latin is used [i.e., the word *penis*]."' I am not trying to claim that dictionary editors did not recognize that medieval readers knew about sex. I am saying that later generations often use their own assumptions about what is acceptable or not as a starting point for interpreting texts created in the past, especially when their meaning is ambiguous. This can create an awkward relationship between the text and reader: sometimes later readers perceive innuendo that was never intended; at other times, later readers fail or refuse to see things that are obvious because they make us so uncomfortable.

We have a great deal of evidence that medieval people knew about sex and enjoyed putting audiences in the awkward position of deciding whether they were reading extended innuendo. Riddle 45 of the Exeter Book, which was compiled around four hundred years before 'I have a Gentil Cock', offers a good example:

> Something's swelling over in the corner,
> Rising and standing, raising its cover.
> A haughty bride grabbed that boneless thing
> With her hands, and the prince's daughter
> Slipped that swelling thing under a cloth.[6]

If one answers 'dough', others might scorn the reader's naivety; if one answers 'penis', others might claim the reader has a dirty mind. Likewise, 'I have a Gentil Cok' leaves

---

[6] 'Riddle 45', in *The Broadview Anthology of British Literature, Vol. 1: The Medieval Period*, 3rd edn. (Toronto, ON: Broadview Press, 2015), 58.

readers wondering whether the speaker is a man obsessed with his anatomy or whether this impression is a product of their own assumptions. In other words, texts like this seem designed to create discomfort by capitalizing on the gap between intention and impact. This gap is always there, and the assumptions we make about other people, especially those who lived in the past, can potentially widen that gap. Contemporary readers almost certainly perceive the sexual innuendo in both texts but may also feel reluctant attributing it to texts written by people who lived many generations ago and were often thought to lead pious lives.

I believe that 'I have a gentil Cock' uses the gap between intention and impact to create a sense of awkwardness in its audience. Reading the word cock as it is often used today transforms the first stanza into a description of a man who is woken each night with an erection. Every monk would have been prepared to handle something like this, though they would have understood this phenomenon as the consequence of unsatiated bodily desire that would eventually need to be quelled. Judd Apatow's *The 40 Year-Old Virgin* plays on the idea that nocturnal arousal is a sign of sexual desire in its opening scene. The scene is almost painful to watch partly because what Andy (played by Steve Carrell) really desires is a chance to empty his bladder. Both 'I have a Gentil Cock' and *The 40 Year-Old Virgin* use their opening scenes to create discomfort by revealing something that is usually kept private: the body is not always subject to the will; sometimes its responses are involuntary. Reading 'I have a Gentil Cock' as sexual innuendo helps to explain the repetition in stanzas two and three, which emphasize the fact that what the speaker is describing has a red crest and is darkly coloured at the other end. Stanza four seems to lead readers away from this line of thought (though it may just be that I don't recognize the innuendo here), but the final image might be the most suggestive of all. Though I acknowledged above that 'myn ladyis chaumbyr' might refer to a chapel or church dedicated to the Blessed Virgin Mary, the word 'chaumbyr' does not quite fit this reading. Chaucer uses this word in *The Wife of Bath's Prologue* for a very different purpose when the wife describes her sexual proclivity by indicating that she had difficulty withdrawing her 'chaumbre of Venus from a good felawe'.[7] This poem literally reaches its climax with the detail that every night the 'gentil cock' perches himself in 'myn ladyis chaumbyr'. If we assume that both these terms are euphemisms, then this poem reaches its climax in the same place as *The 40 Year-Old Virgin*. This seems appropriate since this aspect of the poem seems so closely attuned with the juvenile approach to sexuality espoused by most of the men in Apatow's film. Reading it this way almost certainly confirms my initial assumption that the speaker is male.

Is this poem telling us that its speaker has sex every night with his lady? I hope to have shown that there is good reason to think that it is. I also think there is good reason to think that this was probably not a reflection of the author's lived experience and almost certainly not a reflection of those who encountered the text at Bury St Edmunds. I think we are right to feel discomfort about the idea that this poem may have reflected

---

[7] Geoffrey Chaucer, *The Wife of Bath's Prologue and Tale*, in *The Riverside Chaucer*, 3rd edn., gen. ed. Larry D. Benson (Boston, MA: Houghton Mifflin, 1987), III.618.

one or more monk's desires, but I also believe that we can leverage the awkwardness we feel about this poem in order to develop a more nuanced understanding of medieval attitudes about sex and maybe even the relationship between religious and secular lyrics. On the one hand, I think it helps us to explain why a monk might have compiled it. After all, this poem is not really that riveting as an ode to a rooster, but it takes on new life if the rooster represents a monk's fantasy, combining as it does the impossible goals of becoming an ideal preacher and of enjoying sexual experience. What could an abbot say if he found this poem? He would find himself in the awkward situation I have been describing throughout much of this chapter, forced to decide whether he wants to open himself to the accusation that he is reading something into a poem that connotes but never denotes sex. Our discomfort with this poem reminds us that it is possible, even vital, to imagine that medieval people, including those pursuing devout vocations, might have found it especially awkward to talk about sex openly. Their comfort level likely varied a great deal depending on their circumstances: could they know others' intentions or the impact they would have on others? Was what they were sharing normally kept private? Were they free to express their desires? In other words, while medieval people probably held different beliefs from our own and seem to come from a world that can seem at times more licentious and more chaste than our own, they also challenge our assumptions about previous generations and even the relationship between secular and spiritual concerns. I am not trying to suggest that attitudes towards sex were better or worse in the Middle Ages. I am suggesting that sexual innuendo generated awkwardness and laughter for the same reasons then as it does now: 'sex and sexual behaviour' were 'a natural breeding ground for humour' because they 'are freighted with so many norms and stereotypes'.[8] Acknowledging the awkwardness and uncomfortable laughter elicited by a poem like 'I have a Gentil Cock' can draw our attention to the many levels of norms and stereotypes that it may or may not be violating. It might also help us to become more attuned to the way that other fifteenth-century texts exploit the gap between intention and impact to generate laughter and awkwardness as well as and sometimes instead of irony.

---

[8] Noël Carroll, *Humour: A Very Short Introduction* (Oxford: Oxford University Press, 2014), chap. 1, Kobo.

9

Does this stress make me look fat? Awkward questions in Thomas Hoccleve's *La Male Regle*

At one point in Thomas Hoccleve's first pseudo-autobiographical poem, *La Male Regle* (1405), the speaker reveals that he likely would have blushed to hear someone recite a poem like 'I have a Gentil Cock' aloud. Nonetheless, *La Male Regle* is like 'I have a Gentil Cock' in that it creates discomfort by providing 'too much information' about various aspects of the speaker's life and his needs. In this sense, *La Male Regle* might be understood as a fifteenth-century version of *Fleabag*. Both reveal the less glamorous side of living in London, albeit six centuries apart. Phoebe Waller-Bridge draws from her life experiences in her writing and portrayal of Fleabag, though *Fleabag* does not provide unmediated access to her life. The same holds true for Hoccleve's *La Male Regle*, which it is about a Privy Seal clerk who is identified as Hoccleve by name (351).[1] Both texts feature a wry, self-deprecating narrator who regularly addresses the audience directly. Both texts ask awkward questions of their narrators and the audience to explore the possibility that, in Adam Kotsko's words, 'some social orders […] actually *produce* certain forms of awkward behavior'.[2] Kotsko focuses this part of his argument on the workplace, but *Fleabag* and *La Male Regle* both explore other aspects of social life as well: financial insecurity, communal meals, sex and flattery. By so doing, both texts reinforce a theme central to Augustine and Brené Brown: attempting to go along with certain social norms in order to fit in can often impede opportunities to experience belonging.

Fleabag and *La Male Regle* connect financial instability to 'grief and bisy smert cotidian [anxious daily pain]' (25). Both texts acknowledge that the 'misreule' or lack of regulation of the protagonists may have something to do with their situations, so neither text makes a strong case that they will manage funds especially well. Nonetheless, both texts also invite us to attend the awkwardness that so frequently arises from the need to ask for money. In Season 1, Episode 1, Fleabag applies for a loan from a bank that has recently faced a sexual harassment suit. Having run from the bus to avoid being late, she finds herself in some discomfort at the beginning of the interview. She is further discomfited when the bank manager (played by Hugh Dennis) tells her he finds her application funny. (Spoiler

---

[1] All citations to *La Male Regle* are from Thomas Hoccleve, *'My Compleinte' and Other Poems*, ed. Roger Ellis, Exeter Medieval Texts and Studies, 64–78 (Exeter: University of Exeter Press, 2001).
[2] Adam Kotsko, *Awkwardness: An Essay* (Ropley: Zero Books, 2010), 26.

alert: in the last episode of Season 1, the audience learns this is because she indicated she was seeking the loan to fund a café for guinea pigs rather than the guinea-pig-themed café that she actually runs.) The situation becomes more uncomfortable when he offers her water: she declines, then accepts, but he ignores her. He returns to the application and then says there are 'one or two bits or pieces I'm going to need to see some more of'.³ At this point, Fleabag lifts her jumper over her head to reveal her bra. It is not entirely clear whether she is responding to what she takes to be a suggestion or whether she thought she had a top on, as she tells the manager when he indicates 'that kind of thing won't get you very far here anymore'.⁴ She insists it was a genuine accident and says, 'I'm not trying to shag you. Look at yourself!'⁵ He asks her to leave and the encounter deteriorates into an exchange of insults. She then meets her sister, Claire (played by Sian Clifford), at a lecture where she reveals that she is wearing the top that her sister 'lost' years ago. Fleabag then turns to the camera and claims, 'The only thing harder than having to tell your super high-powered perfect anorexic rich super sister that you've run out of money is having to ask her to bail you out.'⁶ She tries to fortify herself to ask several more times before deciding against it when Claire asks, 'Do you have to borrow money?'⁷

At the end of *La Male Regle*, the reader finds out the whole text has been a petition for funds. It addresses the realm's Treasurer, Lord Furnival, by name to request a token or two of kindness in the form of ten pounds that is owed to him as part of his annuity for work done in the Privy Seal:

> Lo, lat my lord the Fourneval, I preye,
> My noble lord þat now is tresoreer,
> From thyn hynesse° haue a tokne or tweye　　　*greatness*
> To paie me þat due is for this yeer
> Of my yearly x li.° in th'eschequeer°,　　　*ten pounds / the Exchequer*
> Nat but° for Michel° terme þat was last.　　　*Only / Michaelmas*
> I dar nat speke a word of ferne yeer,°　　　*previous years*
> So is my spir[i]t simple and sore agast.°　　　*fearful*
> 　　　　　　　　　　　　　　　　　(417–25)

This kind of thing made early critics – including Hoccleve's early editor, Frederick Furnivall – very uncomfortable, and the way that this stanza causes discomfort merits further analysis. One reason is obvious: Hoccleve has not missed one payment but has apparently not been paid prior to this as well (this happened to Privy Seal Clerks on a regular basis). While the stanza literally says that he is too simple and fearful to ask for the other money that is owed to him, its subtext is that it is shameful that the Clerks keep

---

³ *Fleabag*, season 1, episode 1, directed by Tim Kirkby and Harry Bradbeer, written by Phoebe Waller Bridge, featuring Phoebe Waller-Bridge, Sian Clifford and Olivia Colman, aired 15 September 2016, https://app.primevideo.com/detail?gti=amzn1.dv.gti.14b4ffae-8fb4-a5c4-b768-c7be263546b2&territory=CA&ref_=share_ios_season&r=web.
⁴ Ibid.
⁵ Ibid.
⁶ Ibid.
⁷ Ibid.

having to ask for money that is rightfully theirs. The second potentially awkward element in this address may be less apparent to English-speakers today (unless you have read the chapter on *Cleanness*). Hoccleve risks coming across as overly familiar by addressing the Lord treasurer by using the second-person singular pronoun. As in other European languages, the singular form of the pronoun (thee, thow, thyne) is used in Middle English to express intimacy, informality or to address those of lower status. Hoccleve and Furnivall almost certainly knew each other by name, and they may well have used this more intimate form of address when speaking to each other in person. However, this poem is not an intimate conversation between the two men (it is far easier to make the case this poem is an intimate conversation between Hoccleve and the reader). Nor is this the kind of petition Hoccleve would have made were he formally requesting his salary. Instead, it is a parody of the formal procedures a Privy Seal Clerk might use to request payments that had been withheld. Hoccleve's use of the second-person singular is a violation of formal norms that is analogous to the moment when Fleabag lifts her jumper in her interview with the bank manager. Inadvertent or not, both moves seem presumptuous.

Like Fleabag, Hoccleve also seems to dig himself deeper even when he's ostensibly trying to be polite. Worrying that Furnivall might think he is greedy when asking for his annuity, he insists that he does not want 'to be seen importune' (425). He then suggests the system is corrupt when he notes that 'the shamelees crauour' [craver] has been rewarded ahead of him. As he ends his pitch in the final stanza, he complains that because he is likely to 'sterue' [die] (444) if he does not receive his annuity, it will shame Furnivall's magnificence to refuse the request. This may indicate that Furnivall could become like a God by showing grace, for it calls to mind the poem's appeal to Health, where Hoccleve asks to be shown 'thy mercy and thy grace,' asserting that 'it sit a god been of his grace free' (406–7). The appeal also connects the end of the poem to the beginning, which addresses the 'Eerthely god ... thow helthe' (8). These lines invoke Augustine's appeal to God's mercy at the beginning of the *Confessions*, but *La Male Regle* seems to undermine the allusion because the poem ends not by seeking rest in God but with his request for money from the Treasurer. This request is all the more awkward because Hoccleve's early audience would have known that Furnivall had neither the money nor the freedom to pay him, since there was a profound shortage of funds in the first decade of Lancastrian rule.

La Male Regle is no more designed to make a case that Hoccleve deserves his annuity than *Fleabag* makes a case that Phoebe Waller-Bridge deserves a loan for a guinea-pig café (let alone a café for guinea pigs). Instead, they invite readers to consider what it means to be worthy – of money, certainly, but also of a sense of belonging. Both texts do this by challenging readers with protagonists who repeatedly turn away from reason. Hoccleve blames his youth for his indiscretion, using *kinesic* imagery that echoes Augustine's account of his own mis-spent youth:

> O yowthe, allas, why wilt thow nat **enclyne**
> And vnto reuled resoun **bowe** thee,
> Syn resoun is the verray streighte lyne° *line*
> þat ledith folk unto felicitee?
>
> (69–72)

Hoccleve stresses the fact that 'willfully fro reson me withdrawe' (102). He plays on the multiple meanings of 'enclyne' as he admits that his youth made him unwilling to incline or bow to reason, but he 'was **enclyned**' (125) to go to the tavern when he saw 'The outward signe of Bachus' (121). He keeps going, even though he seems to know he's going too far. By paying attention to the syllables that are stressed in the following passage, it is possible to see how they emphasize the speaker's awkwardness metrically:

> I dare nat telle how þat the fresh repeir
> Of Venus femel lusty children deer
> Þat **so good**ly, **so shap**ly **wer**, and **feir**,
> And **so ples**ant of **port** and **of** ma**neer**e
> And feede cowden al a world with cheere,
> And **of atyr passing**ly **wel** byse**ye**,
> At Poules Heed me maden ofte appeere,
> To talk of mirthe and to disporte and pley.
>
> (137–44)

The unusual stress in two key lines enhances the sense that Hoccleve is moving beyond the line of reason, allowing readers to register awkwardness physically through our sense of rhythm. I have used bold to indicate the stressed syllables, which emphasize the intensifier **so** along with the following syllable in a way that seems sarcastic: these women are '**so good**ly, **so shap**ly' and '**so ples**ant' in the same way that someone's ex-partner might be '**so hap**py' to meet the new partner. This pattern continues in the primary and secondary stress in 'passyngly', which creates a situation where there are three consecutive stressed syllables in the line. Thus Hoccleve reinforces the idea that he turns away from reason by appearing at the Paul's Head tavern to see women by turning away from the line of reason metrically, varying the stress unusually in a decasyllabic line that Nicholas Myklebust has shown is remarkably consistent.[8] This rhythmic production of an awkward mood does not have an exact correlation in *Fleabag*, which achieves a similar effect through other techniques associated with its medium: it regularly creates the sense of awkwardness through smash cuts and scenes that end more abruptly than expected or seem to go on too long.

At a structural level, both *Fleabag* and *La Male Regle* use awkwardness – or wrongwardness – as an organizing principle by going too far or not far enough. Fleabag establishes a kind of conspiratorial intimacy between herself and the audience by addressing the camera directly with her dialogue and facial expressions. Eye rolls, raised eyebrows and asides shape the audience's response by instigating an empathic response: when she raises her eyebrows, I simulate that process and have a pretty good idea about what Fleabag is feeling, whether I sympathize with her or not. Hoccleve does not use his face in this way in *La Male Regle* (though he does in the *Series*, as I shall show in the next chapter), but he does provide extensive commentary on his circumstances as if it is an aside. Like Fleabag, who regularly reveals intimate information or apologizes for

---

[8] Nicholas Myklebust, 'Historicizing Hoccleve's Metre', in *Thomas Hoccleve: New Approaches*, ed. Jenni Nuttall and David Watt, 25-46 (Cambridge: D.S. Brewer, 2022).

having gone too far in some way, Hoccleve keeps on digressing into comments about the way he now feels about his behaviour before he calls himself back to the main line he is trying to maintain through phrases like 'Now wole I torne ageyn to my sentence' (160), 'no force of al this' (305) and 'but to my purpos' (337). He ends a particularly moving passage by asking, 'Ey, what is me, þat to myself thus longe / Clappid haue I?' (393–4). He is essentially asking, 'What is wrong with me that I've jabbered away to myself so long?' Remember, though, this is a decision: Hoccleve is not actually turning back from jabbering away to himself but representing himself doing just that in order to show the 'misrule or misregulation of T. Hoccleve,' as the manuscript heading for the poem indicates. *La Male Regle* and *Fleabag* both use their structure and content to convey what it feels like for those who are not inclined to follow the straight line of reason in the way they experience their relationship with others and themselves. What they both reveal is a profound sense of shame in the way that Brené Brown defines it 'as the intensely painful feeling or experience of believing that we are flawed and therefore unworthy of love and belonging – something we've experienced, done, or failed to do makes us unworthy of connection'.[9] Even the structure of *La Male Regle* and *Fleabag* suggests Hoccleve and Fleabag are unwilling to accept they are worthy of the belonging they seek.

Both Hoccleve and Waller-Bridge reinforce Brown's argument that trying to fit in can impede opportunities for belonging. Drawn in by the beautiful women described a couple of paragraphs ago, Hoccleve goes to the Paul's Head tavern in order 'To talke of mirthe and to disporte and pleye' (144). In other words, he goes to find connection with others through conversation and conviviality. Elsewhere, Hoccleve uses the word 'communing' to describe this kind of sociability, and it is not hard to see how his consumption of 'swet wyn' (145) and 'wafres thikke' (146) might transform his experience in the tavern into a kind of secular communion. But he is also trying to assuage the emptiness he describes experiencing in his current state. He recalls that when he was healthy he felt 'farsed [stuffed] ... with heart's gladnesse' (13), but 'now my body empti is, and bare/of ioie' [joy] (14–15). If it is full, he laments, it is full of 'seekly heuynesse' (15). In other words, he was once full of happiness, but now he feels empty because he is full of grief, just like Fleabag in Season 1. The one advantage, he notes, is that now he can tell 'feeste fro penauce' [feasting from fasting] (23), whereas he did not really understand the distinction before. A clear indication of his 'misreule' occurs when reason bids him 'To ete and drynke in tyme attemprely [moderately]' (106), and he turns away again, doing both 'outrageously,/And out of tyme' (109–10). He uses a lovely little bit of personification to describe how he has been over-indulging for twenty years, explaining that 'Excesse at borde hath leyd his knyf with me' (112). He claims to practise 'repleet abstinence' (113), but that means he only abstains when he is full, and he blames his body, his 'greedy mowth' (114) and 'hondes two' (115), for overpowering his reason. Hoccleve represents eating and a lack of health as a kind of vicious circle. Like Algernon in Oscar Wilde's *The Importance of Being Earnest*, he

---

[9] Brené Brown, 'shame v. guilt', *Brené Brown (blog)*, 14 January 2013, https://brenebrown.com/blog/2013/01/14/shame-v-guilt/#:~:text=I%20define%20shame%20as%20the,makes%20us%20unworthy%20of%20connection.

eats when he is unhappy. Yet Hoccleve's eating also seems to cause unhappiness. Overeating does not provide the sense of fulfilment he hopes it will but only makes him feel more uncomfortable in and about his body. I can certainly sympathize with that.

Food is also unfulfilling in *Fleabag*. The characters share a number of meals together, and these scenes invoke the idea of communion – especially since they are joined at one of the meals by a hot priest who insists on keeping the wine flowing. Yet the knowledge that meals often create a sense of communal connection seems to heighten the sense of awkwardness *Fleabag* establishes because almost all the meals consist of misalignments between people. Sometimes this is a result of misunderstandings, but sometimes it is deliberate. The way characters treat food in general and at these meals is often revealing. When Fleabag's café is not completely out of food in Season 1, she overcharges for what she does have available. When she is tricked into serving drinks at her godmother's 'Sexhibition', she is accused of causing a scene when she drops a tray at a key moment. The claim that her sister is anorexic may well be true, but it also reveals Fleabag's sense that Claire will not accept what Fleabag has to offer her in an emotional or culinary sense because she wants to maintain a sense of distance and control. This changes to some extent in Season 2, especially when Fleabag begins developing her friendship with Hot Priest over drinks (from tea to G & T), and this is largely related to her increasing willingness to be vulnerable.

Both *La Male Regle* and *Fleabag* reveal that sex can be awkward because it seems to promise connection but can sometimes create a profound sense of isolation. Fleabag reveals that she thinks about sex all the time. She says, 'I'm not obsessed with sex, I just can't stop thinking about it: the performance of it, the awkwardness of it, the drama of it, the moment you realize someone wants your body. Not so much the feeling of it.'[10] In Season 1 Fleabag is very much concerned with her desirability and less with her own desires. After all, she is better at satisfying most of her desires than any of the men whom she encounters. What she cannot satisfy by herself is her desire to feel wanted. This shapes almost every aspect of her life, and it often compounds the shame she feels. Hoccleve, in contrast, feels unable to fit in with others because he feels ashamed even talking about sex, let alone having it. When it comes up in conversation at the tavern, he demurs:

> Of loues aart yit touched I no deel.
> I cowed nat, and eek° it was no neede.   *also*
> Had I a kus,° I was content ful weel,   *kiss*
> Bettre than I wolde han be° with the deede.   *would have been*
> Theron can I but small, it is no dreede.
> Whan þat men speke of it in my presence
> **For shame I wexe as reed** as is the gleede.°   *glowing coal*
>
> (153–9)

Often in *La Male Regle*, Hoccleve seems to go too far. Here, he feels ashamed for not wanting to go far enough. Whereas Augustine avoids this kind of shame in the

---

[10] *Fleabag*, season 1, episode 2.

Confessions by bragging about things he hasn't done, Hoccleve experiences shame because he does not try to claim he is more experienced than he is. He suggests he would have been embarrassed to hear Augustine speak the way he did or even to hear a poem like 'I have a Gentil Cock' recited aloud. Moreover, he admits he's more content with a kiss than he would have been with sex since he knows so little about it. Like Fleabag, he seems more interested in feeling like someone else wants him than in sex itself, but this knowledge does not seem to mitigate the shame he feels, and his blush prompts an empathic response that asks readers to decide whether they are embarrassed with him or for him. Either way, the scene both expresses his sense of isolation and puts readers in the awkward position of feeling discomfort about a situation that would, in most circumstances, be totally acceptable. There are very few situations in which we feel less awkward when someone starts bragging about their sexual experiences in a tavern.

Flattery might seem to offer a way of avoiding awkwardness in both texts, and both protagonists are susceptible to it, but it often leads to a greater sense of isolation in the end – especially since the flatterer is more interested in the concept of fitting in than belonging. Fleabag experiences this through her relationship with Arsehole guy that runs through Season 1. While she is flattered to have the attention of such a beautiful man, it turns out that he is really using her as a mirror to reflect on himself and (spoiler alert) another relationship. Hoccleve describes the pleasure he takes from being recognized by tavern-keepers and cooks and being called 'maister' by the boatmen on the Thames. His decline has allowed him to see that these men and those who used to enjoy his largesse out on the town were false friends whom he compares to 'combreworldes' [encumberers of the world] (225), 'enchantours' (225), and 'sotil deceyuou[r]s' (227) who misdirect people through pleasure. He likens them to mythical 'meermaides in the see' (236), who sing sailors to sleep in order to devour them. And yet he realizes that nobody wants to listen to the 'sobre, treewe, and weel auysid [prudent]' (273) person who informs others 'with sad visage' [with a serious face] (274) that their 'gouernance is despysid/Among the peple' (275–6). Those responsible for governance want to be liked. How can anyone speak truth, let alone speak truth to power, when it creates so much awkwardness? Flattery seems to be the only option, but both *La Male Regle* and *Fleabag* suggest that it defers awkwardness rather than addressing the circumstances that make it possible in the first place.

La Male Regle ends by flattering the treasurer, Lord Furnivall, comparing him to the God of Health. This approach, taken in a poem that criticizes flattery, creates an awkward situation in which Hoccleve risks seeming like a hypocrite for employing flattery and Furnivall will risk seeming like a hypocrite if he succumbs to it. While several early readers have pointed out that this does not seem like a good strategy if Hoccleve is asking for money, I would like to return to the point that this poem is not actually the formal mechanism Hoccleve would use to ask for money. Instead, it draws attention to a set of circumstances that often lead to awkwardness: Hoccleve and his fellow clerks find themselves in a position where they have to ask for something they shouldn't have to request: the annuities that are owed to them. This invites other awkward questions: how could Henry IV's administration function if it could not pay its clerks?[11] Why should flatterers and dissemblers flourish while honest men are made to feel guilty when requesting what was owed to them? The text certainly indicates that Hoccleve's personal circumstances have driven these questions, for he acknowledges that his poverty and pain have 'artid [compelled] me speke as I spoken haue' (396). It may be awkward to ask for money, but poverty and pain have become more miserable than asking for relief. Just as importantly, by asking these questions Hoccleve implies there may be someone there to hear these words and the story he needs to tell 'whil my breeth may in my body waue' (399). That person may be Furnivall, but it seems equally likely that he is referring to the reader. This triangulation of Hoccleve's exchanges for the benefit of someone observing the situation helps to explain why Hoccleve copied *La Male Regle* into one of three surviving verse manuscripts that he made in the final years of his life. The one in which *La Male Regle* appears includes the names of other friends and colleagues who likely knew Hoccleve and his work intimately.

Waller-Bridge likewise preserves her story by triangulating Fleabag's exchanges for the benefit of the audience, whom she refers to as her friends in the second season. Fleabag's poverty and pain are compounded by gender differences that make her vulnerable in different ways than Hoccleve: breast cancer, menstruation and menopause figure prominently in the show, as does misogyny. Nonetheless, both *Fleabag* and *La Male Regle* invite readers to imagine how their protagonists have come to a point where they both desire a sense of belonging while they also feel unworthy of it. While their self-deprecating style gestures towards an acceptance of the imperfect, neither text offers clear solutions to the problems their narrators face. Ultimately, they reward those who pay attention to awkwardness as a way of becoming more attuned to others: they promote opportunities to really look at and listen to others, to practise empathy even when the experience causes discomfort and does not necessarily become sympathy.

---

[11] For an excellent account of these troubles, see Jenni Nuttall, *The Creation of Lancastrian Kingship*, Cambridge Studies in Medieval Literature 67 (Cambridge: Cambridge University Press, 2007).

10

You're so vain, you probably think this Psalm is about you: Saving face in Thomas Hoccleve's *Series*

Thomas Hoccleve's *Series* initially seems like it might be a continuation of *La Male Regle*. Its first part, a 'Complaint', echoes *La Male Regle* because it invokes the forms that Hoccleve used in his vocation as a Clerk in the Privy Seal to seek redress for the speaker's current circumstances, which bear a close resemblance to the author's own. Indeed, both texts seem to share a little too much information about the author, inviting comparisons with Augustine's *Confessions*. One of the other ways that Hoccleve adopts Augustine's style in the 'Complaint' is to cite the Psalms in a way that suggests they reveal something about him personally. It might seem vain for these two authors to think the Psalms are about them, but this practice allows them to feel and imagine a connection with others – to know they are not alone. What differentiates Hoccleve's work from Augustine's is that Hoccleve seems to acknowledge that he has exaggerated several of the attributes he shares with the speaker in his poem (whom I will call Thomas). The effect of this exaggeration is almost uniformly to heighten the awkwardness others experience when they encounter Thomas in dialogue or through his text, though it sometimes seems to generate laughter in other ways, too. To explain this aspect of Hoccleve's writing and its implications, I turn now to the UK version of *The Office*.

I am not saying that Thomas is a fifteenth-century version of David Brent, but the two of them do have a number of things in common. David literally pushes paper as the manager of Wernham Hogg paper company at the turn of the twenty-first century. Thomas figuratively pushes paper as a clerk in an important bureaucratic and diplomatic office at the turn of the fifteenth century. Both seem to long for opportunities for self-expression as they fulfil roles where their primary function is to provide other people with the tools they need to express themselves. Hoccleve's approach to self-representation is comparable to the way that Ricky Gervais – who co-created, co-wrote and co-directed *The Office* along with Stephen Merchant – presents a socially awkward version of himself to the world in the form of David Brent through a series of episodes recounting moments in the making of a text about him. More importantly, the genre and mood of *The Office* help explain how and why Hoccleve creates awkwardness in the last of his pseudo-autobiographical texts. Most of the social discomfort that appears in the *Series*, which Hoccleve wrote around 1420, is the result of Thomas's 'Complaint' that others refuse to recognize that he has recovered from a mental affliction. This is no laughing matter, and I do not want to give the impression that I am making light of it, but I do want to contrast these moments with other awkward moments that do generate laughter later on in the text.[1] Ultimately, I hope to show that both *The Office* and *The Series* explore what it means when a desire to fit in and seek approval become barriers to belonging. They get there through slightly different routes, but both texts ultimately encourage their audiences to move from empathy to compassion.

Both Hoccleve's *Series* and *The Office* use innovations in their respective genres to create the paradoxical effect of revealing a lack of attunement in relationships by creating a sense of intimacy. The empathic process that Keysers describes is present in these texts and our interactions with them, but connections fail because the characters either cannot or do not want to know what others feel. *The Office* is credited by many as popularizing the mockumentary (mock documentary) genre for television. The term 'mock' is not meant to imply that all films in this genre are parodies, though many of the most seminal ones are. These include the BBC feature on the Spaghetti Harvest (1957), *The Gods Must Be Crazy* (1980) and *This Is Spinal Tap* (1984). The turn of the twenty-first century marked the arrival of television mockumentaries around the world, from *The Games* in Australia (1998–2000) to *The Trailer Park Boys* in Canada (2001–2008; 2014–2018) and *The Office* in the UK (2001–2002). Early programmes of this kind generally used hand-held cameras and remove the laugh track to create the impression that the audience has unmediated access to regular people who are being filmed in everyday situations and who modify their behaviour accordingly. The camera functions as a proxy for the audience, making it seem as though we are present during many intimate or awkward conversations.

I invite you to imagine *The Series* as a fifteenth-century mockumentary about the making of a book that we now know as *The Series*. Instead of using a hand-held camera, though, Hoccleve uses the technology available to him – parchment, ink and the forms associated with his bureaucratic vocation – to document the making of a book.[2] Hoccleve also engages with a widely disseminated kind of writing that A. C. Spearing calls autography, a form of writing (graphia) that is written in the first person (auto) 'in which there is no implied assertion that the first person either does or does not correspond to a real-life individual'.[3] In Spearing's view, 'the *Series* seems to show autography evolving into autobiography – or better, into what one scholar calls "autobiographical fiction", or better still, what others call "pseudo-autobiography", since we have no reason to believe that the specific events narrated in the *Series* either did or did not occur in reality'.[4] Recent work by Sebastien Sobecki and Misty Schieberle

---

[1] For a very different account of Hoccleve's experience, see Marion Turner, 'Illness Narratives in the Later Middle Ages: Arderne, Chaucer, and Hoccleve', *Journal of Medieval and Early Modern Studies* 46.1 (2016): 61–87.

[2] See Ethan Knapp, *The Bureaucratic Muse: Thomas Hoccleve and Early Fifteenth-Century Literature* (University Park: Pennsylvania State University Press, 2001) for a detailed account of the way that Hoccleve's vocation shaped his poetics.

[3] A. C. Spearing, *Medieval Autographies: The 'I' of the Text* (Notre Dame, IN: Notre Dame University Press, 2012), 7.

[4] Ibid., 173.

suggests much of the *Series* reflects his experience working on other manuscripts that include texts that form part of the *Series*, but Hoccleve is also telling a story about making a book.⁵ Thus his text initially looks like other forms of autography, a kind of supergenre that 'includes dream poems and prologues, along with the group of poems known in French as *dits*', but it differs substantially from them insofar as the *Series* emphasizes the work that goes into putting a book together, from deciding which audience to address to selecting what texts to include to gaining access to those texts and spending the time necessary to copy them.⁶ As he accounts for every component of the *Series* – which is made from a 'Complaint', a 'Dialogue', two tales from the *Gesta Romanorum* with moralizations, a tract called 'Learn to Die', and the ninth lesson read on All Saints' Day – he always keeps the audience in mind. This means that he has made a decision to represent every moment in which he claims to run into trouble, to digress or to do something embarrassing. In other words, the moments of discomfort that Hoccleve shares are as much a *decision* as the uncomfortable situations that Hannah Gadsby points out in her discussion of Renaissance Art in *Douglas*.⁷ It also means that awkward moments are just as carefully staged in the *Series* as they are in *The Office*. Ricky Gervais and Stephen Merchant did not create a sense of verisimilitude by just letting the cameras roll; the social discomfort that permeates the two series of their show required multiple takes. Hoccleve is never just letting the parchment roll, so to speak. He is making decisions about how to document the process of making a book in order to generate certain effects for readers who were familiar with conventional techniques associated with book production and traditional fictions about how books come into being: dreams delivered by muses, spontaneous storytelling competitions or collections of poetry inspired by a lover.

As Hoccleve well knew, those types of poems conventionally establish their mood and atmosphere through weather and music. Dream poems normally open in spring, often with birdsong; the *Canterbury Tales* famously begins on an April day and the Miller's playing of his pipes probably created a certain kind of mood. The opening stanzas of *The Series* offer a sharp contrast to these texts. It opens at 'the ende of Nouembre, vppon a niȝt' [the end of November, upon a night] (17):⁸

Aftir þat heruest inned had hise sheues,°	*brought in / sheeves*
And that the broun sesoun of Mihelmesse°	*Michaelmas*
Was come, and gan° the trees robbe of her leues,°	*began / leaves*
That grene had ben° and in lusty freisshenesse,	*been*

---

⁵ Sebastian Sobecki, 'The *Series*: Thomas Hoccleve's Year of Mourning', in *Last Words: The Public Self and the Social Author in Late Medieval England*, Oxford Textual Perspectives, 65–100 (Oxford: Oxford University Press, 2019); Misty Schieberle, 'A New Hoccleve Literary Manuscript: The Trilingual Miscellany in London, British Library, MS Harley 219', *The Review of English Studies* 70.297 (2019): 799–822.
⁶ Spearing, *Autographies*, 7.
⁷ See David Watt, *The Making of Thomas Hoccleve's Series*, Exeter Medieval Texts and Studies (Liverpool: Liverpool University Press, 2013).
⁸ All citations to the 'Complaint' and 'Dialogue' are from Thomas Hoccleve, '*My Compleinte*' and *Other Poems*, ed. Roger Ellis, Exeter Medieval Texts and Studies, 115–55 (Exeter: University of Exeter Press, 2001).

>   And hem into colour of ȝelownesse°   *yellowness*
>   Had died and doun throwen vndirfoote,
>   That chaunge sanke into myn herte roote.
>
>   (1–7)

The embodied experience that Thomas describes in this passage reinforces Gumbrecht's claim that weather affects the 'inner feelings' of people in the same way that music does:[9] 'Another dimension of reality that happens to our bodies in a similar way and surrounds them is the weather. For this very reason, references to music and weather often occur when literary texts make moods and atmospheres present or begin to reflect upon them.'[10] In this case, the changing atmospheric conditions associated with autumn are closely associated with the change in Thomas's heart and mind, leading him to experience what he calls 'the þouȝtful maladie' (21) or melancholia, which was consistently identified with Autumn in medieval texts. What is happening here is not the pathetic fallacy in action, but a representation of a causal phenomenon identified by Heidegger and translated in paraphrase by Gumbrecht: 'Varied – and constantly changing – moods and atmospheres, Heidegger writes, condition our behavior and feelings in everyday existence; we are not free to choose them.'[11] It also reflects the way that the brain constructs emotions through prediction and simulation: things that are outside seem to move inside because the emotion connected to them is simulated in the brain. Gumbrecht's claims are clinched by the observation that Hoccleve's *Series* is *Canterbury Tales* in a 'bitter' or 'minor key' – a musical metaphor that describes the mood or atmosphere created by weather.[12]

If you are having trouble imagining how this scene establishes its mood and atmosphere, take a moment to look at the opening credits of *The Office*. There are no leaves on any of the trees, the sky is overcast and it seems to be set in very late Autumn or Winter in England. *The Office* further enhances the bleak mood through its representation of banal architectual elements: nondescript office buildings, the Brunel Bus Station and Carpark, a roundabout and the building in which the show is ostensibly set. The only break in brown and grey comes in the form of green in the middle of the roundabout (separated from people), a few cars and a black and white sign for the Slough Trading Estate. The accompanying music, an instrumental version of 'Handbags and Gladrags', matches the somber mood of the images.[13] In the closing credits, the same song includes a chorus that provides a clue about why it was selected for the show. These lines ask what is left when the person addressed

---

[9] Hans Ulrich Gumbrecht, *Atmosphere, Mood, Stimmung: On a Hidden Potential of Literature*, trans. Erik Butler (Stanford: Stanford University Press, 2012), 5.
[10] Ibid., 4.
[11] Ibid., 9.
[12] Ethan Knapp describes these lines as being transposed into a 'bitter key' in *The Bureaucratic Muse: Thomas Hoccleve and the Literature of Late Medieval England* (University Park, PA: Pennsylvania State University Press, 2001), 164. Sebastian Langdell changes this slightly in paraphrase to describe this passage as being 'transposed into a minor key', but both convey the same mood; see *Thomas Hoccleve: Religious Reform, Transnational Politics, and the Invention of Chaucer*, Exeter Medieval Texts and Studies (Liverpool: Liverpool University Press, 2018), 11.
[13] Big George Webley, 'Handbags and Gladrags', by Mike D'Abo, track 1 on *The Office UK Theme Music*, Avant Garde a Clue, Inc., 2006, compact disc.

in the song no longer possesses the titular handbags and gladrags (i.e. fancy clothes), especially since they were purchased through another's labour.[14] The lyrics resonate with the melancholy mood that the music and weather establish during the opening credits. While the credits roll, they give way briefly to a shot of characters still doing something associated with what they were doing during the episode, suggesting that they will not get a break from the drudgery. The sense of melancholy becomes even more acute when we consider what the second verse of the song, not included in the credits, might reveal about David Brent. In this verse, the speaker reflects on a time when he was a young man who thought he could get by on his charm. He then warns young women that the cost they will likely pay to fit in will exceed the cost of the fashionable clothing and accessories they deem to require: fitting in may cost them the opportunity to experience belonging in the way that Brené Brown describes it, as a sense of being valued for who they are.[15] David is no longer a young man, and he cannot get by with a charming smile, though he repeatedly tries to do just that. He would also do well to listen to the advice the song offers to the fashionable young women because, as the show repeatedly shows, the more he thinks he's in, the more he seems to be out – both out of favour with those whom he tries so desparately to impress and out of touch with the way others perceive him. He is so preoccupied with how he is seen that he fails to use his empathic system to see how others respond to him or to comprehend what their responses to him might be revealing.

Thomas is likewise preoccupied with how others see him, though he imagines himself as someone who is out. He also conveys this mood through music, though this might not be immediately evident to modern readers. When we refer to psalms today, we often think of written texts preserved in the biblical book of that name. However, people in the Middle Ages experienced the Psalms as music (as do many people who worship in certain Christian denominations today). It is likely that Hoccleve memorized all 150 Psalms when he was in song school, where many boys received a primary education in Latin grammar as well as knowledge of the psalms that formed the foundation for mass and office in the Church. When Thomas tries to explain the isolation he feels, it seems just as appropriate for him to turn to Psalm 31 as it would be for Ricky Gervais and Stephen Merchant to associate 'Handbags and Gladrags' with David Brent. We do not need to know exactly how the psalm might have sounded to Hoccleve to see why its words appealed to him:

As seide is in þe sauter° mighte I sey,	*Psalter*
'They þat me sy,° fledden awey fro me.'	*saw*
Forʒeten° I was al out of mynde awey,	*forgotten*
As he þat deed° was from hertis cherte.°	*dead / heart's charity*
To a lost vessel lickned° miʒte I be,	*likened*
For many a wiʒt° aboute me dwelling	*person*
Herde I me blame and putte in dispreisynge.	

(78–84)

---

[14] Ibid.
[15] Ibid.

The choice of this psalm seems apt because it allows Thomas to claim that he is like David (King David, to whom the psalm is attributed, not David Brent) in that he is paradoxically both forgotten and the main topic of everyone else's gossip.[16] Later, David (Brent, not the King) insists that he is right to worry about how others see him, 'For I hear the whispering of many … as they scheme together against me as they plot to take my life' (Psalm 31.13). Like David, Thomas imagines that his plight is on everyone's lips: 'Howe it wiþ me stood was in euery […] mouþe' (45). He constantly complains about what people are saying about him (85, 120, 127, 130, 134–5). Thomas's preoccupation with how others see him combined with his inability to discern what they actually think about him makes him very much like David Brent; they differ in that Thomas eventually tries to emulate King David by seeking solace in the fact that he may find belonging with God even if he does not fit in with those around him.

Even if Hoccleve did not have the music associated with the psalm in mind, verse has a rhythmic effect that functions like music. Thomas uses this to great effect as he explains why he thinks the psalm is about him. Paying attention to the way Hoccleve's verses function is one way that we can gain knowledge of how past readers might have experienced the poem: 'The point of departure and catalyst for the experience of historical and cultural alterity lies … in the most objective phenomenal field of literary texts: in their prosody and poetic form.'[17] When Hoccleve explains that Thomas's melancholic mood is a product of his awkward encounters with others, he makes use of his poetic form to draw attention to this transition. Normally, Hoccleve aligns the sense and structure of his seven-line rhyme royal stanza. This means that a high percentage of stanzas in the *Series* are self-contained units of meaning. The tenth stanza initially looks like it ends by concluding a thought, and anyone reading it in a manuscript likely would have thought so, since the punctuation in these manuscripts often relies upon line or stanza breaks as a sign of punctuation against which the practice of enjambment or run-on lines really stands out. The tenth stanza creates an awkward situation by ending on what seems to be the end of the sentence before following up with a relative clause in the following stanza. It describes the fact that nobody will accept that Thomas's wit has returned to him; instead, they continue to disdain him, to consider him a riotous person, to refuse his friendship or to 'make daliaunce' [converse] with him. He seems to sum this all up by saying, 'The world me made a straunge countinaunce' (70). This statement itself is a little ambiguous. It describes either how others show Hoccleve 'the face of a stranger' (Ellis) or suggests that others make him out – perceive him – to be strange. In modern editions, a comma appears, allowing readers to anticipate the relative clause that follows in the next stanza: 'Wi[c]h þat myn herte sore gan to torment' (71). This transition's syntax would have compelled medieval readers to read awkwardly, turning back in order to move forward. The rhythm and form draws readers into the awkward situation that Hoccleve is going to develop in greater detail in the following stanzas.

---

[16] See Knapp, *Bureaucratic*, 18–19.
[17] Gumbrecht, *Atmosphere*, 13.

Both *The Office* and *the Series* draw on weather and music to create mood and atmosphere by using the system the brain uses to construct emotions through simulation. They also engage the empathic system, which uses the same system in the brain to understand what others are feeling by using *kinesic* imagery. The scene depicted in the rest of the stanza I just cited suggests that Thomas is not vain to think the psalm is about him: witnessing others turn away from him, he is left feeling as abandoned as the Psalmist. I think we can understand the visceral force of this scene by turning to another one in *The Office*. In this scene, David pretends to fire Dawn as a prank in the first episode of the first season.[18] The scene is shot as if the person holding the camera has been sitting with the intern Ricky and David, and it focuses on the two of them in one set of shots and Dawn on the other. At the beginning of the episode, David Brent has been told that there will be redundancies at Wernham Hogg. Knowing this, and keen to impress the intern on his first day in the office, David asks his long-serving receptionist to stay when she enters the room to deliver a fax. David reminds Dawn of the need for redundancies at Wernham Hogg, and she smiles when he then says that she has made his life easier. When David then says this is because he's going to let Dawn go first, her face falls as she asks why. David claims he is compelled to act because Dawn has been stealing post-it notes. When she asks how much they're worth, David looks to Ricky, who turns white while turning away. It may seem obvious to say that the audience recognizes Ricky's discomfort because of the look on his face and the posture of his body, but I would like to focus on the way that this process works. According to Feldman Barrett, 'we do not "recognize" or "detect" emotions in others';[19] instead, we perceive an instance of emotion. As we are trying to work out what to feel in response to this scene, 'our own premotor cortex resonates as if it was doing the actions we observe' when we see Ricky contract his body and lower his gaze.[20] We might cringe or we might not, but our brains process the response as if we have done what Ricky has done and we then construct an instance of emotion for him and for others: I associate Ricky's reaction with social discomfort, and it makes me feel awkward to think he feels awkward. Not everyone will feel this way. As Feldman Barrett insists, when it comes to constructing emotions, 'variation is the norm'.[21]

I have focused on Ricky because he is the audience's surrogate in this scene. This is his first day in the office just as this is the audience's first encounter with *The Office*. The audience does experience empathy when watching Dawn and David. Most viewers can tell that Dawn is in distress and that David is being an asshole. We might therefore sympathize with Dawn's sadness or feel angry with David. We might also feel angry with Ricky, since he says nothing to relieve the situation. My own response is to feel the awkwardness he feels. He is clearly embarrassed by David's breach of decorum,

---

[18] *The Office*, season 1, episode 1, 'Downsize', written and directed by Ricky Gervais and Stephen Merchant, featuring Ricky Gervais, Lucy Davis and Oliver Chris, aired 9 July 2001, https://www.netflix.com/title/70136112?s=i&trkid=13747225.
[19] Lisa Feldman Barrett, *How Emotions are Made: The Secret Life of the Brain* (Boston, MA: Mariner Books, 2018), 39.
[20] Christian Keysers, *The Empathic Brain: How the Discovery of Mirror Neurons Changes our Understanding of Human Nature* (Oklahoma, OK: Smashwords, 2011), chap. 4, Kobo.
[21] Feldman Barrett, *Emotions*, 32.

which ultimately causes both Dawn and David to lose face, and he tries to practise what Erving Goffman calls 'tactful overlooking'. Goffman argues that this kind of approach often occurs 'when a person is caught out of face because [s]he had not expected to be thrust into interaction, or because strong feelings have disrupted [her] expressive mask, the others may protectively turn away from [her] or [her] activity for a moment, to give [her] time to assemble [her]self'.[22] Dawn has clearly not expected this conversation and has been overcome by strong feelings. She tries to cover her face and to pull herself together, and Ricky tries to look away. Seemingly oblivious to Dawn's distress, David tries to maintain his line for far too long. Ricky finds himself in exactly the kind of situation in which Goffman suggests people may become embarrassed, 'not because of inability to handle such difficulties, but because for a moment no one knows whether the offender is going to act blind to the incident, or give it joking recognition, or employ some other face-saving practice'.[23] David finally relents, looking down as he admits it was a joke while stealing a glance towards the camera. The audience can see that he finally recognizes the awkwardness of the situation when he starts muttering about practical jokes for the good and becomes engrossed in the fax Dawn delivered at the beginning of the scene. Like Ricky, those watching the scene may find themselves embarrassed because David is not embarrassed enough.

Goffman also helps to explain why the scene ends the way it does. He writes that as part of the process of correcting a situation where someone has lost face, people involved in social interactions sometimes 'find themselves in an established state of ritual disequilibrium or disgrace, and an attempt must be made to re-establish a satisfactory ritual state for them'.[24] That happens in this case when Dawn stops crying and addresses David directly and assertively. 'You wanker', she says, 'Such a sad little man'. David asks, 'Am I?' At this point, the audience finally gets a bit of distance, for a third camera angle, which comes from a perspective outside the circle, is introduced. We therefore see all three of them as we overhear David say to Ricky, 'Didn't know that.' At this point, Dawn gathers herself, stands up and leaves. The chances for future productive social interactions seem bleak insofar as David does not offer an apology, nor does he seem to recognize the need for interaction rituals. Instead, an audio track of him describing the importance of people in the company caps the episode off in a way that seems both unsatisfactory and consistent with David's character. In the American version of *The Office*, Steve Carrell generally portrays the manager Michael Scott as being oblivious to the impact he has on others. Ricky Gervais, on the other hand, plays David Brent as self-conscious and defensive about the possibility that he might misread others or go too far, so he constantly addresses the camera directly in order to reassure himself and the audience about his intentions. This almost always has the effect of highlighting the fact that David is so vain he thinks *The Office* – the workplace and the documentary – is about him. Many audience members recognize aspects of themselves or others in David Brent, yet he seems unable or unwilling to see himself through others' eyes.

---

[22] Erving Goffman, *Interaction Ritual: Essays on Face-to-Face Behavior* (New York: Pantheon, 1967), 18.
[23] Ibid., 27.
[24] Ibid., 19.

In contrast, Thomas consistently attempts to see himself through the eyes of others in the 'Complaint'. The following scene begins in the building where the Office of the Privy Seal was located (Westminster Hall) before moving to where clerks lived together (London). It describes the way that those who once called Thomas to company, his friends and colleagues, respond physically when they see him in places where they have seen him before. Recalling how sad he felt when others made him a strange countenance, he writes,

For ofte° whanne° I in Westmynstir Halle,	*often / when*
And eke° in Londoun, among the prees° went,	*also / crowd*
I sy° the chere° abaten and apalle	*saw / expressions*
Of hem that weren wonte° me for to calle	*were wont*
To companie. Her heed° they caste awry,	*Their heads*
Whanne I hem mette, as they not me sy.	

(72–6)

Those whom Thomas meets embody awkwardness. Like Ricky in *The Office*, the expressions on their faces 'abate' [fall] and 'apalle' [grow pale or subdued] when they recognize him. They cast their heads awry, either cringing or just turning away to pretend not to see him. Their body language conveys the sense that they feel awkward or embarrassed, but it is unclear whether this concerns something Thomas has done (is he David?), something that has been done to him (is he Dawn?) or their failure to intervene (are they Ricky?). They attempt to practise the 'tactical overlooking' Goffman describes as a way for all involved to save face. Perhaps they planned to send Thomas a card later that looked like Figure 11. This scene creates discomfort because the reader knows that Thomas desperately craves the opportunity to converse with others. He constructs a much different emotional experience in response to seeing them turn their backs on him than David Brent does. For Thomas, this is the encounter that leads him to think that Psalm 31 is about him, for his friends' refusal to have an uncomfortable conversation with him is a sign of his social exclusion.

The text raises the possibility that others are genuinely concerned about his behaviour, but Thomas is convinced that the gossip about him is mean-spirited. However, his emotional responses seem misaligned with his bodily expression of them. When Thomas overhears others say that his sickness will return, especially given his age, he claims, 'thanne my visage / Bigan to glowe for the woo [grief] and fere [fear]' (89–90). John Burrow rightly notes that sometimes medieval gestures and looks meant something different than they do today, but the connection between cause and effect here invites readers to question whether Thomas is being honest about what he is feeling: the glowing or reddening of his face seem to suggest that he feels anger or shame, not grief and fear. The four-stanza digression on how others have been wrong about him seems to confirm he is angry about their perception. The misalignment between the expression on his face and his inner state becomes a theme as the 'Complaint' continues. Finding himself shaking with shame and fear (151) because of the way others speak about him, he resolves to 'to peinte [contrive] countenaunce, chere and look' (149). Twenty-first-century neuroscience suggests this

Figure 11 Thanks for Pretending Not To See Me Funny eCard Sign.²⁵

is a good strategy. According to Keysers, 'a substantial number of experiments show that our bodily state, including our facial expression, can influence our feelings'.²⁶ I don't think Keysers was including the experiment Thomas goes on to conduct in the most frequently cited lines in the *Series*. In this scene, Thomas looks into a mirror as he attempts to make sure his expression is appropriate:

And in my chaumbre at home whanne þat I was	
Mysilfe alloone° I in þis wise wro3te.°	*Alone / acted*
I streite° vnto my mirrour and my glas,	*straight*
To looke° how þat me of my chere þou3t,°	*see / thought*
If any othir were it than it ou3t,°	*ought*
For fain wolde I, if it not had bene ri3t,°	*right*
Amendid it to my kunnynge and my3t.°	*might*

(155–61)

Thomas would have done anything to correct his appearance, but it doesn't seem to him that anything is amiss. He concludes that human beings are blind when it comes to their own case and that he needs to do something else. But what? That's the problem he identifies: 'Howe shal I do? Wiche is the beste way / My troublid spirit for to bring in

---

²⁵ https://www.amazon.com/thanks-pretending-funny-sign-aluminum/dp/b012yaxdv6.
²⁶ Keysers, *Empathic Brain*, chap. 6.

rest?' (173–4). Thomas embodies Goffman's observation that fear of the loss of face often leads people 'to seek the safety of solitude rather than the danger of social encounters.'[27] This may help him to conceal his anger and impatience (177–9), but staying home is also wrought with difficulties. He asks to be judged through conversation rather than his 'countynaunce' (214) or the expression on his face: 'By commvnynge is the beste assay [test]' (217). The 'Complaint' repeatedly reminds readers that human beings form judgements based on conversation and body language, and he seems to realize he is sending mixed messages.

The *Series* both recognizes how reluctant people can be to engage in awkward conversations and insists that these conversations are necessary if Thomas is going to feel a sense of belonging again. Thomas feels angry and upset about the way that others have treated him since his recovery, but the 'Complaint' seems to suggest that the social discomfort is mutual. The descriptions of what others are saying about Thomas start to look a little different if we imagine that others might be picking up on the misalignment between what he feels and what he is trying to get his body to express. Thomas uses an apt image to describe the discomfort arising from this process when he explains that he does not know 'hou in my skyn to tourne' [how in my skin to turn] (303). He has repeatedly described the process of trying to turn away from the emotions he is actually feeling, and this image reveals just how awkward – literally awkward in the case that he is moving against the grain of his body – his situation is. This is a powerful *kinesic* image because it seems to describe exactly what it feels like to feel awkward.

The image of turning in one's own skin describes David Brent in many scenes, especially those where he is most uncomfortable with the situation or attempting to make a good impression. This is exactly the position in which Thomas finds himself in the 'Complaint'. While David constantly brags about the type of manager he is, his body constantly belies his confidence. If he were to overhear people talking about him, he might hear them describe how he changes his pace when he walks, that he fidgets, that his feet are constantly moving and that his eyes seem to flit about. In other words, they might say what Thomas hears others say about him:

Chaunged had I m[y] pas° some seiden eek,°	*pace / also*
For here and ther forþe stirte I as a roo,°	*startled as if I was a deer*
Noon abood,° noon areest,° but al brainseke.°	*resting / stopping / brainsick*
Another spake° and of me seide also,	*spoke*
My feet weren ay wauynge° to and fro,	*waving*
Whanne þat I stonde shulde and wiþ men talke,	
And þat myn yen° soȝten euery halke.°	*eyes / corner*

(127–33)

I don't want to downplay the fact that Thomas thinks people are reading his body language as a sign that he is continuing to suffer from some sort of mental illness. But I also want to point out two other things. First, they are engaging their empathic

---

[27] Goffman, *Interaction Ritual* 39.

brain when they notice his behaviour. Second, his body language conveys a sense of social discomfort. When I see David Brent behave in this way in episodes of *The Office* I suspect he feels awkward, and it often makes me feel awkward. Perhaps those who encountered Thomas in Westminster Hall and London feel awkward about the way others perceive him. This would explain why they turn away from him when they meet. This is an example where sympathy – sharing his feeling of discomfort – is less effective than empathy, which might lead others to show him compassion by engaging in conversations with him that might help to relieve his suffering.

The other option Thomas has is to worry less about what other people think. The 'Complaint' ends with his resolution to set 'the lesse / By the peples ymaginacioun, / Talkinge this and þat of my siknesse' (379–81), and to turn to God for 'mercy and grace' (413). Like Augustine, Thomas comes to the decision that belonging with God is more important than fitting in with others, and he sees his illness and isolation as an opportunity sent by God for him to change his life. Thomas reaches this conclusion when reading a copy of Isidore of Seville's *Synonyma*, which has been loaned to him by a friend. Somewhat awkwardly, though, the person who loaned it took it back before Thomas was done with it. Nonetheless, he says, he was able to catch 'sum of the doctrine by Resoun tauȝt [taught] / To þe man' in the book' (376–7). Perhaps this is the reason that he seems to forget his resolution to worry less about what others think the moment a friend shows compassion by arriving at his door to instigate the 'Dialogue', the second part of the *Series*. Thomas is keen to hear what his friend thinks of 'my compleinte' ('Dialogue' 17), and he reads it aloud right away. When the friend confirms that Thomas has made the 'Complaint' to be read by others, the friend warns him against this. He also reluctantly confirms that Thomas wasn't actually vain to think the psalm was about him: throughout the course of their conversation, the friend both insists that nobody was speaking about Thomas's misfortune and that he was the subject of their conversation, albeit for different reasons than Thomas might have thought.

There is a lot of awkwardness in 'the Complaint', but not much laughter. That changes when the friend arrives to start 'the Dialogue', which marks a profound shift in how the text represents social discomfort. Although most of the conversation between Thomas and his friend seems earnest, the incongruity between the initial intentions expressed in this scene and what they end up doing has the potential to generate laughter. The friend starts by sharing the uncomfortable news that he thinks the first part of the *Series* shouldn't be circulated because it reveals that the speaker is both too worried about how others see him and not worried enough about the effect that circulating his 'Complaint' will have on his reputation. He initially insists that Thomas should keep quiet, but he then starts making suggestions about what Thomas should write once he is convinced of his soundness of mind. These exchanges continue throughout the *Series*, culminating in the friend encouraging Hoccleve to add one more tale even when he thought he was finished with the book. Almost all the awkward exchanges concern Thomas's plans to make a book for Humphrey, Duke of Gloucester, King Henry V's brother. As he tries to get Thomas to change his plans, the friend somewhat ineptly cites a passage from Geoffrey of Vinsauf's *Poetria Nova* [The New Poetry] that says authors should make a plan and stick to it. He then cites a fictional character, Chaucer's Wife of Bath, as his authority that women do not like it when men find vice in them, and that's exactly what he thinks Thomas has done with his translation of Christine de Pizan's *Epistre de Cupide* [Letter of Cupid]. The friend insists that the only way to make amends is by writing something that will please women. He then seems to go a little too far when he suggests that women will see the text if it is included in a book for Humphrey because

> His lust and his desir
> Is, as it wel sit to his hy degree,
> For his desport and mirth, in honestee
> With ladyes to haue daliance,
> And this book wole he shewen hem par chance.
>
> (703–7)

This might seem innocuous enough, until we recognize that 'daliance' has a range of connotations in Middle English: it can mean conversation, flirtation or sexual intercourse. In other words, Thomas records his friend's potentially inappropriate comments about his patron liking the ladies in a book being made for Humphrey. Yet he thinks that this is the best way that Thomas can seek mercy. The friend tells him that unless 'to women thow thyn herte bowe [bow], / Axyng [Asking] hir graces with greet repentance / For thy giltes [guilt]' (715–17), Thomas will be asking for trouble.

The friend's insistence that Thomas should write a book to amend for the wrongs he has done to women creates another awkward situation. Thomas insists that he wasn't the author of the offending texts, and he goes on to claim that whoever questions it is 'misauysed' [misadvised] (771) since anyone who has read the whole thing would know it ends by favouring women. Doesn't it, Thomas asks his friend? That question leads to this awkward exchange:

'Thomas, I noot,° for neuere it yit I say.'°	*know not / saw*
'No, freend?' 'No, Thomas.' 'Wel trowe I, in fay,°	*faith*
For had yee red° it fully to the ende,	*read*
Yee wolde seyn° it is nat as yee wende.'°	*see / think*

(781–4)

The conversation grinds to a halt with two caesuras in the second line, when Thomas stops to confirm what he thinks the friend has said. He has *not* read Thomas's other book. Although this admission creates a remarkably awkward situation, at least the friend has the decency to be honest. Thomas seems heartened by the friend's decision to acknowledge his imperfections as a friend, and he allows them both to save face by saying if the friend had read the offending book, he would agree with Thomas's view. The exchange is incongruous not only because the friend has just been insisting on how offensive the text is but also because it is surprising that an author would include an exchange with a friend who hadn't actually read his book. Remember: this exchange is a *decision*. It is a brave one, too. While it is conventional for authors to include conversations about what to write in order to make amends for offending women, there are very few other examples that feature a friend who hasn't read the author's previous work making inappropriate comments about the patron in the book that is ostensibly being made for that person. The awkwardness in the 'Dialogue' seems different in tone than the awkwardness that dominates the 'Complaint'. I think that is because it begins to show how awkward conversations between friends can not only lead to effective collaboration but also create a renewed sense of belonging.

At the end of the Christmas special that caps off *The Office*, David Brent finally rejects the toxic friend whose approval he has sought throughout the two series. David brings a date to the office Christmas party after he has been fired, and it goes surprisingly well; they say an awkward goodbye – handshake, then kisses on the cheek – before she gives him the signal to 'call her' as she pulls away in a cab. He returns to the party feeling more confident and begins to banter with Chris Finch (his disgusting friend at the firm) and Neil Godwin (the new manager). When Chris makes a characteristically inappropriate joke about the David's date, David stands up to him and goes on to chat with Gareth and Tim. It's not much, but it does suggest that he has come to worry less about Chris's approval and to value himself a little more – and he's clearly the better for it. David does not immediately change his cringeworthy behaviour: the joke he is telling with Gareth and Tim does not go as gracefully as he would like. Nonetheless, both *The Office* and *The Series* use awkwardness not to single out an awkward individual but to draw attention to the ways that relationships might break down and be renewed. Sometimes this creates further discomfort and even deep sadness: both Thomas and David are depicted as sad men in a literal sense at one point or another (and, in David's case, a figurative sense as well). Ultimately, Thomas is proven right that Psalm 31 is about him, but a line near the end of the psalm resonates more than the lines he cites after his friend appears in the 'Dialogue':

> I had said in my alarm,
> 'I am driven far from your sight'.
> But you heard my supplications
> When I cried out to you for help.
>
> (Psalm 31.22)

Thomas calls out for a friend with whom he can share a conversation, and this ultimately leads him to include a text later in the *Series* that describes heaven as a place of perfect belonging: of concord, unity, quiet and rest. This is the kind of rest that Augustine imagines in the *Confessions*. *The Office* does not express the Christian worldview of these other texts, but it does ask its audience to explore a question with spiritual implications. Do we want to live in the world that David Brent imagines we live in, where striving to fit in and seeking approval act as barriers to true belonging, or do we want to live in a world where people are willing to risk honest conversation even if it might feel awkward? If it's the latter, then we may want to heed Sennett's call to consider how to use our empathic brain to develop the kind of social empathy that allows us to imagine the way other people are in themselves. Though they take different approaches, *The Office* and *The Series* both encourage this kind of empathy.

11

Great cause to laugh: Conversation and compassion in *The Book of Margery Kempe*

Like *The Office* and *The Series*, *Fleabag* and *The Book of Margery Kempe* use the paradoxical technique of encouraging empathy and compassion by presenting us with protagonists who not only resist sympathy but often cause discomfort both within their texts and for their audiences by violating social norms as they draw attention to the suffering that some norms create. *Fleabag* draws attention to these norms most explicitly in the setting for Episode 4, Season 1, when Fleabag and her sister have driven out to the English countryside to attend a 'Female Only Breath of Silence Retreat' that also seems to have a subtitle: 'Women Don't Speak'.[1] While the women partake in 'menial tasks' in silence, they are subjected to aggressively misogynist shouts that originate from the 'Better Man Weekend Workshop' being run at a neighbouring facility.[2] While the situation initially seems ridiculous, it lays bare the everyday experience of women who often suffer in silence because they deem it safer not to say anything. In this case, the women have paid to attend a silent retreat and are admonished for making any noise at all: one woman is shushed when she is being attacked by a wasp. When Claire laughs loudly at Fleabag's observations about their cleaning tasks, the sisters are confined to the director's office. Perhaps the most demoralizing thing about the way they are explicitly and repeatedly conditioned to remain silent as they complete domestic chores while hearing men's voices insult women is that it has so often been accepted as a cultural norm. *The Book of Margery Kempe*, a text composed between 1436 and 1438 but which recounts events in the previous decades, recounts and embodies Margery Kempe's determination to violate this norm in order to express her understanding of God's love. It also provides an account of how many men (and some women) took her refusal to remain silent as licence to admonish her for being a troublemaker, an awkward individual and even a heretic. Yet she did speak, and her book reveals that she understood and even invited admonishment as confirmation of her merit in the sight of God. Although Fleabag also invites admonishment, it seems to exacerbate her sense of shame or unworthiness. These two women ultimately have

---

[1] *Fleabag*, season 1, episode 4, directed by Tim Kirkby, written by Phoebe Waller Bridge, featuring Phoebe Waller-Bridge, Sian Clifford and Olivia Colman, aired 15 September 2016, https://app.primevideo.com/detail?gti=amzn1.dv.gti.14b4ffae-8fb4-a5c4-b768-c7be263546b2&territory=CA&ref_=share_ios_season&r=web.
[2] Ibid.

quite different experiences, but I think we can learn something by comparing the circumstances in which they speak with other men and women.

Kempe uses a range of evocative words to describe her conversations with others. She sums up the time she spent with Julian of Norwich, whom she met in 1416, in the following way: 'Much was the holy dalliance that the anchoress and this creature had by commoning in the love of our Lord Jesus Christ the many days that they were together' (33).[3] Her choice of the word 'dalliance' describes the sense that Kempe had that they shared a 'serious, edifying, or spiritual conversation' or even 'communion' with each other (*MED* s.v. 'daliaunce'). Her use of the word 'commoning' reiterates this sense of deep connection, for it describes the experience of talking together as being together in other ways. Both words also function in other registers. As noted in the previous chapter, 'dalliance' can connote 'amorous talk', 'flirting' or even 'sexual union' while 'commoning' could be a euphemism for 'sexual intercourse' (*MED*, s.v. 'communen'); in fact, Kempe uses this euphemism elsewhere in her book. The fact that these words both connote love talk is entirely appropriate since Kempe follows Julian of Norwich's central contention that God wants to share love with human beings. The double meaning of these terms is also an appropriate reminder that human communication can be expressed through the body as well as language. Kempe uses these words deliberately to describe her experience of feeling attuned to Julian – a feeling of connection and belonging that differs from everyday experience. Julian's words explain Kempe's decision to foreground episodes in which she seems not to fit in with those around her in order to show that she is more attuned with God's will than the world's. According to Kempe, Julian told her to 'set all your trust in God and fear not the language of the world, for the more despite, shame, and reproof that you have in the world, the greater is your merit in the sight of God' (33). Kempe frequently and repeatedly describes instances where she experiences spite, shame and reproof in order to make a case that she is worthy in the sight of God. Furthermore, she often puts her readers in the awkward position of deciding whether they are more likely to laugh with her or at her. It is not my intention to laugh at Margery Kempe's expense. In fact, I think she and Julian likely had quite a sophisticated understanding of laughter, given the way both use it in their texts. My aim here is to show that Kempe intentionally – wilfully and purposefully – employs a *kinesic* style, drawing on embodied imagery associated with 'dalliance' and 'commoning' in their whole range of connotations, in order to challenge her audience in ways that *Fleabag* echoes.

I use the word intention advisedly here. It is very difficult to make an argument about authorial intentions because of the nature of literary evidence. It is easier to evaluate the (potential) effect words have on readers. Nonetheless, many critics have implicitly or explicitly ascribed intentions to *The Book of Margery Kempe*, profitably considering it to fall under the genre of female sacred biography or auto-hagiography. The *Book*'s first page reveals that its central concern is Kempe's intentions, at least insofar as her aim is to align her will with God's. The opening lines introduce the book

---

[3] All citations are taken from Margery Kempe, *The Book of Margery Kempe*, ed. Lynn Staley, Norton Critical Edition (New York: W. W. Norton, 2001).

as 'a short treatise and a comfortable for sinful wretches, wherein they may have great solace and comfort for themselves and understand the high and unspeakable mercy of our sovereign Savior Christ Jesus' (3). Using verbs associated with movement, she indicates that 'this little treatise shall treat somewhat piecemeal of his wonderful works, how mercifully, how benignly, and how charitably he **moved** and **stirred** a sinful caitif until his love' (3). She explains that the experience moved her sense of will or intention, for 'the sinful caitif for many years was in will and purpose through the **stirrings** of the Holy Ghost to follow our saviour, making great promises of fastings with many other deeds of penance' (3). Kempe understands will as leading to intention and then action; she believes she has good intentions, but she is nonetheless unable to act in alignment with God's will. Instead, she is '**turned** again aback in time of temptation, like the reed stalk which **bows** with every wind and never is stable unless no wind blows' (3). This simile suggests that the will is not responsible for all her actions because it sometimes feels more comfortable simply to go with the flow.

Kempe's natural imagery resonates with Teresa Brennan's claim that 'only the subject of free will differentiates itself from its environment by activity that is at odds with that environment. Intentional activity in harmony with one's surroundings does not stand out from it, in that it is not motivated by a will of one's own'.[4] Kempe understands her 'turning' and 'bowing' as a sign that she is 'wayward' and 'unstable' (3) relative to God, so she seeks the will to turn her intention into action. This seems to confirm Brennan's assertion that 'to be active is to carry out an individual intention, which must, by definition, differ from the intentions of the environment'.[5] Kempe's *Book* reveals that she is no longer like the reed stalk that bows in the wind, for it repeatedly demonstrates that her intentions differ from those in her community by recounting the actions she takes and the aversion to which others respond. She regularly includes passages that describe how she was 'slandered and reproved by many people because she kept so straight a living' (11). It is helpful to consider her use of the word 'straight' here in the context of the reed that otherwise would be blown down: because she will not bend to the intentions of her environment, others reproach her. Yet the *Book* also provides a model for readers who might wish to become more attuned with God through Kempe, for it includes many scenes in which some of those who encounter her are moved and stirred to change their minds about her and thus become aligned with God's intentions.

Kempe repeatedly stages awkward moments, encounters where there is some uncertainty about where intentions should be directed, that ultimately become opportunities for compassion. I will explore a number of these throughout the rest of the chapter, but I want to start by noting that this is a key structural feature of the *Book* and Kempe's experience. She reveals in the Proem to her *Book* that many clerks were convinced that her experience was inspired by God, and 'some offered to write her feelings with their own hands' (4). Kempe demurs, claiming that 'she was commanded in her soul that she should not write so soon' (4). She therefore waited over twenty years before having her 'feeling and revelations' written (4). Her eventual

---

[4] Teresa Brennan, *The Transmission of Affect* (Ithaca, NY: Cornell University Press, 2004), 93.
[5] Ibid.

reliance on two scribes not only allowed her to produce the book but also enhanced its authority in several ways. As Lynn Staley points out, Kempe would have had good reason to invent a scribe even if she hadn't used one, for the scribes offer legitimacy to her narrative, suggesting it has been vetted to some extent.[6] Sebastian Sobecki has shown that Kempe's son was likely her first scribe: he was the Englishman by birth who had wedded in Germany before returning to England, and he is the man whom Kempe trusted implicitly.[7] When her son died before he had completed the book, she brought it to a priest, who found 'the book was so badly written that he could hardly understand it, for it was neither good English nor German, nor were the letters shaped or formed as other letters are' (5). In other words, the book was such a mess the priest couldn't read it; nor could another man who had once read letters from her son sent from Germany. The situation is resolved when Kempe prays to God for the priest to 'purchase him grace to read it and also to write it' (5). When the priest finds that he can now decipher the text, he implicitly confirms Kempe's spiritual authority. This pattern is repeated throughout the *Book*: others doubt Kempe's authority, become convinced of it and eventually bear witness to it. Moreover, Kempe herself is one of those who initially seems to doubt her vocation, becomes convinced of it and eventually voices her certainty.

The Proem ends by explaining that because the *Book* was ultimately written over twenty years after she had first had her feelings and revelations it is structured, like *Fleabag*, around resonant moments rather than chronological order. According to Kempe,

> This book is not written in order, everything after the other as it was done, but as the matter came to the creature in mind when it was written, for it was so long before it was written that she had forgotten the time and the order when things befell. And therefore she had nothing written but that she knew right well for very truth.
>
> (5)

Like *Fleabag*, The Book of Margery Kempe mainly represents its protagonist in the third person with a self-deprecating name: creature. Every once and a while the first person slips in, but this is rare. What is also clear is that the structure gravitates around trauma. The audience learns very early in *Fleabag* that Fleabag is fixated on the trauma caused by two losses and their aftermath: she has lost her mother to breast cancer and her best friend to an accidental death. As the series proceeds, Fleabag slowly reveals why she feels so much guilt regarding her best friend's death. The first chapter in *The Book of Margery Kempe* reveals that Kempe experienced significant trauma during the birth of her first child. Worried for her life, she sent for a priest to confess, 'for she had a thing in conscience which she had never shown before that time in all her life'

---

[6] Lynn Staley, *Margery Kempe's Dissenting Fictions* (University Park, PA: Pennsylvania State University Press, 1994).

[7] Sebastian Sobecki, '"The writyng of this tretys": Margery Kempe's Son and the Authorship of her Book', *Studies in the Age of Chaucer* 37 (2015): 257–83.

(6–7). Unfortunately, she remains unable to confess, for 'when she came to the point to say that thing which she had so long concealed, her confessor was a little too hasty and began sharply to reprove her before she had fully said her intent' (7), so she lives for the rest of her life with the traumatic experience of this birth, the unconfessed sin and the sense that she has been silenced regarding her own experience. This leads her to have a vision of devils who threaten her, to entertain suicidal thoughts and to bite her own hand so violently that the scar can be seen for the rest of her life. She reveals that Christ came to her at the depth of her despair. She recovered, and others came to see her 'to see how our Lord Jesus Christ had wrought his grace in her' (8). There has been a great deal of speculation about what her sin might be, for it is never revealed explicitly in the book, but I want to focus on the way Kempe's insistence on speaking about the conversion from spiritual discomfort to faith invites readers to convert social discomfort to grace.

Throughout her *Book*, Kempe insists that if her actions create social discomfort, it is only because she is more aligned with God's grace than with the world. She wasn't always like this. There was a time when she loved beautiful clothes and, like Augustine, 'all her desire was to be worshipped by the people' (8). Moreover, she was not content with what she had, 'but ever desired more and more' (9). This led her to pursue other ways to make money. She became a brewer for three or four years but ended up losing money because the ale wouldn't proof properly. She bought two horses to mill corn, but the horses wouldn't draw. Her failures in these ventures lead some to say 'she was accursed' (9) while others believe 'it was the high mercy of our Lord Jesus Christ that had summoned and called her from the pride and vanity of the wretched world' (9–10). The adversity she faces eventually leads her to ask for mercy, and she is rewarded by hearing 'a sound of melody so sweet and delectable, she thought, as if she had been in paradise' (10). The music she hears transforms her mood profoundly, for she jumps out of bed and says, 'Alas, that ever I did sin; it is full merry in heaven' (10). She begins thinking about the joy of heaven so much that her former friends become angry with her, 'for she would not hear any speak of worldly things, as they did and as she did before' (10). Similar scenes are repeated throughout the text. For example, when Kempe goes on pilgrimage, her fellowship becomes 'most displeased because she wept so much and spoke always of the love and goodness of our Lord, as well at the table as in other places' (45). They, in turn, 'reproved her and greatly chided her and said they would not suffer her as her husband did when she was at home and in England' (45). Kempe's *Book* reveals that others regard her as the kind of person Sara Ahmed describes when pointing out that 'the female troublemaker might be trouble because she gets in the way of the happiness of others'.[8] Kempe's former friends and companions on the pilgrimage just want to have a good time: thinking about the mirth of heaven or the love and goodness of God can be a real buzzkill for people who just want to enjoy worldly pleasures guilt-free.

There are several illuminating parallels between the way Kempe represents her experience speaking with others and Ahmed's analysis of the way people often respond

---

[8] Sara Ahmed, *The Promise of Happiness* (Durham: Duke University Press, 2010), 60.

to feminists who dare to speak out. 'However she speaks', Ahmed writes, 'the feminist is usually the one who is viewed as "causing the argument", who is disturbing the fragility of peace'.[9] Whether or not we would use the word feminist to describe Kempe, it is not difficult to see that Ahmed's point explains many reactions to Kempe as depicted in the book and the critical tradition. Kempe prioritizes heavenly belonging over fitting in with her earthly companions. Her exchange with her companions on pilgrimage in particular exposes their hypocrisy, and they're not happy about it. Instead of accepting that Kempe is unhappy, a troublemaker or an awkward individual, I think we can learn a great deal by delving deeper into scenes that engender awkwardness and asking what they reveal about the situation. The most interesting of these in the *Book*, from my perspective, occur when there is a legitimate disagreement about what it means to be attuned to God.

Several of these moments are signalled by laughter, which both reveals and creates awkwardness in *The Book of Margery Kempe* as it does in *Fleabag*. Kempe recognizes that laughter can play this role, and she uses it in one story to diffuse a tense situation that has arisen in response to her violation of the norm that held that only men should speak of holy matters. Early in the *Book*, a young monk in Canterbury accosts Kempe after hearing her speak. He says, 'Either you have the Holy Ghost or else you have a devil within you, for what you speak here to us, it is Holy Writ, and that have you not of yourself' (22). The young monk raises the problem known as *discretio spiritii* [discretion of spirits] that was especially pertinent for late-medieval people, especially women who claimed to hear the voice of God – a group as diverse as Bridget of Sweden, Julian of Norwich and Joan of Arc – because it was hard for men to determine whether their experiences were sent by God or the devil. When she is challenged on these grounds, Kempe asks leave to tell a tale, and the people express their desire to hear her speak by proclaiming in a collective voice, 'Let her say what she will' (22). Kempe tells a story about a man who had sinned, confessed and been told by his confessor to hire men to reprove him for his sins for a year. One day, the man 'came among many great men as now are here, God save you all, and stood among them as I do now among you, despising him as you do me' (22). The man's response is unexpected: he laughs or smiles and has 'good game at their words' (22). The greatest man among the crowd asks, 'Why do laugh you, wretch, since you are greatly despised?' (22) The man's reply reveals Kempe's wit: 'A, sir, I have a great cause to laugh, for I have many days put silver out of my purse and hired men to chide me for the remission of my sin, and this day I may keep my silver in my purse. I thank you all' (22). Kempe reveals that she has been talking about her own situation, for she had felt sorrow that she 'had no shame, scorn, and despite as I was worthy' (22). Thanks to the experience she endured that day, she's now had more than enough scorn to remain humble. While Kempe maintains the line that her worthiness increases through the disapproval of others, the monks lose their poise.

What happens next is not funny, for the monks, having lost face, align themselves against Kempe. They now speak in a collective voice, proclaiming she shall be burnt as

[9] Ibid., 65.

a heretic: 'You shall be burnt, false Lollard. There is a cartful of thorns ready for you and a tun [barrel] to burn you with' (22). The monks would have known that they didn't have the legal authority to condemn her to the flames, but that does not stop them from turning against her. Unfortunately for Kempe, the crowd picks up on their discomfort and anger, and they now use their collective voice to condemn her. They say, together, 'Take and burn her' (22). Kempe recognizes the danger that has arisen, and she registers it as discomfort in her body: 'and the creature stood still, trembling and quaking full sorely in her flesh, without any earthly comfort, and knew not where her husband was gone' (22). Whether she was trying to diffuse the awkward confrontation earlier or not, she feels uncomfortable about the way the situation has developed.

Two young men appear, apparently the answer to Kempe's prayers, and they play the same role as the two angels who save Lot from the angry mob in the Book of Genesis and the poem *Cleanness*. These two men 'brought her home to her hostel and made her great comfort, praying her to pray for them, and there found she her husband' (23). Their actions provide insight into the broader exchange and its outcome. While Kempe's book conveys the words spoken in the exchange, those words do not fully convey the anger that the monks direct towards her nor the reason why the crowd so quickly joins in with them. The fact that the monks and bystanders speak collectively provides evidence of the kind of entrainment that Brennan describes. The scene above can best be explained if one imagines what it might have felt like to be there as Kempe, the monks who clearly feel threatened by her or those who participated in the scene in other ways. Entrainment plays a crucial role in this part of Kempe's *Book* as well as Brennan's argument, for it can create 'opposing positions in relation to a common affective thread'.[10] This episode distinguishes between those who are willing to go along with the general sentiment like reed stalks blowing in the wind and those few who attempt to stand up against it. Ahmed's description of the way feminists are often perceived again applies to Kempe here: 'In the thick sociality of everyday spaces, feminists are thus attributed as the origin of bad feeling, as the ones who ruin the atmosphere, which is how the atmosphere might be imagined (retrospectively) as shared.'[11] She is not the one yelling, but the monks identify Kempe as the origin of bad feeling, and the bystanders agree. Their collective speech marks their entrainment even if we cannot sense the atmosphere ourselves. Thankfully,

> despite hormones, pheromones, and wavelengths affecting one's chemistry or nervous system directly, the fact is that people are different. The fact, too, is that even when a strong affect has most people in its collective grip, there are exceptions. A favorite theme of plays and screenplays is the lone resister, the one who holds out against a common affect, usually of persecution.[12]

Initially, Kempe is the lone resister. She holds out against a common affect and considers her persecution as a badge of honour even if, in this case, it has clearly put her in a

---

[10] Brennan, *Transmission*, 9.
[11] Ahmed, *Happiness*, 65.
[12] Brennan, *Transmission*, 11.

precarious situation. But her resistance inspires others, who support her and view her as source of spiritual strength. Kempe invites readers (who may have been reading her book as part of a group) to feel compassion: whether they start out like the crowd, ready to condemn her, or like the two young men who seem to appear on the scene, she provides her audience with an opportunity to feel motivated to relieve the suffering of others.

This becomes evident as the pattern of people turning both away and towards Kempe is repeated and varied throughout the text. She clearly makes men of religion uncomfortable, and they express their concern about her influence in language that describes her effect on other people. A number of clerks, again speaking collectively, tell the Archbishop of York that 'the people have great faith in her dalliance, and perhaps she might pervert some of them' (92). She convinces the Archbishop of her orthodoxy. The famous friar in Lynn takes the same approach. He says, 'I would this woman were out of the church; she annoys the people' (110). This time, 'some who were her friends answered again, "Sir, have her excused"' (110). Unwilling to relinquish his petty grievance, the same friar preaches against her in 'Saint James chapel yard at Lynn' (112), with the result that 'many of those who pretended their friendship turned back for a little vain dread that they had of his words and dared not well speak with her' (112). One of these men was 'the priest who wrote the treatise' (113). In other words, this priest who initially doubted her was eventually 'moved him to give credence to the said creature' (113), to become one of her scribes. His change of heart inspires others: 'and many others who had forsaken her through the friar's preaching **repented and turned again** unto her by process of time …' (113). Throughout the book, people are moved to act not only through words but through a kind of collective re-alignment that we might now understand as entrainment. Those who oppose Kempe, according to the logic of her Book, are focused not on God's intentions but with maintaining their alignment with each other.

Nonetheless, Kempe worries about the level of persecution she experiences, and she repeatedly asks for reassurance. After the episode at Canterbury, she worries that others will 'wonder upon me' (25). Christ confirms that they will, but he also reassures her: 'yes, daughter, the more wondering that you have for my love, the more you please me' (25). Despite Christ's words, Kempe continues to feel discomfort, especially when she feels doubt about what God is telling her to do. While she considers her weeping a gift, her embodied experience often echoes the discomfort Augustine recounts before he came to find rest in God: 'then she fell down and cried with loud voice, wonderfully **turning and twisting her body on every side**' (51). Although it may seem like a stretch to suggest that Kempe might be alluding to Augustine, she later tells a provocative story about a priest who falls asleep in a garden near 'a fair pear tree' and then dreams about a bear who ate all the pears and then 'voided them out again at the shameful part' (93), which is remarkably on the nose as a reference to the pear tree episode in the *Confessions*.

At times, others call Kempe out for not seeming to suffer enough bodily discomfort. On one occasion, a steward grows angry 'because she laughed and made good cheer', and he goes on to tell her, 'Holy folk should not laugh' (99). Her reply echoes the story she told the monks at Canterbury: 'Sir, I have great cause to laugh, for the more shame and despite I suffer, the merrier may I be in our Lord Jesus Christ' (99). When Kempe worries that the discomfort she consistently causes and feels might be a problem, Christ appears to offer reassurance: 'Nay, nay, daughter, for that thing that I love best they love not, and that is shames, despites, scorns, and reproofs from the people, and therefore shall they not have this grace. For, daughter, I tell you, he who dreads the shames of the world may not perfectly love good' (116). At one point, Christ praises how well she has aligned her intentions to his will by using a memorable simile: 'Daughter, because you are so buxom to my will and cleave as sorely unto me as to a man's hands cleaves the skin of dried fish when it is boiled' (66–7). This image is strikingly evocative, appealing as it does to the senses of sight, touch and smell while praising Kempe for acting in a way that not only annoys others but also unites people in their desire to persecute her. Christ reassures her that she belongs to him because she does not care whether she fits in or not: she is worthy because she is willing to be called the problem for naming the problem. She embraces her role as the 'feminist killjoy'. Ultimately, Kempe depicts the awkwardness she is accused of creating as a sign of the grace bestowed upon her.

The remainder of this chapter concerns discomfort associated with the other aspect of communing that Kempe's *Book* explores. This part of the chapter deals with sexual violence, which is an uncomfortable but important part of Kempe's narrative. I do not claim to speak for Kempe. My aim is to understand her intentions as she expresses them in her *Book*. I will therefore provide some contextual information to inform my reading of it. I want to make it clear that by seeking to understand how people in the past thought about their behaviour, I do not condone or apologize for that behaviour then or now. Moreover, I think it is entirely reasonable to describe what Kempe experiences in her relationship with her husband as marital rape even though this is probably not what late-medieval people were likely to have called it. I think it is reasonable to assert that the experience of unwanted sex is traumatic for her while also trying to understand the way that she represents her relationship with her husband.

To explain my approach, I will dwell for a moment on the way that *Fleabag* represents the bank manager who is accused of sexual harassment when he encounters Fleabag while attending the 'Better Man' workshop. When the bank manager recognizes Fleabag and begins a conversation with her, she indicates her lips are sealed because of the retreat. At first, this looks like a miniature version of the overall setup, where women are silent in the face of misogynistic men. But it leads to an expression of vulnerability on his part. He tells Fleabag that he has been acting out of a sense of shame: 'I'm just a very disappointing man.'[13] He reveals that what he wants is to feel a sense of belonging with his wife and family:

> I want to move back home; I want to hug my wife, protect my children, protect my daughter. I want to move on. I want to apologize to everyone. I want to go to the theatre. I want to take clean cups out of the dishwasher, and put them in the cupboard, at home. And the next morning I want to watch my wife drink from them. I want to make her feel good. I want to make her orgasm again, and again. Truly.[14]

---

[13] *Fleabag*, season 1, episode 4.
[14] Ibid.

Fleabag feels moved to respond to his expression of vulnerability with one of her own: 'I just want to cry all the time.'[15] The conversation ends when both indicate their lips are sealed. Kempe claims she feels like she wants to cry all the time as a sign of God's grace, but her incessant crying is like Fleabag's in that it provides a compelling reminder about the vulnerability she experiences. In what follows, I aim to listen carefully to what she has to say about that experience. I also want to suggest that she demonstrates the value of having uncomfortable conversations about the effects of sex and sexual violence.

After Kempe hears heavenly music while she was lying in her bed, she realizes that she no longer wants to have sex with her husband, John. This event took place after the traumatic experience she endured after the birth of her first child, but it is not entirely clear whether it took place before or during the time she bore thirteen more children or at a later date. They certainly had sex against Margery's will at some point, and the imagery she uses to describe her desire to live chastely leaves no doubt about the extent to which she finds the prospect of sex to be distressing:

> And after this time she had never desire to common fleshly with her husband, for the debt of matrimony was so abominable to her that she had rather, she thought, eat or drink the ooze, the muck in the channel, than to consent to any fleshly communing, save only for obedience. And so she said to her husband, 'I may not deny you my body, but the love of my heart and my affection is drawn from all earthly creatures and set only in God.'
>
> (10)

Kempe begins the passage with two euphemisms for sex. As I noted earlier, Kempe uses the word 'common' to describe sex as well as other activities that connect her to others, like sharing a conversation or a meal. She also describes sex as 'the debt of matrimony'. This phrase was understood in the Middle Ages to refer to the mutual obligation spouses had to each other to engage in intercourse. Kempe very clearly tells John that she will not refuse to have sex with him but that she would rather eat or drink the ooze or muck in the channel than to do it out of anything other than obligation. This is worse than it sounds to our ears. The channel she mentions is not the English channel but the 'gutter, drain, or ditch' (*MED*, s.v., 'chanel') where filth and sewage would flow out of a town like King's Lynn. She is literally saying she would rather eat shit than have sex with John. In other words, Kempe feels distressed about being compelled to engage in non-consensual sex. And John knows it. Just because something is legally permissible, it does not mean it is morally permissible, nor that it does not cause trauma. John's refusal to grant Kempe's request for marital chastity is therefore indefensible.

Kempe's *Book* devotes substantial time to the question of what it means for her to live a chaste life, which has an impact on her relationship with John and causes social discomfort as well. I hope it is possible to argue that Kempe makes meaning from her experience in a theologically sophisticated way without equivocating about the

---

[15] Ibid.

distress she experiences or seeming to apologize for how long it takes John to accept her will. The *Book* seems to encourage this approach. For example, Kempe contrasts the revulsion she feels about sex with her husband with the temptation to have sex with another man:

> She lay by her husband, and, whether to common with him, it was so abominable unto her that she might not endure it, and yet it was lawful unto her, at a lawful time, if she had wanted. But ever she was labored with the other man, whether to sin with him inasmuch as he had spoken to her. At the last, through the inopportunity of temptation and the lack of discretion, she was overcome, and **consented in her mind**, and went to the man to learn if he would then **consent** to her.
>
> (13)

Her distress at the prospect of having sex with her husband persists, but she insists this is not because sex is inherently sinful. When she describes sex with her husband being lawful to her and at a lawful time, she is reminding her readers that sex was permitted to medieval Christians only under certain conditions: they had to be married, they could only have sex at certain times (of the day, week, month, year), and their intentions needed to be right (i.e. they were having intercourse to reproduce and not for pleasure). Thus Kempe contrasts her abhorrence of theologically sanctioned sex with her husband with the enticing prospect of sinful sex with another man. While she initially refuses this man's approach and then struggles with temptation, she is eventually overcome. Kempe's use of the phrase '**consented in her mind**' suggests that she has adopted an Augustinian view of sin. In this view, which Augustine proposes in *De Trinitate* and Thomas Aquinas takes up in *Summa Theologica*, there are three stages to sin. The first occurs when one perceives something that causes delight. The second is when the mind delights in the perception and continues to contemplate it. The third is when the will consents. This, for Augustine, is when the sin actually takes place.[16] I think Kempe adopts this view because she seems to imply that she has already sinned with the other man because it was her **intention** to sin. At this point, the man refuses, saying 'he had rather been hewn as small as meat for the pot' than sleep with her, and she goes away 'shamed and confused' (13). Kempe explains that she does not feel ashamed because the man turned her down but because she thought she had developed 'a perfect will never to turn again to her sin', but 'now she saw how she had consented in her will to do sin' (13). This leads her to suffer despair until she is finally able to confess many times, do penance and be governed by the rules of the church once again.

The way that Kempe speaks about consent in this scene also informs the way that she talks about non-consensual sex with her husband. Read in light of Augustine's theory of sin, Kempe's insistence that she would rather eat shit than consent to sex with John can be read as a theologically sophisticated way of allowing her to fulfil her marriage debt, and thus avoid transgressing church doctrine, while not consenting in her mind to the sin of lechery by enjoying sex. This does not mitigate the distress

---

[16] Augustine, *On The Trinity, Books 8–15*, ed. Gareth B. Matthews, trans. Stephen McKenna, Cambridge Texts in the History of Philosophy (Cambridge: Cambridge University Press, 2002), 12.12.

she feels when John compels her to have sex, but it shows that Kempe is capable of drawing on theological language in order to claim agency precisely when it is being denied to her. This, in turn, reveals a bigger theological question: what kind of doctrine repeatedly insists that certain acts are sinful in many instances and then compels people (mostly women, but sometimes men) to engage in those acts against their will at the few times when they are not sinful? Paradoxically, Kempe uses that doctrine's language to convince John to agree to a chaste marriage, but the awkwardness of the exchange draws attention to the fact that the norms in effect here are a more intractable problem than the individuals who ultimately find a way to live with them.

The negotiations that lead Kempe and her husband to live together in a chaste marriage take up a significant portion of the *Book*, and I think they offer a model for helping readers understand how Kempe transforms conversation into opportunities for compassion. The turning point occurs when Kempe and John have a revealing conversation on their way back from York. I cite the exchange at length because it is highly revealing. It begins with a remarkably awkward question:

> 'Margery, if there came a man with a sword and would smite off my head unless I should common naturally with you as I have done before, tell me the truth from your conscience – for you say you will not lie – whether would you suffer my head to be smote off or else suffer me to meddle with you again, as I did at one time?'
>
> 'Alas, sir,' she said, 'why move you this matter, and have we been chaste these eight weeks?'
>
> 'For I will know the truth of your heart.'
>
> And then she said with great sorrow, 'Forsooth I had rather see you be slain than we should turn again to our uncleanness.'
>
> And then he said again, 'You are no good wife.'
>
> And then she asked her husband what was the cause that he had not meddled with her eight weeks before, since she lay with him every night in his bed. And he said was so made afraid when he would have touched her that he dared do no more.
>
> (18–19)

John's question is awkward because it seems to be moving them in the wrong direction, for they have been living chastely for some time. John is implicitly asking her what would compel her to have sex with him again after he has not insisted on it for eight weeks. Intriguingly, he asks what she would do if someone was threatening *him* rather than *her*. As the exchange goes on, Kempe asks him if he is ready to make a vow of chastity yet. He refuses, explaining that 'now may I use you without deadly sin and then might I not so' (19). She ends this portion of the exchange by saying, 'If it be the will of the Holy Ghost to fulfill what I have said, I pray God you may consent thereto; and, if it be not the will of the Holy Ghost, I pray God you never consent thereto' (19). She insists that she is less concerned with what she desires than with aligning her intentions with God's will. Nonetheless, she feels worried about her chastity again.

The relationship takes a different turn when they take a break under a cross on the way to Bridlington. John says that he will make a deal with Margery: if she grants his desire, he will grant hers. This seems rather ominous until the terms of the deal are revealed. John wants three things. First, to 'lie still together in one bed as we have done before' (19); that is, to sleep together but not to have sex. Second, he asks that she pay his debts before she leaves on pilgrimage to Jerusalem; that is, he asks her to pay his financial debts rather than the marriage debt. Third, he asks her to 'eat and drink with me on Fridays as you were wont to do' (19). Having committed herself to fasting, Kempe initially refuses, and John threatens to 'meddle you again' (19). She prays for guidance, and Christ tells her to take the deal. In fact, Christ reveals, fasting was a means to an end: it was the leverage he knew she would need to negotiate her way to a chaste marriage. When John hears that she agrees to his conditions, he says, 'As free may your body be to God as it has been to me' (20), which might not seem that generous to us but is actually quite revealing. Whatever we have thought of him up to this point, he has come to understand that what he really craves isn't 'fleshly commoning' but other types of communing: being close, eating together and sharing conversation.

Kempe does make her body as free to God (or Christ, anyway) as she was with her husband. At one point, Christ uses a telling simile when he tells her that he fares 'like a man who loves well his wife' (60). Elsewhere, he describes how she should know his love:

> For it is suitable for the wife to be homely with her husband. Be he never so great a lord and she so poor a woman when he wedded her, yet they must lie together and rest together in joy and peace. Right so must it be between you and me, for I take no heed what you have been but what you would be. And oftentimes have I told you that I have clean forgiven you all your sins. Therefore must I needs be homely with you and lie in your bed. Daughter, you desire greatly to see me, and you may boldly, when you are in your bed, take me to you as your wedded husband, as your most worthy darling, and as your sweet son, for I will be loved as a son should be loved by the mother and will that you love me, daughter, as a good wife ought to love her husband. And therefore you may boldly take me in the arms of your soul and kiss my mouth, my head, and my feet as sweetly as you will.
>
> (66)

Although the simile seems to get muddled here when Christ suggests that she should love him as a husband and son, it actually suggests that she imagines communing with Christ in the same way that her husband wants to commune with her: by sharing her bed but not 'meddling'. Near the end of Book Two, Christ confirms that John was right to release Kempe from her marriage debt and pursue her dream of becoming wedded to Christ, at least figuratively. At the same time, he points out the larger structural problem with medieval Christian doctrine on marriage:

> Daughter, if you knew how many wives there are in this world who would love me and serve me right well and duly, if they might be as freely from their husbands as you are from yours, you would say that you were right much beholden unto me. And yet **are they put from their wills** and suffer full great pain, and therefore shall they have right great reward in heaven, for I receive every good will as for deed.
>
> (154)

Christ's words to Margery identify the problem clearly: women suffer because their husbands fail to acknowledge they have a will of their own, especially when it comes to sex. For Christ, as for Kempe, women should have the freedom to devote themselves body and soul to God. Christ tries to mitigate this problem by indicating that these women will be rewarded in heaven for having the right intentions. He insists they will be rewarded for their 'good will' rather than being held accountable for acts they were compelled to do against their will.

Kempe also creates social discomfort when she finally manages to exert her will by taking a vow of chastity with her husband. She is frequently reprimanded for wearing white, which was reserved as a sign of virginity or chastity, since people do not believe she is really living chastely. Near the end of her life and the *Book*, this leads to serious problems when Kempe and John take separate living quarters because people doubt they are living chastely. Kempe reminds readers that 'both **with one assent and with free will of the other** had made a vow to live chaste' (131). While they are separated, John falls down the stairs and injures himself quite seriously. Many people blame Kempe for the incident because they believe they should have been living together. However, Kempe takes this as an opportunity for penance, for her husband (now sixty years of age) has become like an infant who does not have the ability to control basic bodily functions:

> Then she took her husband with her and kept him years after, as long as he lived, and had full much labor with him, for in his last days he turned childish again and lacked reason so that he could not do his own easement by going to a stool, or else he would not, but, as a child, voided his natural digestion in his linen clothes where he sat by the fire or at the table, whether it were, he would spare no place. And therefore was her labor much the more in washing and wringing and her expense in making fires and hindered her full much from her contemplation, so that many times she should have been irked at her labor save she bethought herself of how she in her young age had full many delectable thoughts, fleshly lusts, and inordinate loves for his person. And therefore she was glad to be punished with the same person and took it much the more easily and served him and helped him, as she thought, as she would have done Christ himself.
>
> (132)

The final line not only alludes to the maxim one should see Christ in the lowest but also alludes to Christ's injunction for Kempe to love him like a husband and a son. As in Julian of Norwich's *Revelations*, excrement can be seen as a sign of sin. But Kempe transforms the figurative into the literal as a way of doing penance for the desires she had felt when they were young together by suffering the indignities of old age with her husband.

Throughout her *Book*, and rather frequently in the criticism, Kempe is identified as an awkward person. I hope to have shown, though, that one of her most remarkable achievements is to use awkward situations in order to reveal the potential that dialogic conversation, which she also describes as 'comoning' and 'daliaunce', might have for overcoming the hypocrisy, injustice and miscommunication that create the conditions for awkwardness. If we persist in seeing her as an awkward individual, the norms that precipitate her trauma – those pertaining to marriage and gender – will remain unchallenged and unchanged. Many of those norms have persisted over time, and *Fleabag* reveals that many remain today. It is therefore valuable to shift the mode of analysis to consider the circumstances and norms as the cause of awkwardness. *The Book of Margery Kempe* provides a glimpse into the historical dimension of Ahmed's argument that the person who identifies the problem is often identified as the problem. One reason that so much early criticism of Kempe's *Book* focused on diagnosing her may be because what she had to say was profoundly troubling for the critics at that time. Rather than asking what institutions or norms she was calling out, it was more expedient for scholars who wanted to maintain those institutions and norms to explain why she was the problem. It was often beneficial to say she was hysterical than to critique the way that theological norms associated with marriage have long justified non-consensual sex. Kempe often creates discomfort by violating norms associated with theological discourse, but that should not distract us from asking whose interests are served by identifying Kempe as the awkward individual, troublemaker or feminist killjoy, rather than accepting the invitation to practise the empathy and compassion needed to challenge norms that do violence.

12

Sing with us, with a merry cheer! The awkwardness of going along with it in *Mankind*

Like *The Book of Margery Kempe*, *Mankind* puts its audience in the awkward position of deciding whether to show compassion for its main character or to go along with those who seem to be having much more fun perverting Mankind to entertain mankind. Before going any further, I should explain that I use the words '*Mankind*' to denote the play, 'Mankind' to denote the character and 'mankind' to denote those people who identify themselves with this term. I do not adopt gender-neutral terms because while I acknowledge that *Mankind* assumes the masculine subject position is the norm, it also raises questions about Mankind's misguided sense of masculinity. Boiled down to its basic elements, this is a play about a man who is lost and refuses to ask for help. The other benefit of maintaining the term Mankind is that it is one of many puns that the playwright uses to draw attention to the duplicity of language, which can both reveal and conceal or give and take.[1] Ultimately, this is what the play does in that it invites its audience to feel part of a collective embodied experience while also making them feel uncomfortable about fitting in with other people. *Mankind* helps those audience members who identify as part of mankind to witness the shame and spite that Mankind suffers when others not only fail to show him compassion but laugh at his condition. It also reminds the audience how hard it is to remain aligned with God when it feels so good to fit in with others while laughing, singing and watching a play together.

Mankind was likely written around 1470, and the only surviving copy was made by a monk named Thomas Hyngman, who made a copy of the play *Wisdom* around the same time. These two plays were later bound with another play, *The Castle of Perseverance*, and the book in which they appear together is now known as the Macro manuscript, after its eighteenth-century owner, and held at Folger Shakespeare Library in Washington, D.C. These plays have come to be called 'morality plays', though this is a later description. They differ in tone, but they all personify concepts in the same way that Disney's *Inside Out* personifies emotions. The process is sometimes spelled out for the audience. Here is what the protagonist of *Mankind* says when he introduces himself:

---

[1] For a more detailed discussion of language in *Mankind*, see Kathy Cawsey, *Images of Language in Middle English Vernacular Writings* (Cambridge: D. S. Brewer, 2020).

> My name is 'Mankind.' I have my composition
> Of a body and of a soul, of condition contrary –
> Betwix them twain is a great division.
> He that should be subject, now he hath the victory.
>
> (194–7)[2]

Mankind therefore shows how the potential for misalignment between body and soul makes Mankind vulnerable to being seduced by vices like Mischief, Nought, New-Guise and Nowadays as well as the demon Titivillus. This is why, the play insists, he should listen to Mercy, even if that character is less interesting than the vices. All the characters would have been distinguished from the audience by their costumes, but they also interact with those watching the play directly and at some points seem to emerge from among them. The audience was likely mixed in terms of its social background and physical situation at the play. Mercy distinguishes patrons based on whether they were sitting or standing: 'O ye sovereigns that sit, and ye brothern that stand right up' (29). This line along with other aspects of the play and developments in theatrical history suggest that it might be helpful to imagine that the play was performed in an innyard or manor hall, which established in turn some of the general principles used to design theatres like Shakespeare's Globe.[3] *Mankind* was written by a skilled playwright to be performed where cast members could mingle with a gathering of people who were likely inclined to laugh and sing together while paying to see some drama unfold.

Mankind is often read as a religious allegory in which Mercy teaches Mankind and mankind about mercy. This is an important aspect of the play, but I will focus on the way that the play consistently figures its audience's desire to fit in and seek approval as an impediment to compassion. The lack of compassion leads Mankind – and perhaps mankind – to feel unworthy of God's mercy and unwilling to ask for it. In the play, the character Mercy explains that 'mankind was dear bought' through the death of Christ. He preaches about 'the great mercy of God' that is given thanks to 'meditation of Our Lady' (21–2). Early in the play, Mankind's alignment with Mercy is expressed through both his words and their form: he imitates Mercy's stanza form, four lines rhyming abab. Mercy is nonetheless worried, and he insists that Mankind will find trouble if he does not ask for mercy as soon as he goes astray: 'If ye displease God, ask mercy anon, / Else [Otherwise] Mischief will be ready to brace [take] you in his bridle' (304–5). The bridle imagery reflects Mercy's view that Mischief, the character and the concept introduced early in the play, will turn Mankind away from God. Even though the play is missing a leaf of the manuscript that clearly includes further conversation between Mischief and Mankind as well as the introduction of New-Guise, Nowadays and Nought, one thing is clear: they are more appealing than Mercy. They certainly have a better sense of rhythm than him, as far as we can tell, for Mercy refuses to dance. As their names suggest, they are also more attuned to the times than Mercy, too.

---

[2] All references to *Mankind* Are from the *Broadview Anthology of British Literature: The Medieval Period*, 3rd edn., ed. Joseph Black et al., 753–73 (Peterborough, ON: Broadview Press, 2015).

[3] Lawrence M. Clopper, 'English Drama: From Ungodly Ludi to Sacred Play,' in *The Cambridge History of Medieval English Literature*, ed. David Wallace, 739–766 (Cambridge: Cambridge University Press, 1999), 755.

New-Guise is basically a devil wearing Prada (Guise means fashion); in other words, New-Guise is a personified version of the men who set the world 'aukewarde' in *The Pricke of Conscience*.[4] Nowadays doesn't need much modernizing, though perhaps 'Newfangled' would capture its tone. Nought translates as Nothing, but perhaps a better name would be Idleness in the double sense of 'not doing anything' and 'doing nothing meaningful'. These three are different manifestations of the desire to be of the world, to fit in with other people and to march (or dance) to the beat of the same drummer.

One way that the vices align themselves with the audience is through laughter. You may not laugh aloud at the citations in this chapter, and that is why you should imagine it being performed in a social setting. As Robert Provine has shown, people are far more likely to laugh when they are with others than when they are alone.[5] In fact, people often laugh at things other than jokes or formal attempts at humour, so the lines I cite here are only one aspect of communal laughter that probably took place during the play. Provine's findings are important because they demonstrate that laughter plays a 'nonlinguistic role in social bonding, solidifying friendships and pulling people into the fold. You can define "friends" and "group members" as those with whom you laugh. But laughter has a darker side, as when group members coordinate their laughter to jeer and exclude outsider'.[6] The vices in *Mankind* exploit both of these functions in order to ensure that the audience laughs with them and at Mercy. To be fair, the vices are much funnier than Mercy, especially when they make jokes at his expense. Many of their jokes probably resonated well with medieval audiences who were familiar with the sounds of Latin from the mass but not fully conversant in it. Such an audience may well have seen their own priests in the depiction of Mercy as a pompous preacher who uses big words to tell people what is good for them. *Mankind* relies on this image to set Mercy up as a stooge from the moment he is introduced:

MERCY. 'Mercy' is my name by denomination.
    I conceive ye have but a little favour in my communication.
NEW-GUISE. Ey, ey, your body is full of English Latin!
    I am afeard° it will brest.°   *afraid / burst*

(122–5)

New-Guise is right that words like denomination, conceive and communication are derived from Latin, and that this leaves the audience with the impression that Mercy is a little more inflated than he should be. Nowadays extends New-Guise's critique by asking Mercy to translate a traditional riddle – one spoken in the voice of the thing to be identified – from English into Latin:

'I have eaten a dish-full of curds,
And I have shitten your mouth full of turds.' –

---

[4] *Prik of Conscience*, ed. James H. Morey, TEAMS Middle English Texts Series (Kalamazoo, MI: Medieval Institute Publications, 2012), 2.592.
[5] Robert Provine, *Laughter: A Scientific Investigation* (London: Penguin, 2001), chap. 3, Kobo.
[6] Ibid.

> Now, open your satchel° with Latin words   *bag*
> And say me this in clerical° manner.   *learned*
>
> (131–4)

Nowadays does not answer his own riddle, but he reinforces its tone when he exclaims, in Latin, '*Osculare fundamentum!*' [Kiss my ass!] (142). The banter goes on and on, in a stanza form that differs from Mercy's (eight lines rhyming aaabcccb). The vices are funny in part because of their incongruous use of Latin, the elevated language, to express base subject matter. Paradoxically, their use of Latin in this register makes Mercy seem like an elite snob for his use of long words even though Mercy's message – anyone can ask for God's grace – is more democratic. Mercy doesn't really endear himself to the audience when all he can muster to interrupt the banter is to say,

> This idle language ye shall repent!
> Out of this place I would ye went.
>
> (147–8)

It sure feels disappointing when the vices, who seem like the kind of guys you'd like to have a beer with, leave a few lines later.

Some members of the audience may have felt awkward about laughing at a play while Mercy explicitly tells them that they will need to account for every idle word, those heard and spoken. Mercy himself seems to think that the humour the vices employ is entirely reliant on the superiority theory of laughter. After they leave, he points out that 'their joy and delight is in derision / of their own Christ' (168–9). They are therefore worse than beasts, who just follow their desires, because they are condemning themselves on judgement day, 'When for every idle word we must yield a reason' (173). This is again a reminder to the audience that they may need to account for the words they say and hear, and it creates incongruity by inviting the audience to feel remorse for taking part in the laughter and idle speech that the play works to elicit. The lines provoke laughter, and they create an awkward situation.

Mercy's warning about idle words gets lost somewhat when Mankind appears on stage with a spade to stave off Idleness through his labour. Nonetheless, Mercy takes the time to warn Mankind – somewhat dryly it must be said – about the vices:

> Moreover, in special I give you in charge:
> Beware of New-Guise, Nowadays, and Nought!
> Nice° in their array, in language they be large.   *unrestrained*
> To **pervert** your conditions, all their means shall be sought.
>
> Good son, intromit° not yourself in their company!   *put*
> They heard not a mass this twelmonth, I dare well say.   *year*
> Give them none audience; they will tell you many a lie.
> Do truly your labour, and keep your holy day.
>
> (293–9)

Mercy is profoundly worried that the vices will pervert Mankind by turning him away from Mercy in the same way that Augustine feels he is being perverted by his flesh. He is right to worry. That is exactly their goal. Mercy thinks labour will help Mankind, and his spade is therefore an important prop throughout the play. In fact, Mischief returns, identifying himself in case audience members have forgotten him – 'I, Mischief, was here at the beginning of the game, / And argued with Mercy' (416–17) – and correctly identifies the spade as a weapon that Mankind can wield against New-Guise, Nowadays and Nought. Mankind even uses it for this purpose, keeping them at bay through hard work for a while and then literally beating them with it, producing laughter through slapstick comedy.

Nobody in the audience seems to have brought a spade to help Mankind do his work. In fact, the play relies on the fact that they have come to the place where the play is being performed to take a break from their labour. They have come to an inn or tavern to be idle for a time. According to one of the texts in the thirteenth-century collection known as the *Carmina Burana*, people who go to taverns rarely think about the kinds of things Mercy wants them to think about: 'In taberna quando sumus / non curamus quid sit humus' [When we are in the tavern / we do not think how we will go to dust].⁷ This poem also reveals what people do when they go to the tavern:

Bibit hera, bibit herus,	The mistress drinks, the master drinks,
Bibit miles, bibit clerus,	the soldier drinks, the priest drinks,
Bibit ille, bibit illa,	the man drinks, the woman drinks,
Bibit servus cum ancilla	the servant drinks with the maid,
bibit velox, bibit piger,	the swift man drinks, the lazy man drinks,
Bibit albus, bibit niger,	the white man drinks, the black man drinks,
Bibit constancs, bibit vagus,	the settled man drinks, the wanderer drinks,
Bibit rudis, bibit magus.	The stupid man drinks, the wise man drinks.
Bibit pauper et egrotus,	The poor man drinks, the sick man drinks,
Bibit exul et ignotus,	the exile drinks, and the stranger,
Bibit puer, bibit canus	the boy drinks, the old man drinks
Bibit praesul et decanus,	the bishop drinks, and the deacon,
Bibit soror, bibit frater,	the sister drinks, the brother drinks,
Bibit anus, bibit mater,	the old lady drinks, the mother drinks,
Bibit ista, bibit ille,	that woman drinks, that man drinks,
Bibunt centum, bibunt mille.	a hundred drink, a thousand drink.⁸

Everyone drinks. This may be why everyone seems to ignore Mankind when he tries to tell himself and others, '*Memento, homo, quod cinis es, et in cinerem reverteris*' [Remember, man, that you are dust and to dust you will return] (320). It is pretty hard to think about such serious matters when everyone is not only drinking but singing so passionately about it, as they do in Carl Orff's musical arrangement of this text.⁹ The expectations associated with what is done in taverns makes it pretty difficult for

---

⁷ 'In Taberna Quando Sumus'. Classical Net, 19 May 2020, http://www.classical.net/music/comp.lst/works/orff-cb/carmlyr.php#track14, 1–2.
⁸ Ibid., 33–48.
⁹ itswhatwelooklike, 'Carmina Burana – "In taberna quando sumus" – Carl Orff', 13 May 2011, video, https://www.youtube.com/watch?v=HTfCkCnGRsU.

those in attendance not to give Nought, New-Guise and Nowadays an audience, even though Mercy warns them against doing exactly this.

Not only do the vices find an appreciative audience, they manage to get everyone to sing along with their Christmas song. What follows is a master class in the way that repetition and rhythm can generate a collective experience. Nought asks everyone to sing, and they apparently oblige, first in response and then all together. I include the passage as a whole to do it justice:

> Nought. Now I pray all the yemandry° that is here   *free-born men*
> To sing with us, with a merry cheer!
>
> [*He sings each line; New-Guise and Nowadays encourage the members of the audience to sing along in response.*]
>
> Nought. It is written with a coal, it is written with a coal,
> New-Guise *and* Nowadays. It is written with a coal, it is written with a coal,
> Nought. He that shitteth with his hole, he that shitteth with his hole,
> New-Guise *and* Nowadays. He that shitteth with his hole, he that shitteth with his hole,
> Nought. But he wipe his arse clean, but he wipe his arse clean,
> New-Guise *and* Nowadays. But he wipe his arse clean, but he wipe his arse clean,
> Nought. On his breech it shall be seen, on his breech it shall be seen,
> New-Guise *and* Nowadays. On his breech it shall be seen, on his breech it shall be seen.
>
> (*Cantant omnes:*)
> Holyke, holyke, holyke! Holyke, holyke, holyke!
>
> (330–42)

Every time I have tried this song as a call and response with my classes nearly everyone is singing along by the end. True, I remind them that participation grades are at stake, but the conditions in a twenty-first-century classroom are far less felicitous for collective song than they are in the middle of a play, especially if that play were being performed in venue where they may have been accustomed to singing a new, repetitive, song to the tune of another.

The practice of setting one set of lyrics to the tune of another is known as *contrefactum*. There are several medieval examples of this, but I think 'Bring us in Good Ale' is the most illuminating in this context since it is the kind of song that might have been sung in an inn or tavern and one of its manuscripts suggests it could be sung along to the tune of a Christmas song. 'Bring Us in Good Ale' is eight stanzas long in Oxford, Bodleian Library MS Eng. Poet. E.1 (fol. 41v) and six stanzas long in London, British Library MS Harley 541 (fol. 214v). In the Oxford manuscript (Figure 12) it appears at the bottom of a leaf that includes the music and lyrics of a Christmas song that begins with the words, 'Nowell, Nowell, Nowell'[10] as well as a note that claims, 'Thys is þe tewyn [tune] for þe song folwyng [fo 10] yf so be that ye wyll have a notther tweyn it may be at yowr plesur

---

[10] DIMEV 5952.

Figure 12 Oxford, Bodleian Library, MS Eng. Poet. E. 1, fol. 41v. Reproduced by permission of the Bodleian Libraries, University of Oxford.

for I haue set all the song.' There are some rhythmic difficulties that arise from using this music for 'Bring us in Good Ale', which is something the person who wrote 'fo 10' likely realized: that's where the rest of the song known as 'The salutacyon' actually appears. Having said that, the initial scribe seemed pretty open to the idea that tunes and lyrics could be interchangeable, since he invites those using the manuscript to choose another at their pleasure. For an indication of how this would sound, I invite you to consider listening to a version of it on YouTube, which you can find by searching 'Bring Us in Good Ale (bray harp)'.[11] In case you would like to sing along, here are the lyrics:

Bring us in good ale, and bring us in good ale,
Fore our blessed Lady sak,° bring us in good ale.   *sake*

Bring us in no browne bred, fore that is mad of brane;°   *made of bran*
Nor bring us in no whit bred, for therin is no game:
But bring us in good ale, and bring us in good ale,
Fore our blessed Lady sak,° bring us in good ale.

Bring us in no befe, for ther is many bones;
Bring us in good ale, for that goth downe at ones,°   *once*
And bring us in good ale, and bring us in good ale,
Fore our blessed Lady sak,° bring us in good ale.

Bring us in no bacon, for that is passing fat;
But bring us in good ale, and give us inought° of that,   *enough*
And bring us in good ale, and bring us in good ale,
Fore our blessed Lady sak,° bring us in good ale.

Bring us in no mutton, for that is ofte lene;
Nor bring us in no tripes, for they be seldom clene:
But bring us in good ale, and bring us in good ale,
Fore our blessed Lady sak,° bring us in good ale.

Bring us in no egges, for ther are many shelles;
But bring us in good ale, and give us nothing elles,°   *else*
And bring us in good ale, and bring us in good ale,
Fore our blessed Lady sak,° bring us in good ale.

Bring us in no butter, for therin ar many heres;°   *hairs*
Nor bring us in no pigges flesh, for that will mak us bores:°   *boars*
But bring us in good ale, and bring us in good ale,
Fore our blessed Lady sak,° bring us in good ale.

Bring us in no podinges,° for therin is all gotes blod;°   *puddings / goat's blood*
Nor bring us in no venison, for that is not for our good:
But bring us in good ale, and bring us in good ale,
Fore our blessed Lady sak,° bring us in good ale.

---

[11] IPMusic, 'The Salutation / Bring us in Good ale (bray harp)', 22 November 2016, video, https://www.youtube.com/watch?v=d9Sx9nmKxYM. Bring us in Good Ale begins at 2:17.

Bring us in no capon's° flesh, for that is ofte der;° *fowl's / costly*
Nor bring us in no dokes° flesh for they slobber in the mer:° *duck / pond*
But bring us in good ale, and bring us in good ale,
Fore our blessed Lady sak,° bring us in good ale.[12]

My hunch is that you did not actually sing along, whether you were alone or in company. I suspect that you may have felt more inclined to sing along if you had been in a group in which others were singing. An experienced song leader, like one of the vices in *Mankind*, would likely increase your likelihood of joining in by indicating very clearly when you were expected to join in on the highly repetitive chorus.

The other reason you would be more likely to join in if you were part of a group who were singing it has to do with the way that rhythm functions. Rhythm is what makes it possible not only to sing along with others but also to feel a sense of alignment with others. This is one way in which people can experience what Teresa Brennan calls 'socially induced affect'.[13] As Brennan shows, affective states can be communicated through a variety of means between humans in proximity with each other, and they have an effect from within each person: 'The transmission of affect, if only for an instant, alters the biochemistry and neurology of the subject. The "atmosphere" or the environment literally gets into the individual.'[14] Brennan notes that the faculty of smell is especially critical in the way that we 'feel the atmosphere':[15] As we think about the way that 'Bring Us in Good Ale' and the song in *Mankind* establish mood or atmosphere, then, we will need to consider the fact that it was likely sung in a setting where people could see, hear, feel and smell each other. Since 'pheremones are literally in the air', according to Brennan, touch is less important: 'No physical contact is necessary for a transmission to take place.'[16] Entrainment functions by other means, but it is nonetheless an embodied experience. Rhythm merits special attention, according to Brennan:

> Rhythm is a tool in the expression of agency, just as words are. It can literally convey the tone of an utterance, and, in this sense, it does unite word and affect. Rhythm also has a unifying, regulating role in affective exchanges between two or more people. The rhythmic aspects of behavior at a gathering are critical in both establishing and enhancing a sense of collective purpose and a common understanding. This can be done consciously whereas chemical entrainment works unconsciously. That is to say rhythm unites within a more conscious frame of reference, which is why it may transmit more complex states.[17]

Rhythm can be scaled up and down. It describes the ebb and flow of verbal exchange, the beat in a poem or song, the experience of moving together in time or even the

---

[12] I have drawn on the edition in *The Broadview Anthology of British Literature: The Medieval Period*, 3rd edn., ed. Joseph Black et al., 258–9 (Peterborough, ON: Broadview Press, 2015).
[13] Teresa Brennan, *The Transmission of Affect* (Ithaca, NY: Cornell University Press, 2004), 1.
[14] Ibid.
[15] Ibid., 9.
[16] Ibid., 69.
[17] Ibid., 70.

marking of seasons of rites of passage. Brennan writes that the sense of alignment created through rhythm can create a sense of well being:

> The sense of well being that comes with a rhythmic entrainment with one's fellows (in dancing for instance) is entirely compatible with mutually directed activity of a most intelligent order. By contrast, nonrhythmic or dissonant sound also separates. It leads people to stand apart from one another and generates unease.[18]

Rhythm can establish a powerful sense of connection even when we feel most disconnected. The many videos of people singing together during the Coronavirus lockdowns, either on Zoom or from their balconies, attest to this. Brené Brown provides another example of the sense of connection that singing together can create in *Braving the Wilderness*.[19] She concludes that 'the power of collective joy can transcend that division' that we often feel.[20] That does not mean that everyone in the audience of *Mankind* would have felt entirely comfortable singing along. But the sense of connection the song establishes would have made them feel equally awkward about not joining in or stopping.

While the song in *Mankind* likely helped members of the audience feel connected through their proximity and shared sense of purpose, it likely caused a sense of awkwardness as members of the audience began to register the meaning of the lyrics. Something similar happens in a scene from an episode in the second season of *Arrested Development*, which explores ways that members of the Bluth family feel that they are pulling away from each other. The loss each one feels leads them to seek new connections with other family members. This explains why Michael Bluth and his niece, Maeby, are so excited about the opportunity to sing together when she learns they can set up a 'Karaoke thing' at the Bluth Company Christmas party. Michael tells her to put on the first song in the book, then joins her on stage to sing 'Afternoon Delight'. Their singing isn't entirely in tune or time, but Michael and Maeby clearly enjoy doing it together (yes, that is where the joke is heading): they start out by smiling widely, and the employees at the party smile in turn, some even nodding along. This makes George Michael (Michael's son) and Lindsay (Maeby's mother) stand out, for they believe the performance reveals they aren't needed. They leave. 'Had George Michael and Lindsay stayed', the narrator reveals, 'they might have discovered what Michael and Maeby did: that "Afternoon Delight" was more adult-themed than its innocent melody would have you believe'.[21] As they get into the second stanza, the expression on Michael's face and that of others in the room change from delight to discomfort as they take in the meaning of the words: 'Rubbin' sticks and stones together make the sparks ignite /

---

[18] Ibid.
[19] James DeWeaver, 'Liverpool F.C. & 95,000 Australian Fans Sing "You'll Never Walk Alone" FULL Dolby MCG 24 July 2013', 5 Aug 2015, video, https://www.youtube.com/watch?v=5iLL57puZPM.
[20] Ibid.
[21] *Arrested Development*, season 2, episode 6, 'Afternoon Delight', directed by Jason Bateman, written by Abraham Higginbotham and Chuck Martin, featuring Jason Bateman, Alia Shawkat, Michael Cera and Portia de Rossi, aired 19 December 2004, https://www.netflix.com/title/70140358?s=i&trkid=13747225.

and the thought of rubbin' you is getting so exciting.'²² Realizing what the words are about, Michael stops singing while Maeby carries on alone for a moment: 'Skyrockets in flight! Afternoon Delight!'²³ Thankfully, Michael comes to his senses at this point, stopping the music and announcing he is going to get more punch because it is time for toasts before he insists that Maeby go in a different direction from him when they leave the stage because it will look even worse if she doesn't. Moments earlier, everyone in the room was smiling and nodding along in time. Now, they cringe, turn away and frown. They remain aligned with each other, but now it is in their discomfort.

Some members of *Mankind*'s audience likely reacted in the same way as the characters in *Arrested Development* as they realized what they were singing. Some people might have stopped singing or stopped a loved-one from singing, but it seems likely to me that most audience members continued to sing, at least in part, because that's what everyone else was doing. Like Michael Bluth, *Mankind*'s audience members probably had an uncomfortable moment as they recognized the incongruity between what they thought they were about to sing and what they were actually singing. This would have been enhanced by the fact that Nowadays suggests that they are about to sing 'a Christmas song' (331). Familiarity with the tune might have helped the audience to sing collectively quickly, but it is also likely to have heightened the audience's sense of dissonance when they contrasted the well-known lyrics with the new ones, which make the song literally about assholes. While these audience members might have been shocked or surprised, they could hardly complain if they continued participating to the end of the song when *sanctus, sanctus, sanctus* [holy, holy, holy] is translated as 'hole-lick, hole-lick, hole-lick'. Unlike Michael and Maeby, though, many audience members would have found it difficult to stop once they had gotten going: it seems likely that those who had chosen to go to a performance of this kind would have laughed at the incongruity of their expectations about the song and the reality of the lyrics and kept singing along with the group. They would want to fit in, after all.

As incongruous as the song might have seemed in comparison to the Christmas song that was promised, it reinforces the play's major theme. As the song in *Mankind* explains, it is written that anyone who does not wipe their bottom clean after defecating will leave traces of it in their underwear. Everyone poops, so the song's message applies to everyone at a literal level. It also applies to everyone if we understand defecation as a metaphor for sin. The question is not to poo or not to poo, but what can be done afterwards so it doesn't become a shameful mess. The song effectively provides audience members an embodied example of the point that it is making. Through its use of repetition and rhythm, it has enticed audience members to adopt the 'large' [unrestrained] language they were warned that Nought, New-Guise and Nowadays would use. They not only enjoy the idle words that the vices offer but participate in singing them while also failing to speak at other times.

The audience's participation in the song represents a broader pattern in the play insofar as it reveals how other human beings – mankind in the play's language – might collude in Mankind's fall from grace. In other words, the act of singing together

[22] Ibid.
[23] Ibid.

embodies the paradox that people seeking to fit with each other seem to be actively preventing others amongst them – the character named Mankind or anyone who kept singing despite being uncomfortable about the song's content – from seeking Mercy. This is the paradox that Brené Brown describes when she notes that fitting in and seeking approval 'are not only hollow substitutes for belonging, but often barriers to it'.[24] In this play, Mankind struggles to accept that he is worthy of Mercy. One of the reasons that he struggles so much is that the play makes it far easier for members of the audience to align themselves with the vices, led by Mischief, than with Mercy, who is a killjoy (though not a feminist). They're fun, they're funny and they let audience members fit in and seek approval rather than presenting their authentic, imperfect selves to the world.

While the part of mankind in the audience might have gone along with the song, Mankind the character has been eschewing idleness by working the soil instead of joining in the song. His labour allows him to eschew vice. After he manages to fend off Nought, New-Guise and Nowadays, Mischief helps them to come up with a new plan. They will bring in another demon, one with a powerful (or perhaps just a great big) head, but they need to entice him with money. The vices begin their collection by indicating that nobody will see this new marvel if they don't pay up:

> NEW-GUISE Yea, go thy way, we shall gather money unto –
> Else there shall no man him see.
> Now ghostly° to our purpose, worshipful sovereigns.   *devoutly*
> We intend to gather money, if it please your negligence,
> For a man with a head that is of great omnipotence.
>
>   (456–60)

Knowing again how the general will can be turned, they start taking up the collection by turning to a leader in the audience:

> NEW-GUISE. At the good-man of this house first we will assay.
> God bless you, master! Ye say us ill, yet ye will not say 'nay.'
> Let us go by and by, and do them pay.
> Ye pay all alike. Well mut ye fare!°   *Good luck to you*
>
>   (466–9)

The vices use people's desire to fit in and seek approval against them: like street performers today, they know that people will feel awkward about not paying up if everyone else seems to be doing it. They also know that people *say* they don't like the vices, but they'll pay up quickly enough to witness the drama of someone else being tempted. By paying at this point, the audience members have done exactly what Mercy warned them not to do: they have given Nought, New-Guise and Nowadays an audience. In fact, they have just paid to continue serving as that audience.

The playwright clearly expected the audience to pay, for a demon shows up after the collection and announces, '*Ego sum dominantium dominus* [I am the lord of lords],

---

[24] Brené Brown, *The Gifts of Imperfection* (Center City, MN: Hazelden Press, 2010), 26.

and my name is Titivillus' (474). Particularly alert audience members might have recognized already that Mercy had also warned Mankind about this demon, who is the worst of all:

> MERCY. Beware of Titivillus – for he leseth° no way –   *loses*
> That goth° invisible and will not be seen.   *goes*
> He will round° in your ear, and cast a net before your eye.   *whisper*
> He is worst of them all, God let him never theen!°   *thrive*
>
> (300–3)

Having successfully resisted temptation so far, Mankind will face increased challenges because that's what the audience has paid to see. In fact, Titivillus sets out to do exactly what Mercy warned he would. The first thing he says is that he will 'hang my net / To blench his sight' (530–1). Having blinded Mankind to his actions, Titivillus puts a 'bourd' [board] under the earth and steals his sack of seed. Laura Kendrick has pointed out that the word 'bourd' is a play on 'board' and 'joke', and this scene 'tricks the character Mankind into idleness and the audience-as-mankind into idle laughter'.[25] As she explains, 'the devil's practical joke on Mankind has serious consequences, for it is the beginning of Mankind's diversion into idleness and sin – and the audience's as well. To the extent that we laugh at Mankind and enjoy the devil's joke, the joke is on us, and not merely because Mankind symbolizes us'.[26] This is significant because Titivillus is a demon associated with idle words. Kendrick is right about everything here, though this is not the first time the joke has been on the audience, something that would be both enjoyable and a little awkward for audience members who had begun to see the pattern. It would be especially awkward for those who realized they paid for Titivillus to be there even though they were just warned he would invite them to collude with him. Titivillus continues to get the audience's help when he asks for silence: 'Whist! Peace! I shall go to his ear and tittle therein' (557). Titivillus whispers that nature calls, so Mankind goes, leaving his prayer beads behind. Mankind says he's tired, so he decides to sleep. Titivillus again asks the audience to collude with him:

> TITIVILLUS. [*To the audience.*] And ever ye did, for me keep now your silence!
> Not a word, I charge you, pain of forty pence!
> A praty° game shall be showed you, or ye go hence.   *crafty*
> Ye may hear him snore – he is sad asleep.
> Whist! Peace! The devil is dead, I shall go round in his ear.
>
> (589–93)

Presumably the audience remains silent as Titivillus tells a sleeping Mankind that Mercy cannot be trusted. Titivillius, not to mention the playwright and actors, are relying on the conventions of theatrical productions: outside of Pantomime performances, it is pretty hard for audience members to fit in if they are constantly shouting warnings

---

[25] Laura Kendrick, '"In Bourde and in Pleye": *Mankind* and the Problem of Comic Derision in Medieval English Religious Plays', *Études Anglaises*, Tome 58, n. 3 (2005): 261–75, 261.
[26] Ibid, 262.

to characters on stage. By asking audience members to stay silent – twice, in almost the same way – and then doing exactly what Mercy warned everyone he would do, Titivillus makes those watching his accomplices, which they surely are.

Titivillus elicits in Mankind the kind of shame that Brené Brown describes insofar as he does not feel worthy of love or belonging. Brown defines shame 'as the intensely painful feeling or experience of believing that we are flawed and therefore unworthy of love and belonging – something we've experienced, done, or failed to do makes us unworthy of connection'.[27] This is exactly what Mankind feels and exactly what Titivillus set out to make him feel. Believing that he has done enough to tempt Mankind – both the character and the people at the play – Titivillus takes his leave:

> For-well, everychone, for I have done my game,
> For I have brought Mankind to mischief and to shame!
>
> (605–6)

Mankind's subsequent despair leads him to try to fit in with New-Guise, Nowadays and Nought, who cleverly make him feel part of their community. They clothe him by offering him a jacket so fashionable it is not fit for purpose. They make a phony contract with him, which reads 'Blottibus in blottis / Blottorum blottibus istis' [Nonsense words that allude to the blotting of ink] (680–1). They then have him go through a kind of counter-baptism, where he must answer, 'I will, sir', to a series of statements: he agrees that he will believe lechery doesn't count as a deadly sin and that he will rob, steal and kill; he agrees that he will go to the ale-house early to dine rather than going to mass on Sundays; he agrees that he will carry a dagger to rob or cut throats. At the end of the liturgy, they all say 'Amen' as one, sealing their commitment to one another. Not only is he saying their words at this point, he has also adopted the repetition and rhythm of their speech. Whereas Mankind employs Mercy's four-line abab stanzas early in the play, he adopts the eight-line aaabcccb form after the audience has sung the Christmas song with the vices. He has become more attuned to them from the moment the audience as a whole demonstrated their willingness to repeat their words and adopt their rhythms.

When Mercy returns near the end of the play, it is clear that Mankind has become perverted in the Augustinian sense of turning away from God. Recognizing this, Mercy uses a pun that works in exactly the opposite way than those used by the Vices, for its potential meaning enhances rather than effaces meaning. He calls, 'Man un-kind, wherever thou be!' (742). 'Un-kind' suggests initially that Mankind has turned away from 'kind', a word that has several valences. It could mean kindness in the way we would expect it to be used today, but it also means both Nature as an abstract entity and one's own nature, as it does in *The Pricke of Conscience*. What could have made Mankind turn against his own nature? For Mercy, and for the audience, the answer seems pretty clear: he has fallen in with vicious friends. But perhaps the vices aren't Mankind's only problem: in fact, Mankind had defeated them through labour before the audience paid

---

[27] Brené Brown, 'Shame v. Guilt', Brené Brown, 14 January 2013, https://brenebrown.com/blog/2013/01/14/shame-v-guilt/#:~:text=I%20define%20shame%20as%20the,makes%20us%20unworthy%20of%20connection.

good money to have Titivillus show up with his 'bourde'. It turns out, then, that the worst company Mankind can keep is the kind of person who would come to a play like *Mankind*, for their desire to fit in and go along with the conventions of being in a theatrical audience is what leads him to feel shame. To be fair, Mankind bears some responsibility here, since he was so quick to fall in with a bad crowd, but it doesn't help that the audience laughs at his suffering rather than expressing compassion for him.

Mankind's shame becomes despair, and he attempts to end his own life because he does not believe he deserves Mercy: 'A rope, a rope, a rope! I am not worthy' (800). At this point, Mercy shows up to insist that Mankind is, in fact, worthy, but to no avail. Mankind repeats his claim:

> MANKIND. Alas, I have be so bestially disposed I dare not appear!
> To see your solacious° face I am not worthy to desire.   *comforting*
> (813–14)

He then reveals why despair was thought to be related to pride in the Middle Ages, for he presumes to understand God's justice, which he claims 'will not permit such a sinful wretch / To be revived and restored again; it were impossible' (831–2). Mercy says that it is possible, but that Mankind must bend: **'Incline** your capacity; my doctrine is convenient' (844). Mercy insists that Mankind will have what he seeks, but he must ask for it before he dies: 'Ask mercy, and have, while the body with the soul hath his annexion' (863). Mankind might ask, but he is too busy castigating himself for his own lack of wisdom:

> A, it swemeth° my heart to think how unwisely I have wrought!   *grieves*
> Titivillus, that goeth invisible, hing his net before my eye,
> And by his fantastical visions seditiously sought,
> To New-Guise, Nowadays, Nought caused me to obey.
> (875–8)

He sees what he has done clearly enough, but his shame makes him unwilling to accept that he is worthy of God's grace. The language of inclining leads back to language of the will when Mankind repeats his advice to beware of Titivillus's 'envious will' and to remember, 'Your body is your enemy. Let him not have his will!' (897). Ultimately, Mankind asks God to send everyone mercy, and Mercy proclaims that he has been delivered. Sarah Beckwith rightly points out that this is the point where Mankind's language ceases to be idle.[28] Whereas he could talk all he wanted about asking for mercy earlier in the play, this request matters because he really means it. He really means it now because this is the moment when he needs mercy the most.

Just before the end of the play, Mercy helpfully explains to Mankind and the audience that there are several levels of figurative meaning at work within the play. The characters are clearly allegorical, but they also signify other things. New-Guise, Nowadays and Nought represent the world, Titivillus is the devil, and Mankind's

---

[28] Sarah Beckwith, 'Language Goes on Holiday: English Allegorical Drama and the Virtue Tradition', *Journal of Medieval and Early Modern Studies* 42.1 (2012): 107–30.

body is the flesh. All three have brought Mankind to Mischief, Mercy notes, 'as it hath been showed before this worshipful audience' (890). Having suddenly remembered the audience's presence, Mercy turns towards them: 'Search your conditions with due examination!' (908). He goes on to say that 'the world is but a vanity, / As it is proved daily by diverse transmutation' (909–10). The phrase 'diverse transmutation' may mean 'many changes', but it could also refer to other kinds of transformations, like the way that an actor might transform into a character. Or perhaps the way that a Christian in an audience might transform into someone who might collude with the vices to join in song and continue singing even when the lyrics turn out to be inappropriate. Or perhaps the way a Christian might turn into someone who would pay good money to see Titivillus make Mischief for Mankind. Or perhaps the way a Christian might turn into the kind of person who laughs with others at Titivillus's jokes even when they create shame. While the play is raucously funny at times, the ending is powerful because it asks the audience to reflect on an awkward question: to whose will have they been inclined throughout the play, Titivillus's or God's? In the final stanza, Mercy offers some reassurance. 'Mankind is wretched', he says, but nonetheless he asks that 'God grant you all *per suam misericordiam* [by his mercy] / That ye may be play-feres [*playmates*] with the angels above' (912–13). In other words, Mercy ends the play by insisting that if those at the play can worry a little less about fitting in with the kind of people who go to plays like *Mankind*, they might find they belong in heaven. As audience members reflect on the laughter they shared with others throughout the play, they might experience discomfort and even awkwardness as they reflect on the incongruity between what Mercy has told them and how they behaved. This raises yet another compelling paradox: if *Mankind*'s laughter ultimately causes audience members to reflect on their desire for belonging in heaven, perhaps it is not so idle after all.

Laughter may also play a key role in this play's treatment of gender. I noted at the beginning that *Mankind* is an extended meditation on what happens when a man gets lost and refuses to ask for help. Over and over again, from the slapstick comedy (which includes a number of man-gets-hit-in-groin bits) to the verbal exchanges between characters, the audience is invited to laugh at the way men act. No women appear in the play. It is entirely reasonable to read this as an implicit or explicit expression of deep-seated misogyny: there was plenty of that to go around in the Middle Ages, as there is today. *Mankind* seems to be doing something different, though, insofar as Mankind seems particularly susceptible to temptation because he so often behaves like a stereotypical man, thinking he has to do everything by himself. He consistently fails to call on others when he is in need, either to seek help or compassion. Whereas the script seems to suggest that Mankind stands alone while being assailed by demons, the performance repeatedly shows that any individual man assailed by temptations is actually surrounded by others. Those people, the audience, might be part of the problem. However, they also have the potential to be part of the solution. Mankind's tragedy isn't that those around him compel him to fall: his tragedy is that he doesn't recognize that he could ask those who are near him – maybe even the audience – for help. He learns a great deal from the vices, who repeatedly ask the audience to aid and abet them, but he fails to follow their lead in this regard. He feels not only completely alone but unworthy of love. In this respect, Mankind differs profoundly from Noah's wife, whom we will meet in the following chapter. She values friendship and can't understand why Noah is willing to forsake all other human beings so quickly and entirely. So perhaps *Mankind* also calls on Mankind (i.e. men) to question behaviour that both protects male privilege and repeatedly condemns men to feel shame. As Mankind learns in the end, asking for mercy might feel awkward or like an admission of weakness, but it requires the strength to accept that he is worthy of grace despite his imperfection. It remains an open question whether the audience also learns this and whether they can show compassion for themselves after laughing at Mankind's shame.

13

Ever froward: Standing up for the audience in the Chester *Play of Noah's Flood*

The Chester *Play of Noah's Flood* was performed from around 1422 to 1575. This means that it may have been written nearly fifty years before *Mankind*. I have decided to include it after *Mankind* for three reasons. First, the earliest manuscripts that preserve it were made around 1600 and likely reflect a later stage of the play's performance. Second, as in the case of *Mankind*, we need to imagine how this play brought people together in a literal and spiritual sense to grasp how it generated laughter, awkwardness and social discomfort. *Noah's Flood* was the third of twenty-four plays in the Chester cycle, a series of plays that tell the Christian story from Creation to Judgment Day. Unlike *Mankind*, this play was performed once a year in Chester at Whitsun or Pentecost, a movable feast that takes place either at the end of May or in early June. Like other plays in the cycle, *Noah's Flood* was performed by a trade guild. In this case, as in the others, there was a close association between the play and the guild's specialized skills. As Ernst Gerhardt has shown, the Drawers were fishermen who practised their trade using nets and boats. This piece of information might change our view of some aspects of the play: 'Noah's oared ark, for instance, looks very much like the Drawers of Dee's oared cock-boats, and the pageant engages in divine product placement when God institutes a new post-Flood carnivorous dietary regime and emphasizes the diet's inclusion of fish.'[1] The Waterleaders provided water, often in leather bags, 'but of particular interest is their involvement in Chester's burgeoning sixteenth-century beer-brewing trade, an involvement reflected in the Good Gossips drinking episode' that takes place near the end of the play.[2] Preparations for the play brought members of these two guilds together to prepare for the play and to coordinate their performances on the day. *Noah's Flood* also brought people together through the repetition of familiar story and the rhythms of its verse, its place in the cycle during the day and its performance each year. The third reason that I wanted to consider this play after *Mankind* is that I believe that the embodied relationship between the performers and audience members can help us to understand that Noah's wife's namelessness makes her function like an allegorical

---

[1] Ernst Gerhardt, 'Salmon-Fishing and Beer-Brewing: The Waterleaders and Drawers of Dee and Chester's Corpus Christi and Whitsun Plays', *Medieval English Theatre* 41 (2019): 134–65, 137.
[2] Ibid.

representation of womankind. I hope to show that Noah's wife not only stands in for her gender but ultimately stands up for the audience as a whole, representing all of humanity in a way that Mankind does not.

Although some guilds may have hired actors to play major roles in the cycle dramas, the characters in *Noah's Flood* were played by people who likely had some relationship with members of the audience. Chester was a reasonably important regional town, but its population probably did not exceed around 4,000 people. Even if audience members did not know those who played the members of Noah's family by name, they likely recognized the actors as people from the area through their dialect. This recognition is important for thematic and theological reasons. After all, Noah builds an ark to save his family and select animals while every other human being will be wiped from the face of the planet in a flood. The play in performance makes a point that is perhaps easy to miss when we read the story: there is a relationship between Noah and those who will be left behind. Even if that relationship is based on proximity alone, these are people who had something to do with one another's lives before the world as they knew it came to an end. If we start by assuming that the relationship between performers and audience would have reminded them, as it reminds us, of the relationship that Noah and his family must have had to those they left behind, the play's awkwardness becomes more pervasive and significant.

The play text emphasizes Noah's attunement with God, so it is not entirely obvious what an awkward position he is in until we take a step back and imagine the situation envisioned by the performance. I am going to spend this paragraph and the following one describing this situation. If you would rather not read these two paragraphs, you can get the same general idea by watching the first part of the film *Evan Almighty*, in which Steve Carrell fully embodies the awkwardness of Noah's situation in his depiction of a weatherman who gets elected to congress and is then asked to build an ark.[3] Like *Evan Almighty*, medieval English play cycles are pretty unabashedly anachronistic. We don't have much information about costumes in the cycle plays, but it seems likely that audiences would have found it difficult to distinguish the performers from the audience at some points in the play regardless of their costumes because of the sight lines. God, on the other hand, is immediately recognizable. In *Evan Almighty*, this is because he's played by Morgan Freeman, who introduces himself to Evan when he is sitting on top of a pile of wood and then says, 'I am God.' In *Noah's Flood*, it is because God speaks from 'some high place – or in the clouds, if it may be' and identifies himself: 'I, God, that all this world hath wrought' (1).[4] In both *Evan Almighty* and *Noah's Flood* God identifies himself clearly to command Noah to build an ark.

Evan Almighty and *Noah's Flood* diverge a little in their characterizations of the person receiving instructions. Evan is reluctant at first, but Noah agrees immediately. He thanks God for sparing his household and then starts commanding his family to get building:

---

[3] *Evan Almighty*, directed by Tom Shadyac (Burbank, CA: Universal Pictures, 2007), DVD.
[4] All citations to the Chester *Play of Noah's Flood* are taken from *The Broadview Anthology of British Literature: The Medieval Period*, 3rd edn., ed. Joseph Black et al., 741-7 (Peterborough, ON: Broadview Press, 2015).

> NOAH. A, lord, I thank thee loud and still
> That to me art in such will
> And spares me and my household to spill,
> As I now smoothly° find.   *truly*
> Thy bidding, lord, I shall fulfill
> Nor never more thee grieve ne grill,   *offend*
> That such grace hath sent me till
> Amonges° all mankind.   *amongst*
>
> Have done, you men and women all.
> Hie° you, lest this water fall,   *hurry*
> To work this ship, chamber and hall,
> As god hath bidden us do.
>
> (41–52)

Evan's family is also reluctant to support him while Noah's family members respond immediately to the request. They seem to have heard God's instructions and gotten right down to business, so Noah doesn't need to have any awkward conversations with his family at this point. What might make the audience feel awkward, in retrospect, is just how quickly Noah agrees with God's plan and springs into action. He's so grateful to be singled out for grace that he doesn't pause to ask if there's any chance of saving anyone else or even if he feels happier about the grace he's been offered or the fact that he's been singled out. Whereas Evan's reluctant response makes him seem awkward in his relationship with God, Noah's overly eager response to the news that God will destroy the rest of the world might also create some discomfort amongst the audience members, especially if they recognize their role in the play as those in Noah's community who are about to be destroyed. Eventually, both Noah and Evan appear awkward because they are more attuned to God than to those around them. They are like other people who have had the experience of speaking directly with God in that they struggle mightily to share that experience.

   Noah's Flood also creates awkwardness for the audience by shifting their orientation. On the one hand, the discomfort audience members might have felt about Noah's attunement with God would likely be mitigated by the way they conceived of their place in biblical history. As Noah's descendants, they can view this as a literal story about their past. However, the ark has other meanings in medieval theology: it is often considered to be a figure for the Church, which is meant to carry worthy Christians away from this world to the next, leaving sinners behind. Are audience members certain they have a place on that figurative ark? I'm not sure, and I think that Noah's wife invites them to take this question seriously. She is the first woman to speak in the play, and she claims to speak on behalf of all women, almost certainly for comedic effect:

> NOAH'S WIFE. And we shall bring timber too,
> For we mon° nothing else do –   *can*
> Women been weak to underfoe°   *undertake*
> Any great travel.°   *work*
>
> (65–8)

The labour described in this play is divided along gender lines that would have been recognizable to the medieval inhabitants of Chester, but I think the final two lines must have been delivered in a sarcastic tone. Read in this way, they point out the paradoxical situation in which women were not usually permitted to learn a craft protected by the guilds (though they were able to take over businesses bequeathed to them by their husbands), but they often end up doing unrecognized work to ensure the enterprise is a success. In this play, Noah's wife describes carrying the timbers, which must have been pretty substantial if they were being used to build an ark or even the kind of boat that the Drawers would have used. Noah's wife literally says she's on board with Noah's project, but she also suggests that Noah is getting credit for the unacknowledged labour of others, especially women, just as Abraham relied on Sarah's labour in Genesis and *Cleanness*. If you're not sure whether this critique should or would have rung true, consider the fact that all the men are named in the bible story and play while the women are only known as those men's wives. Whether or not these lines were played for comedic effect, they probably elicited at least a little uncomfortable laughter and possibly some awkward glances between husbands and wives.

Noah's wife is increasingly identified as an awkward individual as the play continues, and I will spend the rest of the chapter exploring why her expression of wilfulness is so powerful. When Noah insists that his wife enter the ship with his children upon its completion, she rejects the idea: 'I will not do after thy rede [advice]' (101). When he insists that she should 'do now as I thee bid' (102), she says, somewhat anachronistically, 'By Christ, not or [before] I see more need, / Though thou stand all day and stare' (103–4). Her insistence that she will not act until she sees the need sends Noah into a misogynist rage in which he takes his wife as an example of all women's willfulness:

NOAH. Lord, that women been crabbed aye°   *all ill-tempered*
And none are meek, I dare well say.
That is well seen by me today
In witness of you each one.

(105–8)

While it seems fair to say that the audience would also have been split between those who are laughing at or with Noah, the play's staging undermines his claim in several ways. First, Noah's argument is clearly specious: Noah's wife is one of four women we have met at this point in the play, and the other three are not ill-tempered at all. Second, Noah turns to the audience to back him up as witnesses – but these are the same people who are about to be destroyed for their wickedness if we imagine them as those in the community. Even the most hardened misogynist must have realized that something has gone awry here.

After a brief interlude in which God gives further instructions and Noah's family begins boarding, Noah's wife again resists his commands and Noah doubles down on his claim that she is the problem. He is particularly upset that she is unwilling just to go with the flow:

NOAH. Wife, come in. Why stands thou there?
Thou art ever **froward**; that dare I swear.

Come, in God's name; half time it were,
For fear lest that we drown.

(193–6)

The word 'froward' is similar to the word *awkward* insofar as the prefixes, *fro-* and *awk-*, both indicate 'wrong' in some sense, though 'froward' has connotations that connect it more specifically to error or contrariness. It also seems to have had a gendered meaning at the time this play was transcribed: Shakespeare uses it several times to describe Katherine in *The Taming of the Shrew* (1590–2). These women are often identified as troublemakers, but as Ahmed notes, 'the female troublemaker might be trouble because she gets in the way of the happiness of others'.[5] To Noah, it seems as though he and everyone else in the family are aligned with God's will, so he blames his wife for creating awkwardness. 'To create awkwardness', according to Ahmed, 'is to be read as being awkward. Maintaining public comfort requires that certain bodies "go along with it." To refuse to go along with it, to refuse the place in which you are placed, is to be seen as trouble, as causing discomfort for others'.[6] Noah calls his wife 'froward' because of the discomfort she causes him by refusing to align herself with his will. The script seems to treat her like a woman who is just causing trouble for the sake of it, who doesn't know what is good for her, but the play in performance offers the audience a different perspective.

There is a moment when Noah's wife decides that she is not getting on that boat. She conveys this very clearly to Noah using atmospheric imagery:

NOAH'S WIFE. Yes, sir, set up your sail
And row forth with evil hail;
For withouten any fail
I will not out of this town.

(197–200)

At this point, she seems like she is just insisting on having her own way because she is wilful, which is a word that Ahmed notes is most often associated with subjects 'at the point that her will does not coincide with that of others, those whose will is reified as the general or social will.'[7] But then Noah's wife goes on:

But I have my gossips everyichone°   *every one*
One foot further I will not gone.   *go*
They shall not drown, by saint John,
And° I may save their life.   *If*
They loved me full well, by Christ.
But° thou wilt let them into thy chist°   *Unless / vessel*
Else row forth, Noah, when thy list°   *desire*
And get thee a new wife.

(201–8)

---

[5] Sara Ahmed, *The Promise of Happiness* (Durham: Duke University Press, 2010), 60.
[6] Ibid., 68–9.
[7] Ibid., 64.

Unlike Noah, who didn't miss a beat before he agreed to be part of God's plan to destroy everyone else on the planet, Noah's wife invokes imagery used by heroic warriors when she says she will not move one foot from the place where she stands without her friends (this looks back to the Old English 'Battle of Maldon' and ahead – or perhaps sidelong – to Henry Howard, Earl of Surrey's 'Love that Doth Reign'). While she might seem 'froward' relative to God and Noah, those in the audience might think she has a point. She shows compassion for those being left behind and speaks up for them.

Those being left behind are represented in the play by the gossips, who speak in a collective voice. As we saw in *The Book of Margery Kempe* and will see again in *The Morte Darthur*, collective speech is often used to represent a sense of shared identity and alignment amongst characters. In this case, the gossips express their shared sense of fear and solidarity by speaking three stanzas together and shifting from the first person singular to the first person plural:

> THE GOOD GOSSIPS. The flood comes fleeting in full fast,
> On every side that spreadeth full far.
> For fear of drowning I am agast;
> Good gossip, let us draw near.
>
> And let us drink or we depart,
> For oftentimes we have done so.
> For at one draught thou drink a quart,
> And so will I do or I go.
>
> Here is a pottle° full of malmsey good and strong;   *pot*
> It will rejoice both heart and tongue.
> Though Noah think us never so long,
> Yet we will drink atite.°   *quickly*
>
> (225–36)

The final lines of the final stanza are often translated in a way that suggests that the women think Noah is waiting for them but they get distracted by one last round of drinking: though Noah will think we're taking a long time, yet we'll have one last drink. If that is how we read the line, what responsibility do the Waterleaders, whom Gerhardt notes were also involved in brewing ale, bear for their circumstances? I think the line could be read as a condemnation of the women and their role as those who provide drink to others. It is also possible to read the passage as the moment when they recognize that they have missed the boat, not because they are 'froward' but because they know Noah won't give a moment's thought to them. That is, after all, what is really happening here. At what point do members of the audience realize they have also missed the boat? They are, after all, part of the group who is not getting on the ark. I think it happens at this moment, when the repetition and rhythm of these stanzas seem to insist on the shared realization that this is goodbye. The gossips and audience alike might want to think it is still possible to get on that ark, but they know in their hearts that ship has sailed.

I find it both troubling and heartening to note that Noah's wife and her female friends represent those that are about to be obliterated in the flood. On the one hand, this seems to convey a misogynist message: these women might seem nice enough, but if we're sympathetic to them we're aligning ourselves with the worldly values that God sets out to destroy. In this reading, it is hard to decide what affective response the audience is supposed to have when Noah's sons finally force her aboard the ark:

> JAFFETT. Mother, we pray you all together –
> For we are here, your own childer –
> Come into the ship for fear of the weather,
> For his love that you bought.
> NOAH'S WIFE. That will I not for all your call
> But I have my gossips all.
> SEM. In faith, mother, yet thou shall,
> Whether thou will or not.
>
> (237–44)

If the action is not clear at this point, the stage direction reveals what is happening: '*He forcibly leads her onto the boat, leaving the gossips behind.*' This forcible removal is uncomfortable at several levels. It might show the generosity of God's grace, which can be given even to those who turn away from it. But it also seems to suggest that Noah's wife doesn't know what's best for herself. More powerfully, though, this passage consolidates the audience's sense of just how wilful Noah's wife is. Whether her wilfulness is understood as a positive or negative trait depends on the values of the person passing judgement, but I want to point out here that the text clearly marks it out as active. According to Teresa Brennan, 'To be active is to carry out an individual intention, which must, by definition, differ from the intentions of the environment.'[8] The intentions of the environment are expressed here by Jaffett and Sem through their actions, but Jaffet's words also draw attention to the fact that she is also experiencing atmospheric pressure. As Gumbrecht notes, weather is a 'dimension of reality that happens to our bodies,'[9] and this is precisely the point Jaffett makes through his imperative: 'Come into the ship for fear of the weather' (239). Of course, the audience knows that the pressure here is not only coming from Jaffett, or even Noah, but from God, who is responsible for this particular weather. For Noah's wife, to be 'froward' means that she is acting under and against considerable pressure. The play could be performed so as to invite us to read Noah's wife's wilfulness in the same way that Sara Ahmed says feminists are often read, 'as being unhappy, such that situations of conflict, violence, and power are read as *about* the unhappiness of feminists'.[10] However, I think the play also offers the audience an opportunity to consider what Ahmed says is too

---

[8] Teresa Brennan, *The Transmission of Affect* (Ithaca, NY: Cornell University Press, 2004), 93.
[9] Hans Ulrich Gumbrecht, *Atmosphere, Mood, Stimmung: On a Hidden Potential of Literature*, trans. Erik Butler (Stanford: Stanford University Press, 2012), 4.
[10] Ahmed, *Happiness*, 67.

often neglected: 'What feminists are unhappy *about*.'[11] And this is the more heartening reading of Noah's wife I would like to suggest. Surely members of the audience recognized the compassion she shows for those who are being left behind – for them – and the concern she expresses about God's desire to destroy most of creation because humans are behaving as he thought they would. Ultimately, the play presents a familiar story, Noah's Flood, and introduces a novel character, Noah's wife, whose behaviour as a 'froward' woman seems to be consistent with the misogyny we expect of the Middle Ages. Read in this way, she figuratively represents the Augustinian flesh that threatens to turn the soul, Noah, away from God and back to the world. But it probably wouldn't feel that way to audience members, whose discomfort would compel them to reconsider their perspective and their assumptions about their own place in the world.

This may even apply to God, who implicitly admits to feeling some discomfort about the way he enacted vengeance. While praising Noah for being 'true and stable' (271), in contrast to others, who have 'been **inclined** to sin' (275–6) since their inception, God nonetheless decides to make a covenant, a '**forward**' (301), with Noah not to take vengeance in this way again. God then switches pronouns from the singular to the plural to indicate a turn to the audience when he explains that a (rain)bow will be set in the clouds to mark this covenant:

> Where clouds in the welkin been,
> That ilka° bow shall be seen,   *same*
> In tokening that my wrath and teen *annoyance*
> Shall never thus worken be.
> The string is turned towards you
> And towards me is bent the bow,
> And such weather shall never show;
> And this behett I thee.
>
> (317–24)

The diction and imagery in God's closing remarks draw together various strands in the play. The passage transforms 'froward' (awkward, wayward, contrary) behaviour into a 'forward' (covenant, agreement) between human beings and their God marked by a change in the atmosphere: whereas humans have been *inclined* towards sin, now God promises to *turn* his bow in the clouds away from earth as a sign he will not use the weather in this way again to enact vengeance when human beings do not align entirely with his will. God does not explain his change of heart, but the diction in this passage makes it seem plausible that the compassion shown by Noah's wife was what moved the needle. After all, it was compassion that gave her the strength to set her will against her husband's, her family's and God's. While some have dismissed her as a 'froward' woman, the play's diction subtly suggests that it is her willingness to stand up for those left behind that leads to the covenant, the 'forward' between God and humanity. Noah's wife may not have been able to avert the flood, but she may have helped to ensure that the play's audience won't suffer in the same way that her friends once did.

---

[11] Ibid.

14

Disappointing expectations: Laughter, awkwardness and the end of Sir Thomas Malory's *Morte Darthur*

I now turn to Sir Thomas Malory's *Morte Darthur* to show how being attuned to laughter and awkwardness might allow us to perceive their presence in unexpected places. I think it's fair to say that few readers would expect to find much to laugh about at the end of a text that reveals in its title that it is about the death of a renowned king. Yet when it comes to reporting Arthur's death, Malory equivocates. On the one hand, he claims to have heard the following inscription is written on Arthur's tomb: 'Hic iacet Arthurus, rex quondam rexque futurus' [Here lies Arthur, the once and future king] (689). On the other hand, he seems to acknowledge that reports of Arthur's demise may have been greatly exaggerated: 'Yet I woll nat [will not] say that hit [it] shall be so; but rather I wolde sey, here in thys worlde he **chaunged** hys lyff [life]' (689).[1] Arthur's wife, Guinevere, changes her life in the text's final scenes, too. Believing Arthur to be dead, she turns her attention to God. Guinevere makes her way to Amesbury, 'and there she lete make herselff a nunne [nun], and wered [wore] whyght clothys and black, and grete penaunce she toke uppon her as ever ded [did] synfull woman in thys londe' (689). We learn that nobody can 'make her myry [merry], but ever she lyvyd [lived] in fastynge, prayers, and almes-dedis [alms-deeds], that all maner of people marveayled [marvelled] how vertuously she was **chaunged**' (690). Malory leaves Queen Guinevere in Amesbury and turns his attention to her lover, Sir Launcelot du Lake. There is little doubt that they will be reunited, but their final encounter is surprisingly awkward. Paradoxically, a familiarity with Malory's sources and the conventions of Romance enhances the sense of surprise and awkwardness the ending creates. The climax of the *Morte* works in the same way as the ending of Disney's *Frozen* insofar as it invites the audience to reflect critically on a sense of disappointment that can arise when expectations are unmet.

I will start with the most awkward encounter between Launcelot and Guinevere before moving both forward and backward in the plot from that point in order to explain why Malory's style can help us to understand its awkwardness as a sign of grace

---

[1] All citations to the *Morte* are taken from Sir Thomas Malory, *Le Morte Darthur*, ed. Stephen H. A. Shepherd, Norton Critical Edition (New York: W. W. Norton & Company, 2004).

both in a literary and a theological sense. Often considered to be the ideal romantic relationship, the connection between Launcelot and Guinevere is awkward from the outset because Launcelot is both a French knight and sworn to be loyal to Arthur, Guinevere's husband and the British King. It becomes even more awkward when their affair leads first to her conviction for treason and then – after Launcelot kills two of Gawain's brothers while rescuing her in his own particular idiom – to Arthur's demise. Both Launcelot and Malory are keen to point out just how indirect the causal chain actually was, and they suggest that others bear some responsibility for the tragedy as well. Launcelot is devastated by news of Arthur's death, and he grieves upon Arthur's tomb for two nights. He then spends 'seven or eyght dayes' looking for Guinevere, who responds to his appearance by claiming responsibility for the realm's destruction. Their souls are in peril, she insists, and she makes her intentions as clear as they possibly can be when speaking to him and others who bear witness to the scene:

> Thorow [Through] thys same man and me hath all thys warre be wrought, and the deth of the moste nobelest knyghtes of the worlde; for thorow oure love that we have loved togydir ys my moste noble lorde slayne. Therefore, Sir Launcelot, wyte thou wel [know you well] I am sette in suche a plyght to gete my soule hele [healthy]. And yet I truste, thorow Goddis grace and thorow Hys Passion of Hys woundis wyde, that aftir my deth I may have a syght of the blyssed face of Cryste Jesu, and on Doomesday to sytte on Hys ryght syde; for as synfull as ever I was, now ar seyntes in hevyn. And therefore, Sir Launcelot, I requyre the and beseche the hartily, for all the love that ever was betwyxt us, that thou never se me no more in the visayge. And I commaunde the, on Goddis behalff, that thou forsake my company, and to thy kyngedom loke **thou turne agayne**, and kepe well thy realme frome warre and wrake. For as well as I have loved the heretofore, myne harte woll nat serve now to se the; for thorow the and me ys the floure of kyngis and knyghtes destroyed. And therefore go thou to thy realme, and there take ye a wyff and lyff with hir with joy and blys – and I pray the hartely to pray for me to the everlastyng Lorde that I may amende my mysselyvyng.
>
> (691–2)

Guinevere's earnest honesty might have made Lancelot and even the ladies who were watching uncomfortable, and I will explore the reasons for that throughout the rest of this chapter. I also want to suggest it is not even the most awkward part of this conversation.

The exchange becomes increasingly awkward as it becomes clear that neither Lancelot nor Guinevere believes the other truly intends to do what they say they will do. From a *kinesic* perspective, the scene draws on the image of turning that is so frequently associated with awkwardness and repeated throughout this section. Launcelot picks up on Guinevere's imagery and asks, incredulously, 'Now, my swete madame ... wold ye that **I shuld turne agayne** unto my contrey and there to wedde a lady?' (692). He says that he can't believe she is asking this because it implies she does not trust the vow he has made to her. He insists he cannot leave, 'for I shall never be so false unto you of that I have promised' (692). He does not pursue her aggressively; instead, he proclaims that he will commit his life to prayer as she has done. Guinevere responds by saying what everyone is thinking, using the turning imagery in the same way that Augustine uses it, to distinguish between an orientation towards God or the world: 'A, Sir Launcelot, if ye woll do so and holde thy promyse! But I may never beleve you ... but that **ye wol turne to the worlde agayne**' (692). Launcelot insists that he will follow her example and do penance as he has promised, but his words reveal the contrast between his intentions and his understanding of her intentions.

Lancelot then makes things awkward by asking for one last kiss: 'But sythen [since] I fynde you thus desposed [disposed], I ensure you faythfully, I wyl ever take me to penaunce and praye whyle my lyf lasteth, yf that I may fynde ony heremyte [hermit], other graye or whyte, that wyl receyve me. Wherefore, madame, I praye you kysse me, and never no more' (692–3). Launcelot's request is awkward because it makes it hard to tell whether he has fully grasped the situation or not understood it at all. Does he hope a kiss will change Guinevere's mind or does he realize this is goodbye? Launcelot's awkwardness becomes even more apparent when Guinevere provides her decisive answer: '"Nay," sayd the Quene, "that shal I never do, but absteyne you from such werkes"' (693). Guinevere has already turned away from the world, and she reminds him that he has just vowed to do the same. Guinevere's actions reflect her intentions, but Launcelot has not yet aligned his actions to his own intentions let alone to hers.

The incongruity between the line Launcelot is trying to hold as the greatest knight in the world and the vulnerability he inadvertently reveals makes me laugh. His vulnerability is not funny. It is what makes him human. What does make me laugh is the fact that Launcelot is so desperate to conceal his vulnerability that he behaves in a manner unbecoming of a man of his age and stature. There is a comparable scene in the cringe comedy *Forgetting Sarah Marshall*, where Sarah (played by Kristen Bell) breaks up with Peter Bretter (played by Jason Segel).[2] Peter's vulnerability in the situation is expressed through his literal nakedness, which helps the audience to understand not only why Sarah refuses his claim that she needs to be held but also the fact that he is projecting his needs onto her. When Launcelot asks Guinevere to kiss him, he is figuratively naked, having given up his identity as a knight of the Round Table. In both cases the men seem oblivious to a situation that the women and the audience perceive clearly: the affair is over whether or not they are ready for it to end.

Malory compensates for the ambiguity created in this awkward exchange by invoking the power of others' feelings to encourage the audience to grieve the end of the love affair between Launcelot and Guinevere. When we read about others crying, we recognize an instance of sadness and our empathic response is engaged:

> And they departed; but there was never so harde an herted [hearted] man but he wold have wepte to see the dolour that they made, for **there was lamentacyon as they had be stungyn [pierced] wyth sperys**, and many tymes they swouned; and the ladyes bare the Quene to hir chambre; and Sir Launcelot awok, and went and took his hors, and rode al that day and al nyght in a forest, wepyng.
>
> (693)

---

[2] *Forgetting Sarah Marshall*, directed by Nicholas Stoller, featuring Jason Segel, Kristen Bell (Burbank, CA: Universal Pictures, 2008), DVD.

The simile in this scene is unusual for several reasons. First, as Terence McCarthy notes, Malory rarely offers readers 'an exceptional detail of information or an unusual comparison'.[3] When he uses similes, they usually appear again: at first, it seems surprising when knights come together like two boars, but then it happens so often that it bores some readers. Second, the simile here connects this scene to very different kinds of encounters: Lancelot and Guinevere lament as if they have been stung with spears. In other words, Malory thinks he can only convey the extent of their emotional pain through language associated with warfare. Malory seems to imply he knows exactly what he is doing when he shapes the reader's emotional reaction by eliciting an empathic response through his description of characters who weep and swoon. As he notes, even a hard-hearted man might weep when witnessing the emotions of others even if the circumstances themselves did not produce this response. Few readers seem ready to identify themselves as so hard-hearted that they do not find this moving. I certainly don't. And this creates an additional level of awkwardness for me because I worry that my sadness during this scene is the result of mis-directed compassion. After all, we have just learned that Guinevere and Launcelot are dedicating their lives to God. It is possible that I have misunderstood the reasons for the emotions being experienced here. Maybe the tears are for their past sins, but many readers infer that the tears are being shed for the end of the relationship.

Ultimately, Launcelot and Guinevere do change their lives. When Launcelot learns that Guinevere is near death through a vision that appears to him three times in one night he obeys the vision, which instructs him to go to her. She dies before Launcelot arrives, and when he sees her face 'he wepte not gretelye, but syghed' (694). He shows more emotion when she is buried, for we hear 'Syr Launcelot swouned, and laye longe stylle' (694–5). This show of emotion does not impress a hermit, who tells Launcelot, 'ye dysplese God with suche maner of sorow-making' (695). Launcelot responds by saying he does not displease God, 'for he knoweth myn **entente**; for my sowrow was not, nor is not, for ony rejoysyng of synne – but my sorrow may never have ende' (695). Having emphasized the importance of his intentions rather than his embodied response, Launcelot reveals that he is sorrowful for his own faults, especially for his pride, and he could not support himself when he thought of the 'kyndenes' of others and his own 'unkyndenes' (695). When Launcelot calls himself 'un-kind' here he is drawing on the double meaning of the word, suggesting that he is both not kind and acting against nature. Recognizing his need to atone for past sins, Launcelot turns completely away from the world: he eats and drinks little, dwindling away until his death. If this seems like a sad way for a great knight to die, it may be even more surprising to learn that the moment of his death is marked when the bishop, who is also a hermit, 'fyl [fell] upon a grete **laughter**' while he was sleeping (696). The bishop laughs so loudly that he wakes everyone else, and they wake him in turn. The bishop asks why they woke him, for he had never been 'so mery and so wel at ease' (696). He reveals that he had seen Launcelot taken up to heaven by more angels than he had ever seen before in one day and the gates of heaven open to him (how many angels

---

[3] Terence McCarthy, *An Introduction to Malory* (Cambridge: Brewer, 1988), 128.

does he usually see each day?). The others find Launcelot dead, but 'he laye as he had **smyled**, and the swettest savour aboute hym that ever they felte' (696). If readers find it difficult to reconcile their empathic response to the bishop's laughter and Launcelot's smile, it might help to think back to Julian of Norwich's conception of heaven as the joy of communal laughter. In this scene, the laughter associated with their spiritual transcendence offers a stark contrast to the fact that when others hear of Launcelot's death, 'the grettest dole they made that ever made men' (696). The 'wepyng and dolour out of measure' (697) they make is awkward in the sense in which that word is used in the *Pricke of Conscience* in that it is more aligned with worldly than spiritual concerns. This is especially true when we consider the laughter and sweet smells that seem to signal that Launcelot and Guinevere were ultimately saved in a spiritual sense. Why, then, does the end of their relationship seem both so disappointing and so sad?

As a Romance, the *Morte Darthur* creates expectations for medieval readers that differ from those modern readers might have. Medieval romance describes a genre that is so diverse that Rosalind Field suggests it might better be described in terms of the role it served for its audience as secular reading material (though often with some religious themes).[4] Helen Cooper points out that readers of prose Romance like the *Morte* may have been anticipating a tragedy of some kind, since they likely connected different outcomes to the use of prose and verse in this context.[5] Readers who knew the French Vulgate version of Launcelot and Guinevere's story, which is also written in prose, would have been surprised to see them get back together, so this may have raised their hopes that Malory's version was one in which lovers overcome a great many obstacles to reunite at the end. This seems to be the type of ending that Malory's source, the *Stanzaic Morte Arthur*, leads its readers to expect when it reunites Launcelot and Guinevere in verse, so readers may have been surprised to see them parted by religious vows rather than through death.[6] In order to explain why the disappointment of expectations might have provoked an additional level of discomfort, I turn now to the 2013 Disney film *Frozen* because its ending has helped me to empathize with medieval readers who expected Launcelot might save Guinevere and then felt uncomfortable about the fact that they initially held that expectation. It turns out that Guinevere is not only fully capable of taking care of herself but is also responsible for Launcelot's salvation. If you would like to have your expectations raised and then confounded by *Frozen*, skip the following paragraph until after you've seen the film.

Like the *Morte Darthur*, *Frozen* raises expectations associated with its genre. In this case, that genre is the Disney Princess film. Until at least the 1990s, Disney Princess

---

[4] Rosalind Field, 'Romance in England, 1066–1400', in *The Cambridge History of Medieval English Literature*, ed. David Wallace, 152–76 (Cambridge: Cambridge University Press, 2008), 152.
[5] Helen Cooper, 'Counter-Romance: Civil Strife and Father-Killing in the Prose Romances', in *The Long Fifteenth Century: Essays for Douglas Gray*, ed. Helen Cooper and Sally Mapstone, 141–62 (Oxford: Oxford University Press, 1997).
[6] The relevant passage appears in the the *Stanzaic Morte Arthur*, lines 3638–721. It seems unlikely that many readers of Malory would have known this version, since only one manuscript survives: London, British Library, MS Harley 2252, fols 86a–133b. *King Arthur's Death: The Middle English Stanzaic Morte Arthur and Alliterative Morte Arthure*, ed. Larry D. Benson, rev. Edward E. Foster, TEAMS Middle English Texts Series (Kalamazoo, MI: Medieval Institute Publications, 1994).

films tended to reach their climax when a man – often a prince (e.g. *Snow White, Cinderella, Sleeping Beauty, The Little Mermaid*) but sometimes a 'fair unknown' (e.g. *Aladdin*) – saved a woman with whom he would go on to have a romantic relationship. The emotional impact of *Frozen*'s climax relies on the fact that audience members expect the film to meet expectations raised by its genre while also violating the norms of that genre to some extent, since this has become common in more recent Disney Princess films like *Mulan, The Princess and the Frog, Tangled* and *Brave*. The conflict in *Frozen* begins when Elsa (voiced by Idina Menzel) involuntarily reveals to her kingdom that she has magical powers. This revelation takes place when she loses control upon learning that her sister Anna (Kristen Bell) has become engaged to Hans (Santino Fontana). Elsa flees Arendelle, building an ice fortress in the mountains, and Anna pursues her with the help of Christophe (Jonathan Groff), the reindeer Sven (Frank Welker) and the magical snowman Olaf (Josh Gad). After Elsa accidentally strikes Anna in the heart with an icy blast, echoing a mishap that occurred when the two were young, Christophe takes Anna to the trolls who had both raised him and healed Anna when she was younger. However, the grandfather troll has grim news: he can heal heads but the ice has gone to Anna's heart: 'Only an act of true love can thaw a frozen heart.'[7] The trolls suggest that perhaps true love's kiss is the answer, and Christophe decides to take Anna back to Hans. Unfortunately, we soon learn, Hans doesn't love Anna. He has used her naivety to secure a position in Arendelle because he is thirteenth in line for the throne in his own kingdom. He leaves Anna to die alone, but Olaf helps her to realize that Christophe's actions revealed his love for her. Olaf sees Christophe on his way back for her, and they set out through a storm to meet him. Just before they embrace, Anna turns to protect Elsa from Hans, who is overcome when Anna turns to ice just as his sword strikes her hand. Anna releases a final breath, and Elsa embraces her fully frozen sister as Christophe, Sven and Olaf watch. After a time – what seemed like an eternity when I first saw this film in a cinema with two young children – Anna begins to thaw. Olaf realizes that the sacrifice Anna made for her sister was the act of true love needed to thaw her frozen heart. Elsa then realizes that love is the answer to the eternal winter she has unleashed, and she quickly thaws her realm (neatly tying together the mood and atmosphere thread with the vulnerability thread of this book). The ending is a revelation, but it raises an awkward question: why was I so quick to share Anna's assumption that her survival depended on a heteronormative relationship, first with Hans, then with Christophe? To be fair, Anna moves quickly from awkwardness to attunement with Hans. After using the word awkward to express her feelings during their initial encounter, she seems so attuned with Hans by the end of the night that they sing a duet in which they finish each others' sandwiches. She takes longer to warm up to Christophe, but the mood between them changes substantially by the end of the film. By implying that first Hans, then Christophe, can save Anna, *Frozen* invites its audience to activate expectations associated with the film's genre, then offers a script in which one powerful woman can save another powerful woman. Whereas one sister responds to her sense of vulnerability by closing doors and the other by opening them

---

[7] *Frozen*, directed by Chris Buck and Jennifer Lee (Burbank, CA: Walt Disney Pictures, 2014), DVD.

too quickly, they both find the sense of belonging they seek when they stop trying to fit in with what others expect of them. Anna no longer imagines she needs a man and Elsa no longer imagines she needs to conceal her strength.

Frozen does not set its audience's expectations at odds with each other in quite the same way that the *Morte Darthur* does. Anna gives up the life she knows out of love, but she does not have to endure that loss beyond the film's climax. When Guinevere becomes a nun, she is like Anna in giving up the life that she knows out of love, but that choice will endure for the rest of her life. The *Morte* suggests that Guinevere's sacrifice saves her soul as well as Launcelot's, but it demands that Guinevere's sacrifice be ongoing. There are historical reasons for the differences between Anna and Guinevere, and these are partly reflected by women like Julian of Norwich and Margery Kempe, for whom turning away from the world required astonishing courage because the costs borne by both women were exceptionally high. These differences are linked to genre as well. Readers of the *Morte Darthur* may well have recognized that Malory follows his source, the *Stanzaic Morte Arthur*, when he switches from Romance to Sacred Biography in the exchange between Launcelot and Guinevere. This switch helps to explain the awkwardness between them and the audience's sense of discomfort regarding the grief they might feel when Guinevere refuses Launcelot's advances. Sacred Biographies sometimes acknowledge the grief that can be felt when worldly pleasures are given up, but they tend to emphasize the fact that heavenly rewards are worth any cost. The bishop's reaction to Launcelot's death emphasizes that ideal and warns against misplaced compassion, but other characters seem to resist the shift from Romance to Sacred Biography, both drawing the audience with them and raising questions retrospectively about Malory's intentions at the end of the *Morte*.

Given that the bishop's joyous laughter implies that Launcelot's turn away from worldly matters was successful, Sir Ector's threnody (or memorial) for Launcelot seems incongruous. When Ector sees the face of his dead brother, he swoons. When he wakes, Ector praises Launcelot for those aspects of his life he has renounced, completely ignoring his final days as a religious man. He lauds Launcelot as the head of all Christian Knights, the truest friend, and 'the trewest lover, of a synful man, that ever loved woman' (697). As Ector continues, the two sides of Launcelot's identity seem increasingly incongruous: 'thou were the kyndest man that ever strake wyth sword; and thou were the godelyest persone that ever cam emong prees of knyghtes; and thou was the mekest man and the jentyllest [gentlest] that ever ete in halle emonge ladyes; and thou were the sternest knyght to thy mortal foo that ever put spere in the reeste' (697). As Terence McCarthy notes, Malory frequently uses the superlative; in this case, though, readers may well take Ector's claims at face value.[8] Lancelot really was the best for most of the *Morte*. But problems arise when these claims are examined more closely: what does it mean to say that Launcelot was the kindest person that ever struck with a sword? When he says kindest, does Ector mean most natural or graceful? How does that fit with him also being the sternest knight to his foes?

---

[8] McCarthy, *Introduction*, 129–30.

These elements are held in tension throughout the text, but Malory brings them into sharp focus structurally at the beginning of the end of the *Morte*, where he juxtaposes the Grail Quest with his Tale of Launcelot and Queen Guinevere. The Grail narrative belies Ector's claim that Launcelot was the Godliest knight that ever came amongst a press of knights. That title belongs to Galahad, Launcelot's son. Moreover, Malory reminds readers that Launcelot was not the Godliest knight because his will was not aligned with God's: 'had nat Sir Launcelot bene in his prevy thoughtes and in hys myndis so sette inwardly to the Quene as he was in semynge outewarde to God, there had no knyght passed hym in the Queste of the Sankgreall' (588). While Launcelot was able to align his bodily actions with God's will during his Quest, his thoughts were directed elsewhere: 'ever his thoughtis prevyly were on the Quene, and so they loved togydirs more hotter than they dud toforehonde, and had many such prevy draughtis togydir that many in the courte spake of hit – and in especiall Sir Aggravayne, Sir Gawaynes brothir, for he was ever opynne-mowthed' (588). If readers align themselves with Ector's view of Launcelot's death, then Aggravain has a lot to answer for. However, if readers align themselves with the bishop's view of Launcelot's death, then the actions taken by Aggravain and Guinevere take on a different meaning.

Malory repeatedly suggests that Aggravain's open mouth causes many problems, not least of which is heightened awkwardness between Launcelot and Guinevere. These encounters suggest that the awkward exchange at the end should not be as surprising as it is, for it is part of a pattern in which the two lovers constantly seem to be speaking at cross-purposes.[9] Launcelot's character remains constant throughout these scenes while Guinevere's does not. She is a dynamic character who learns something and changes her life. After the Grail quest, Launcelot tries 'to do for the plesure of Oure Lorde Jesu Cryst; and ever as much as hy myght he withdrew hym fro the company of Quene Gwenyvere for to eschew the sclawndir [slander] and noyse – wherefore the Quene waxed wrothe [grew angry] with Sir Launcelot' (588). Launcelot is not avoiding Guinevere because of any guilt he might have felt about his failure in the quest for the grail but to quell rumours about their relationship. Upset by his behaviour, Guinevere calls him to his chamber and complains about how much time he is spending with other women. He defends himself at length while she 'stoode stylle and lete Sir Launcelot sey what he wolde' (589). She then bursts out weeping and discharges him from court, telling him that she doesn't ever want to see him again. Guinevere's response is understandable and a signal that their relationship is a worldly one at this point. As he does so often in this part of the text, Launcelot fails to discern Guinevere's intentions, and he plans to leave for France. Yet it is clear to Sir Bors (and to most readers) that Guinevere is actually telling Launcelot to go away in this scene because she is frustrated they cannot be closer. This may be what Launcelot thinks she's telling him in the final scene, but at that point Guinevere has recognized their proximity to each other is preventing them from being close to God. As these scenes and several others reveal, Launcelot is consistently not attuned to his lover's

---

[9] See Catherine La Farge, 'Conversation in Malory's "Morte Darthur"', *Medium Aevum* 56.2 (1987): 225–38.

intentions: he decides to leave when she doesn't really want him to leave and to stay when she really wants him to leave.

The last two books of the *Morte* offer a remarkably unified narrative in comparison to the rest of the text, but three features really stand out: Launcelot fails to be attuned to the intentions of others, he thinks only he can rescue Guinevere and only she seems capable of adapting to changing circumstances. To be fair to him, Launcelot does rescue Guinevere several times, and it does often seem like he's the only one who can. First, he rescues her by taking her part in trial by combat at the end of the episode precipitated by her sending him out of court in the first place. He takes her part in the trial by combat against Sir Mador de la Porte who has accused her of killing Sir Patryse of Ireland with a poisoned apple, and all is forgiven. He then comes to her rescue twice in an episode involving the knight Mellyagaunt, who kidnaps her and then accuses her of sleeping with one of the knights in her chamber – an accusation which is technically wrong, 'but only technically' because she had actually slept with Launcelot, who was not one of the knights in the chamber and whose arrival at Mellyagaunt's castle led him to beg for Mercy.[10] Once again, Launcelot takes her part in trial by combat and prevents her from being sentenced to death. Finally, he rescues her directly from execution for treason after he and Guinevere have been caught together in her chamber. It is not surprising that Launcelot anticipated that he would need to rescue her again at the end of the *Morte*, but he may have found it more helpful to reflect on the fact that he is often responsible for the danger in which she finds herself because he fails to understand either her intentions or those of others.

I think contemporary readers are likely to cut Launcelot a bit of slack in the first episode, for he does exactly what Guinevere tells him to do by leaving court. After that, though, he seems repeatedly to disappoint expectations. He and Guinevere have a misunderstanding that ultimately leads both Elayne (the Fair Maiden of Ascolat) and her brother, Sir Lavayne, to fall in love with him. At first, Guinevere is furious to hear that Launcelot is wearing Elayne's red sleeve at the jousts, but she relents when she reads the letter on her corpse in a barge and Launcelot insists that Elayne loved him out of measure. At this point, Guinevere turns to Launcelot and says, in an inscrutable tone, 'Sir … ye myght have shewed hir som bownté and jantilnes [bounty and gentleness] whych myght have preserved hir lyff' (617). Launcelot seems baffled by her assertion that he should have shown compassion. Once again, he has misjudged the situation.

In a later episode, Launcelot repeatedly misjudges Mellyagaunt, who not only kidnaps Guinevere but orders his men to kill Launcelot's horse with arrows when he pursues them. Both acts surprise Launcelot because they are so shameful. When Launcelot arrives at the castle, Mellyagaunt begs Guinevere to intervene on his behalf, and she again confounds Launcelot when she asks, 'Sir Launcelot, why be ye so amoved?' (631). He wants to know why she is asking this, for he believes she should be more angry than he is about the shame they have suffered. She says that he's right, but now everything has been 'put in myne honde' (631), so he should come

---

[10] See Paul Strohm, 'Mellyagant's Primal Scene', in *Theory and the Premodern Text*, 201–14 (Minneapolis, MN: University of Minnesota Press, 2000).

peacefully. Launcelot and Guinevere do manage to align their intentions that night. Taking advantage of their time away from Arthur's court, Launcelot climbs a ladder to Guinevere's window. After some conversation, 'Sir Launcelot wysshed that he might have comyn in to her' (633). She responds, 'I wolde as fayne as ye that ye might com in to me' (633). Just in case he has misunderstood, Launcelot makes sure he has her consent: 'Wolde ye so, madame ... with youre harte, that I were with you?' (633). She says this is what she wills, and he pulls the iron bars clean out of the window, cutting his hand deeply in the process. This scene is unusually explicit in its approach to consent and sexuality, for it is clear they are not just talking about entering his lady's chamber (or maybe that's exactly what they are discussing if the euphemism at the end of 'I have a Gentil Cock' is anything to go by). The episode becomes even more uncomfortable in the morning, when Launcelot's blood is discovered because he has, unsurprisingly, misjudged Mellyagaunt, who acts shamefully by violating the norms of hospitality when he opens the curtains of Guinevere's bed and accuses her of having slept with one of the wounded knights who were located in her chamber. Unfortunately for Launcelot and Guinevere, the shame that the other knights feel when they see the blood outweighs the shame Launcelot thinks Mellyagaunt should feel for opening the curtains of Guinevere's bed, an act that King Arthur himself would only have done if it 'had pleased hym to have layne hym downe by her' (634). Mellyagaunt feels confident about his accusation, and he challenges Launcelot to trial by combat. Launcelot accepts the challenge, then literally falls into a trap (i.e. through a trapdoor) because he is, according to Malory, too noble: 'for ever a man of worship and of proues [feats] dredis [dreads] but lytyll of perels [perils], for they wene [believe] that every man be as they bene' (635). Launcelot only escapes from the dungeon into which he has fallen once he agrees to kiss one of Mellyagaunt's ladies (but only to save the queen, both he and Malory insist), though he arrives in time to save the queen through trial by combat.

Launcelot doesn't seem to have learned anything from this episode since he and Guinevere are caught in her chamber shortly thereafter, thanks to a plan hatched by the very knight whose shameful open-mouthedness had them worried in the first place. The final book in Malory's *Morte Darthur* begins with Sir Aggravain again speaking 'opynly' about the shame they should all feel about the affair between Launcelot and Guinevere. He appeals to his brothers for help, but Gawain, Gaheris and Gareth refuse to join him. His half-brother, Mordred, will take his part, and this gives Aggravain confidence to announce that he will 'disclose hit to the Kynge' (646). Neither Gawain nor his other brothers deny the affair is happening, but they want to avoid the shame that will arise if it becomes known. When Arthur arrives, Gawain again advises the brothers to be quiet. Then Aggravain and Mordred speak together, saying, 'That woll I nat' (647). Gawain and Gareth then speak together at greater length, saying, 'Alas ... now ys thys realme holy destroyed and myscheved, and the noble felyshyp of the Rounde Table shall be disparbeled' (647). Terence McCarthy notes that this kind of collective speech seems completely unrealistic to us, but it is often designed to show the knights being attuned both with each other and the idea of what it means to be a knight. Normally, most or all of the knights involved in a scene will speak in unison, sometimes at length. Collective speech in this scene marks the divisions between the knights. Moreover, it is marking the way that public knowledge shapes the way that the characters will respond. Arthur is reluctant to hear what Aggravain and Mordred want to tell him, 'For the Kynge had a demyng [sense] of hit, but he wold nat [would not] here [hear] thereof, for Sir Launcelot had done so much for hym and for the Quene so many tymes that, wyte you well, the Kynge loved hym passingly well' (647). Arthur insists that he will only be compelled to act if the affair is revealed publicly, which would be shameful, rather than if they are found to be guilty, which he suspects to be the case but will not cause anyone to lose face if it is not acknowledged openly.[11] Aggravain and Mordred think that guilt matters, and their plan to take Launcelot 'with the dede' (647) according to Arthur's wishes is set in motion, precipitating an end to the Round Table as Gawain and Gareth predicted as well as an end to Arthur's kingdom as they know it.

Malory does not seem very sympathetic to Aggravain and Mordred, and my experience of teaching this text has led me to believe that these two characters are not well-liked even today. When Malory describes them as 'two unhappy knyghtis' (646), he likely had two senses of the adjective in mind. The two knights are obviously unhappy in the sense that we understand the word today, but Malory may have chosen this particular word to reveal that they are knights who cause the 'unhap' [misfortune] (646) that will befall in the rest of the *Morte* or to whom 'unhappy' [unfortunate] things were about to happen. Aggravain and Mordred function as paradigmatic examples of Sara Ahmed's claim that 'the troublemaker is the one who violates the fragile conditions of peace'.[12] Thus Ahmed encourages readers to re-think their judgement of Aggravain and Mordred, especially since Malory seems so keen to help readers form a particular judgement. As I have noted before, Ahmed points out that feminists are often misconstrued because they 'are read as being unhappy, such that situations of conflict, violence, and power are read as *about* the unhappiness of feminists, rather than being what feminists are unhappy *about*'.[13] Aggravain and Mordred are by no means feminists, but they reveal something about a power structure in which everyone focuses on their unhappiness rather than what they are unhappy about. If we focus on that, we may see something different in this situation. First, they're right. Launcelot and Guinevere are having an affair. Second, this affair has some serious implications for the realm. What is preventing Launcelot, a French knight, from laying claim to the English throne, through Guinevere or even a child, before or after Arthur's death? Third when they speak up, they create awkwardness. Aggravain and Mordred are identified as awkward because they create an enormous amount of discomfort for others, both within this scene and throughout the end of the *Morte*. While they certainly seem to kill joy in the *Morte*, Aggravain and Mordred aren't exactly killjoys in the sense that they are not seeking to disrupt norms that are unjust. Instead, they are seeking to reinforce the norms to their advantage: Mordred, as Arthur's son and nephew (he is the product of incest between Arthur and his sister), has a claim to the throne, and he attempts to claim legitimacy through marriage to Guinevere when Arthur leaves

---

[11] For an excellent account of the distinction between shame and guilt in this context, see Mark Lambert, *Malory: Style and Vision in 'Le Morte Darthur'* (New Haven and London: Yale University Press, 1975), esp. 179–94.

[12] Sara Ahmed, *The Promise of Happiness* (Durham: Duke University Press, 2010), 60–1.

[13] Ibid., 67.

the country to pursue Launcelot. Mordred's plot doesn't work out well for anyone, but that doesn't mean that he was wrong to ask why Launcelot and Guinevere were free to violate norms that everyone else was expected to maintain.

By refusing to go along with the affair between Launcelot and Guinevere, Aggravain and Mordred provide Guinevere with an opportunity to show compassion for herself by recognizing that she may be preventing herself from caring for her own soul by orienting her will according to the needs of the men around her. When Mordred seizes her and attempts to wed her against her will, she outwits him and flees to the Tower, where the bishop of London helps to protect her. When she hears that Arthur and Mordred have slain each other, she takes holy orders, and then convinces Launcelot to do the same. Although the text never says so explicitly, its structure implies that Guinevere would not have recognized her guilt, and therefore her need to atone for her actions, if Aggravain and Mordred had not spoken out. Moreover, the threats instigated against her by Mador, Mellyagaunt and Aggravain likely helped her to learn enough about men's intentions to escape Mordred. At the end of the *Morte Darthur*, Guinevere realizes that she is the only one who can save herself, both literally and spiritually, and she takes decisive action. From this perspective, Guinevere can be seen as the most dynamic and influential character in the closing act of the *Morte Darthur*. While she cannot undo the devastation that has come about, she can not only change her life but save herself and Launcelot in the process. Perhaps this is what William Caxton had in mind when he quoted Paul's letter to the Romans in his prologue to the 1485 edition of that 'all is wryton [written] for our doctrine and for to beware that we falle not to vyce ne synne, but t'exersyse and folowe vertu, by whyche we may come and atteyne to good fame and renomme in thys lyf, and after thys shorte and transytorye lyf to come unto everlasting blysse in heven' (817).[14] Whereas Ector focuses on the fame and renown Launcelot earned through a lifetime of action, he completely fails to acknowledge that Guinevere is the one who ultimately saves him in a Christian sense, allowing him to attain everlasting bliss in heaven. This raises a profoundly awkward question: why have so many readers over time adopted Ector's interpretation of events, reading the end of Malory's text as a tragedy for Arthur's realm rather than a story about Guinevere's spiritual triumph? I am not sure any answers to this question will be comforting, but I do take some solace in the fact that the structure of the *Morte Darthur*, like the structure of *Frozen*, seems to invite us to ask why we might be disappointed when it does not meet the conventional expectations it initially seems to raise in terms of gender and genre.

---

[14] William Caxton, 'Prologue and Epilogue to the 1485 Edition', in *Le Morte Darthur*, ed. Stephen H. A. Shepherd, 814–19 (New York: W. W. Norton, 2004).

Conclusion: An awkward age?

In the introduction, I suggested that contemporary readers might be particularly attuned to awkwardness in late-medieval England because we are living in what Adam Kotsko calls 'an awkward age'. When I first noticed resonances between the late-medieval and contemporary texts I discuss here, I thought I would make a case that English society in the later Middle Ages was going through the same 'state of cultural awkwardness' that Kotsko claims has proliferated since the turn of the twenty-first century.[1] Kotsko argues that the rise of awkwardness in North American culture is correlated to the fact that 'mainstream middle-class social norms are not remotely up to the task of minimizing awkwardness' in a diverse society.[2] He does not advocate for a return to so-called 'traditional' norms, and I don't either. As I hope to have shown here, such calls are often used to oppress and silence those who are most vulnerable. I think it is therefore valuable to heed Kotsko's warning that societies that perceive themselves as undergoing a great deal of change sometimes 'become strongly tempted by the fascist promise of a clear set of values and expectations and have found themselves willing to live with the inevitably tragic means used to establish those norms.'[3] Unfortunately, Kotsko seems to have been prescient on this point: a number of early-twenty-first-century politicians have flourished by evoking nostalgia for a time of greater certainty about cultural norms while ignoring the norms that normally apply to governance. There are many examples of people using nostalgia or violating customs for political gain in late-medieval England, so my invitation to focus instead on texts that encourage empathy is a *decision* (with the emphasis Hannah Gadsby places on it). I am interested in how late-medieval and contemporary texts engage with their historical contexts, but I also hope to have shown that these texts provide a strong reminder that norms are constantly being negotiated and renegotiated, so the idea that one could return to a set of stable norms can only be maintained if one has a superficial understanding of the past. I hope to have shown that paying attention to laughter and awkwardness in late-medieval literature and the twenty-first century can help to enrich our understanding of both societies by inviting us to consider fundamental questions about social and political life: How do we live with other people? How do we live with ourselves?

---

[1] Adam Kotsko, *Awkwardness: An Essay* (Ropley: Zero Books, 2010), 17.
[2] Ibid.
[3] Ibid., 25.

What strikes me most strongly about the resonance between the late-medieval and contemporary texts is the way that they use laughter and awkwardness to contemplate belonging. This speaks directly to the question of how we live with other people, for it invites us to recognize that our brains seem to be designed for profound social connection (something many of us have come to recognize during the Covid-19 pandemic). It is less surprising in this context that so many of the texts under my consideration here anticipate Brené Brown's distinction between fitting in and belonging.[4] The medieval texts generally depict fitting in as the pursuit of worldly values and belonging as a sense of communion with God or one's fellow Christians, but we need not adopt a religious or even a spiritual worldview to see how much these concepts matter in Hoccleve's *La Male Regle* and *The Office*. Fitting in and belonging are especially challenging because we may simulate our experience using similar cognitive processes, but variation is the norm when it comes to the way we encounter the world and others within it.[5] Nevertheless, our capacity for entrainment makes us remarkably well-equipped to align ourselves with others. Texts as varied as Augustine's *Confessions* and *The 40-Year-Old Virgin* reveal that aligning ourselves with others can be a double-edged sword: it can lead people to seek fitting in when they really crave belonging. Just as troubling, belonging is often impeded by shame, which is often connected to a lack of worthiness. We have seen how hard it is for Gawain and Fleabag to live with others – to have a sense of belonging with them – when they can't even live with themselves. While not all of the texts under my consideration have happy endings, most seem to demonstrate Brené Brown's view that it is only once we accept our imperfections – once we learn to live with laughter, awkwardness and social discomfort – that we can begin to gain a sense of belonging.

Reading empathetically is a social and political act because it insists upon the importance of interpersonal connection. It may not necessarily lead to the kind of moral goods that many associate with reading, but it can provide opportunities to practice 'the skills of cooperation needed to make a complex society work'.[6] At the most basic level, reading empathetically allows us to practise cooperation with an author or a text. The process of determining what a character is feeling has a great deal in common with the process of identifying instances of emotions in social interactions. At a broader level, it can help us to practise 'imagining the specifics of another human being's experience'.[7] Empathetic reading allows us to engage without embracing the other's view, so it promises to help us to engage with those who make us profoundly uncomfortable as well as those with whom we agree. I am not saying anyone should have to accept the legitimacy of reprehensible views or endure belittlement. What I am saying is that practising empathy while reading about laughter and awkwardness can help us to discern intentions in the face of ambiguity, uncertainty and discomfort

---

[4] Brené Brown, *The Gifts of Imperfection* (Center City, MN: Hazelden Press, 2010).
[5] See Lisa Feldman Barrett, *How Emotions are Made: The Secret Life of the Brain* (Boston, MA: Mariner Books, 2018) and Christian Keysers, *The Empathic Brain: How the Discovery of Mirror Neurons Changes our Understanding of Human Nature* (Oklahoma, OK: Smashwords, 2011).
[6] Richard Sennett, *Together: The Rituals, Pleasures and Politics of Cooperation* (New Haven, CT: Yale University Press, 2012), 9.
[7] Ibid., 21.

in social interactions. For example, I have suggested that David Brent is the kind of person whom Aaron James identifies as an asshole because he violates norms that he expects others to follow.[8] We don't need to sympathize with him to see that part of the reason he behaves this way is that he has been consistently rewarded for behaving in this way. This does not excuse his behaviour. Instead, it focuses our attention on the structures that empower men like him. In contrast, I suggested that Margery Kempe might be seen as the kind of person whom Sara Ahmed identifies as a feminist killjoy because she draws attention to the fact that some norms cause violence.[9] Readers might not sympathize with Kempe, who employs a sophisticated style to provoke her audience (since both Julian of Norwich and Christ assure her that the more people laugh at her, the more God loves her), but they can certainly understand why she feels the need to speak the way she does. Thus awkwardness can both signal the need for uncomfortable but necessary conversations and help us to avoid blaming individuals for causing discomfort when they draw our attention to injustice.

One of those conversations concerns norms associated with gender. A great deal of the awkwardness I have described in this book occurs when men act like adolescents: Augustine, The *Pearl*-maiden's father, Jonah, Gawain, Thomas Hoccleve, Mankind and Launcelot. In contrast to those men, most of the women in this book behave maturely: Monica (Augustine's mother), the *Pearl*-maiden's daughter, Sarah, Julian of Norwich, Margery Kempe and Guinevere. This distinction may seem unfair given that Augustine and others represent their awkwardness as a kind of spiritual adolescence that will transform into spiritual maturity upon conversion. What is notable about these men is they get many chances to change their behaviour. That is not the case for the wives of Noah, Lot or Bertilak, none of whom are even named (though the unnamed abbess in 'The Abbess Delivered by Our Lady' does seem to be an exception). The heightened punishment of women for violating norms is consistent with late-medieval texts I have not included here, including the two tales from the *Gesta Romanorum* that Thomas Hoccleve includes in the *Series*. One of these tales ends with a sinful man recovering from leprosy while the other ends with a sinful woman being consumed by it. The stories are unsettling on their own, but they are alarming when set in contrast to each other.

Awkwardness arising from the violation of norms associated with gender roles is also a key feature of many of the contemporary texts under my consideration. Ricky Gervais explicitly acknowledges, 'One of the main themes of *The Office* is men as boys and women as adults.'[10] Kotsko picks up on this idea when he argues that Judd Apatow films represent the cultural awkwardness experienced by early-twentieth-century men who behave like overgrown adolescents because they are living in circumstances in which 'women are newly competent and self-assured, while men have followed the opposite trajectory'.[11] I think Kotsko makes a reasonable argument about these films,

---

[8] Aaron James, *Assholes: A Theory* (New York: Doubleday, 2012).
[9] Sara Ahmed, *The Promise of Happiness* (Durham: Duke University Press, 2010).
[10] TheFbiFilesRepeat, 'A Night at the Office – Ricky Gervais', 23 January 2001, video, 31:30, https://www.youtube.com/watch?v=akNwLopEda0.
[11] Kotsko, *Awkwardness*, 51.

but it is important to acknowledge its limitations. He is drawing on television and film made exclusively by and about white men, so his argument really applies to their experience of cultural change in the twenty-first century. These texts deal with issues ranging from employment, ideas of masculinity and cultural diversity, but these issues are generally explored from the perspective of the most privileged. To claim these texts represent the spirit of the age seems presumptuous to me, and it is why I resist the temptation to claim that awkwardness is a defining feature of late-medieval literature based on the limited range of experiences represented by the texts I have considered.

I nonetheless hope to have shown that when we consider a wider range of texts, the experience of awkwardness starts to become more nuanced without becoming too diffuse. When we consider the relationship between laughter and social discomfort in *The Office* alongside *Fleabag*, for example, issues of shame and belonging come to the fore. These nuanced representations of awkwardness can also be read as a response to nostalgic calls for a return to cultural norms that often never really existed. Hannah Gadsby offers an especially strong and urgent critique of the way such norms work insidiously to generate a sense of shame in those who are perceived or perceive themselves to violate them. Her case is urgent because the way that norms of the past are perceived today matters a great deal to those who want to impose them on others. All too often those views are based on severely limited evidence. Kotsko's claim that we are currently in an awkward age reflects the fact that men with access to the means of production have now started to represent their sense of awkwardness about a range of issues. But we could easily trace a history of 'froward' women who resist aligning themselves with gender norms from Margery Kempe to the Chester *Play of Noah's Flood* through Shakespeare's *Taming of the Shrew* and on. There is also a literary tradition that represents women who feel awkward in ways that would be familiar to viewers of Judd Apatow's films. Three authors spring immediately to mind. Lady Mary Wroth (1587–1651) uses *kinesic* imagery to describe her sense of disorientation as she struggles to decide which way to turn in the maze of love where marriage means an end to freedom.[12] Jane Austen (1775–1817) repeatedly describes Fanny Price as awkward in *Mansfield Park*, and she is.[13] But she is in an awkward position, after all, financially insecure and in love with a second son who is also her cousin. Anita Brookner's (1928–2016) first three novels (*A Start in Life*, *Providence* and *Look at Me*) deal with protagonists who see themselves as awkward because they are unsure of the role they are to play in post-war British society insofar as the gender norms they thought they knew no longer apply.[14] These three authors explore weighty issues, yet all three also use the awkward incongruity generated by their protagonists' positions to generate laughter.

---

[12] Lady, Mary Wroth, 'In this Strange Labyrinth' is widely anthologized, but I would suggest you read it as Poem 1 in Carol Rumen's article, 'Poem of the Week: From A Crown of Sonnets Dedicated to Love by Lady Mary Wroth', *The Guardian*, 28 January 2019, https://www.theguardian.com/books/booksblog/2019/jan/28/poem-of-the-week-from-a-crown-of-sonnets-dedicated-to-love-by-lady-mary-wroth.

[13] Jane Austen, *Mansfield Park*, ed. Jane Sturrock (Peterborough, ON: Broadview Press, 2001 [1814]).

[14] Anita Brookner, *A Start in Life* (London: Penguin, 1991 [1981]); *Providence* (London: Penguin, 1991 [1982]); *Look at Me* (London: Penguin, 1993 [1983]).

I could go on, but my point is that awkwardness is not exclusively a contemporary phenomenon any more than it is a late-medieval one. Different people feel awkward at different times. To be blunt: people who feel different (or who have been made to feel different) have usually borne the burden of awkwardness, being identified as awkward individuals. What is new in the twenty-first century, I hope, is that more people have become uncomfortable about insisting that others adhere to norms that work to the benefit of the few. While he does not say this specifically, Kotsko seems to acknowledge this is the implication of his argument. It certainly seems to be what the texts under his consideration are demonstrating, for they consistently generate laughter by pointing out the incongruities associated with cultural and social norms that have served to preserve the privilege of white men. While some of the characters behave in ways that suggest they are nostalgic for a past that never existed, the texts themselves consistently reveal that the illusion of social cohesion is often achieved through the imposition of norms that benefit some groups at the expense of others.

There is plenty of evidence that late-medieval writers felt nostalgic for a simpler past, but I find those elements less appealing as a reader than moments when texts engage with and reconsider the norms governing social interactions through laughter and awkwardness. For example, Malory openly complains that people in the present are inconstant compared to people in the past. His sense of nostalgia makes a great deal of sense given that he mostly wrote while imprisoned during the conflict we now know as the Wars of the Roses (1455–87) and in the aftermath of substantial English losses in France. Yet the *Morte* ultimately demonstrates that Guinevere's dynamic character and her willingness to be awkward ultimately save her and Launcelot. In contrast, *The Book of Margery Kempe* openly depicts its challenge to early-fifteenth-century norms about the access lay people, especially women, could have to religious texts. Kempe regularly creates discomfort amongst the clergy because what she has to say seems to violate the norms that Arundel's Constitutions (1409) had been designed to impose by reverting to practices that pre-dated the Papal Schism (1378–1417) and the translation of texts and preaching associated with John Wyclif.[15] I hope this book prompts further inquiry along those lines, though there are already many excellent studies devoted to these concerns.

My aim here has been to try to understand those moments in late-medieval texts when a mis-alignment or lack of attunement has the potential to be resolved productively. These moments are often marked by laughter. In some cases, laughter signals social discomfort; in some cases, laugher creates discomfort; and in some cases laughter becomes a metaphor for the sense of belonging that Brené Brown claims we desire but often feel unworthy to attain. I have tried to avoid claiming that either awkwardness or alignment are ideal end goals. I don't think many of us would want to live in a world in which we always felt awkward. I also think there is a case to be made

---

[15] Fiona Somerset, 'Censorship', in *The Production of Books in England 1350–1500*, ed. Alexandra Gillespie and Daniel Wakelin, 239–59 (Cambridge: Cambridge University Press, 2011) 242. See also Nicholas Watson, 'Censorship and Cultural Change in Late Medieval England: Vernacular Theology, the Oxford Translation Debate, and Arundel's Constitutions of 1409', *Speculum* 70 (1995): 822–64.

that many of us – and here I am thinking especially of white men like myself – need to sit with social discomfort long enough to ask what is really causing it or even 'am I the asshole'? The benefit of this, from my perspective, is that it will enable me to focus my attention on empathy in order to engage in the radical act of working in cooperation with others to understand what they are thinking and feeling even if I don't share their views or experience. In terms I have used throughout the book, I hope this will allow me to identify when assholes are taking advantage of others and to understand what killjoys are angry about rather than becoming fixated on the discomfort caused by their anger. Moreover, I hope it will give me the courage to call out assholes and to be the killjoy when necessary.

Throughout this book, I have drawn on authors who insist that human beings are designed to connect with others empathically and empathetically. The social discomfort often associated with awkwardness and laughter in both late-medieval and contemporary texts provide us with an opportunity to practise empathy while encountering others. Will we turn away from or towards them?

References

1 Primary texts

1.1 Manuscripts

London, British Library, MS Additional 42130.
London, British Library, MS Cotton Nero A.x.
London, British Library MS Harley 541.
London, British Library, MS Harley 978.
London, British Library, MS Harley 2252.
London, British Library, MS Sloane 2593.
Oxford, Bodleian Library, MS Eng. Poet. E. 1.
Washington, Folger Shakespeare Library, Macro MS 5.

1.2 Printed texts

Augustine. *Confessions*, translated by Henry Chadwick. Oxford World's Classics. Oxford: Oxford University Press, 1992 (Reissued 2008).
Augustine. *On The Trinity, Books 8–15*, edited by Gareth B. Matthews, translated by Stephen McKenna, Cambridge Texts in the History of Philosophy. Cambridge: Cambridge University Press, 2002.
Austen, Jane. *Mansfield Park*, edited by Jane Sturrock. Peterborough, ON: Broadview Press, 2001 [1814].
'Bring Us in Good Ale'. In *The Broadview Anthology of British Literature: The Medieval Period*, 3rd edn., edited by Joseph Black et al., 258–9. Peterborough, ON: Broadview Press, 2015.
Brookner, Anita. *A Start in Life*. London: Penguin, 1991 [1981].
Brookner, Anita. *Providence*. London: Penguin, 1991 [1982].
Brookner, Anita. *Look at Me*. London: Penguin, 1993 [1983].
Chaucer, Geoffrey. 'The Wife of Bath's Prologue and Tale'. In *The Riverside Chaucer*, 3rd edn., edited by Larry Benson, 105–22. Boston: Houghton Mifflin, 1987.
'Chester *Play of Noah's Flood*.' In *The Broadview Anthology of British Literature: The Medieval Period*, 3rd edn., edited by Joseph Black et al., 741–7. Peterborough, ON: Broadview Press, 2015.
The Complete Works of the Pearl *Poet*, edited by Malcolm Andrew and Ronald Waldron, with Clifford Peterson, translated and with an introduction by Casey Finch. Berkeley, CA: University of California Press, 1993.
Hoccleve, Thomas. '*My Compleinte' and Other Poems*, edited by Roger Ellis, Exeter Medieval Texts and Studies. Exeter: University of Exeter Press, 2001.

'I have a Gentil Cock'. In *The Broadview Anthology of British Literature: The Medieval Period*, 3rd edn., edited by Joseph Black et al., 257. Peterborough, ON: Broadview Press, 2015.

Julian of Norwich. *The Showings of Julian of Norwich*, edited by Denise N. Baker. Norton Critical Editions. New York: W. W. Norton and Company, 2004.

Kempe, Margery. *The Book of Margery Kempe*, edited by Lynn Staley. Norton Critical Editions. New York: W. W. Norton, 2001.

King Arthur's Death: The Middle English Stanzaic Morte Arthur *and* Alliterative Morte Arthure, edited by Larry D. Benson, revised by Edward E. Foster. TEAMS Middle English Texts Series. Kalamazoo, MI: Medieval Institute Publications, 1994.

Malory, Sir Thomas. *Le Morte Darthur*, edited by Stephen H. A. Shepherd. Norton Critical Editions. New York: W. W. Norton & Company, 2004.

'Mankind'. In *The Broadview Anthology of British Literature: The Medieval Period*, 3rd edn., edited by Joseph Black et al., 753–73. Peterborough, ON: Broadview Press, 2015.

Prik of Conscience, edited by James H. Morey. TEAMS Middle English Texts Series. Kalamazoo, MI: Medieval Institute Publications, 2012.

'Riddle 45'. In *The Broadview Anthology of British Literature: The Medieval Period*, 3rd edn., edited by Joseph Black et al., 58. Peterborough, ON: Broadview Press, 2015.

Wright, Thomas, ed. *A Selection of Latin Stories, from Manuscripts of the Thirteenth and Fourteenth Centuries: A Contribution to the History of Fiction during the Middle Ages*. London: The Percy Society, 1842.

Wroth, Lady Mary. 'In this Strange Labyrinth'. In Carol Rumen. 'Poem of the Week: From A Crown of Sonnets Dedicated to Love by Lady Mary Wroth'. *The Guardian*. 28 January 2019. https://www.theguardian.com/books/booksblog/2019/jan/28/poem-of-the-week-from-a-crown-of-sonnets-dedicated-to-love-by-lady-mary-wroth.

1.3 Other media

Apatow, Judd, dir. *The 40-Year-Old Virgin*. 2005; Burbank, CA: Universal Pictures, 2005. DVD.

Apatow, Judd, dir. *Knocked Up*. 2007; Burbank, CA: Universal Pictures, 2007. DVD.

Brown, Brené. 'shame v. guilt'. *Brené Brown* (blog). 14 January 2013. https://brenebrown.com/blog/2013/01/14/shame-v-guilt/#:~:text=I%20define%20shame%20as%20the,makes%20us%20unworthy%20of%20connection.

Buck, Chris and Jennifer Lee, dirs. *Frozen*. 2013; Burbank, CA: Walt Disney Pictures, 2014. DVD.

Docter, Pete, dir. *Inside Out*. 2015; Burbank, CA: Walt Disney Pictures, 2015. DVD.

TheFbiFilesRepeat. 'A Night at the Office – Ricky Gervais'. 23 January 2001, video, 31:30, https://www.youtube.com/watch?v=akNwLopEda0.

Gadsby, Hannah, writer. *Nanette*. Directed by Madeleine Parry and Jon Olb. Featuring Hannah Gadsby. Aired 19 June 2018, https://www.netflix.com/title/80233611?s=i&trkid=13747225.

Gadsby, Hannah, writer. *Douglas*. Directed by Madeleine Parry. Featuring Hannah Gadsby. Aired 26 May 2020, https://www.netflix.com/title/81054700?s=i&trkid=13747225.

Gervais, Ricky, writer. *After Life*. Directed by Ricky Gervais. featuring Ricky Gervais, Tom Basden, Tony Way, Kerry Godliman. Aired 8 March 2019. https://www.netflix.com/title/80998491?s=i&trkid=13747225.
Gervais, Ricky and Stephen Merchant, writers. *The Office*. Directed by Ricky Gervais and Stephen Merchant. Featuring Ricky Gervais, Lucy Davis and Oliver Chris. Aired 9 July 2001, https://www.netflix.com/title/70136112?s=i&trkid=13747225.
Gilliam, Terry and Terry Jones, dirs. *Monty Python and the Holy Grail*. 1975; Burbank, CA: Sony Pictures Home Entertainment, 2001. DVD.
Higginbotham, Abraham and Chuck Martin, writers. *Arrested Development*, season 2, episode 6, 'Afternoon Delight'. Directed by Jason Bateman. Featuring Jason Bateman, Alia Shawkat, Michael Cera and Portia de Rossi. Aired 19 December 2004. https://www.netflix.com/title/70140358?s=i&trkid=13747225.
'In taberna quando sumus'. Classical Net. Accessed 19 May 2020. http://www.classical.net/music/comp.lst/works/orff-cb/carmlyr.php#track14.
IPMusic. 'The Salutation/Bring us in good ale (bray harp)'. 22 November 2016. Video. 4: 48. https://www.youtube.com/watch?v=d9Sx9nmKxYM.
Itswhatwelooklike. 'Carmina Burana – "In taberna quando sumus" – Carl Orff'. 13 May 2011. Video. 4: 05. https://www.youtube.com/watch?v=HTfCkCnGRsU.
Shadyac, Tom, dir. *Evan Almighty*, 2007; Burbank, CA: Universal Pictures, 2007. DVD.
Stoller, Nicholas, dir. *Forgetting Sarah Marshall*. 2008; Burbank, CA: Universal Pictures, 2008. DVD.
Starland Vocal Band. 'Afternoon Delight'. Written by Bill Danoff. Recorded April 1976. Track 8 on *Starland Vocal Band*. Windstar Records, LP.
Waller-Bridge, Phoebe, writer. *Fleabag*. Directed by Tim Kirkby and Harry Bradbeer. Featuring Phoebe Waller-Bridge, Sian Clifford, and Olivia Colman. Aired 15 September 2016, https://app.primevideo.com/detail?gti=amzn1.dv.gti.14b4ffae-8fb4-a5c4-b768-c7be263546b2&territory=CA&ref_=share_ios_season&r=web.
Webley, Big George. 'Handbags and Gladrags'. By Mike D'Abo. Recorded 2006. Track 1 on *The Office UK Theme Music*. Avant Garde a Clue, compact disc.

2 Secondary texts

Ahmed, Sara. *The Promise of Happiness*. Durham: Duke University Press, 2010.
Barr, Jessica. *Willing to Know God: Dreamers and Visionaries in the Later Middle Ages*. Columbus, OH: The Ohio State University Press, 2010.
Beard, Mary. *Laughter In Ancient Rome: On Joking, Tickling, and Cracking Up*. Berkeley, CA: University of California Press, 2014.
Beckwith, Sarah. 'Language Goes on Holiday: English Allegorical Drama and the Virtue Tradition'. *Journal of Medieval and Early Modern Studies* 42.1 (2012): 107–30.
Bolens, Guillemette. *The Style of Gestures: Embodiment and Cognition in Literary Narrative*, Rethinking Theory. Baltimore, MD: The Johns Hopkins University Press, 2012.
Brown, Bill. 'Thing Theory'. In *Things*, edited by Bill Brown. Chicago: University of Chicago Press, 2004.
Brown, Brené. *The Gifts of Imperfection*. Center City, MN: Hazelden Press, 2010.
Brown, Brené. *Braving the Wilderness: The Quest for True Belonging and the Courage to Stand Alone*. New York: Random House, 2017.

Brown, Michelle. *The Luttrell Psalter: A Facsimile*. London: The British Library, 2006.
Cawsey, Kathy. *Images of Language in Middle English Vernacular Writings*. Cambridge: D. S. Brewer, 2020.
Carroll, Noël. *Humour: A Very Short Introduction*. Oxford: Oxford University Press, 2014. Kobo.
Coley, David. *Death and the Pearl Maiden: Plague, Poetry, England*, Interventions New Studies in Medieval Culture. Columbus, OH: The Ohio University Press, 2019.
Cooper, Helen. 'Counter-Romance: Civil Strife and Father-Killing in the Prose Romances'. In *The Long Fifteenth Century: Essays for Douglas Gray*, edited by Helen Cooper and Sally Mapstone, 141–62. Oxford: Oxford University Press, 1997.
Cooper, Helen and Sally Mapstone, eds. *The Long Fifteenth Century: Essays for Douglas Gray*. Oxford: Clarendon Press, 1997.
Dahl, Melissa. *Cringeworthy: A Theory of Awkwardness*. New York: Portfolio/Penguin, 2018.
Denny-Brown, Andrea. 'The Provocative Fifteenth Century'. *Exemplaria* 29.4, *The Provocative Fifteenth Century, Vol. 1* (2018): 267–79.
Feldman Barrett, Lisa. *How Emotions are Made: The Secret Life of the Brain*. Boston: Mariner Books, 2018.
Felski, Rita. *Uses of Literature*. Oxford: Blackwell Publishing, 2008.
Field, Rosalind. 'Romance in England, 1066–1400'. In *The Cambridge History of Medieval English Literature*, edited by David Wallace, 152–76. Cambridge: Cambridge University Press, 2008.
Gerhardt, Ernst. 'Salmon-Fishing and Beer-Brewing: The Waterleaders and Drawers of Dee and Chester's Corpus Christi and Whitsun Plays'. *Medieval English Theatre* 41 (2019): 134–65.
Gumbrecht, Hans Ulrich. *Atmosphere, Mood, Stimmung: On a Hidden Potential of Literature*, translated by Erik Butler. Stanford: Stanford University Press, 2012.
Huizinga, Johan. *The Autumn of the Middle Ages*, translated by Rodney J. Payton and Ulrich Mammitzsch. Chicago: University of Chicago Press, 1996.
James, Aaron. *Assholes: A Theory*. New York: Doubleday, 2012.
Karras, Ruth Maro. 'The Virgin and the Pregnant Abbess: Miracles and Gender in the Middle Ages'. *Medieval Perspectives* 3 (1991): 112–32.
Kearney, Richard. *Anatheism: Returning to God After God*, Insurrections: Critical Studies in Religion, Politics, and Culture. New York: Columbia, 2011.
Kendrick, Laura. '"In bourde and in pleye": *Mankind* and the problem of comic derision in medieval English religious plays.' *Études Anglaises*, Tome 58, n. 3 (2005): 261–275.
Keysers, Christian *The Empathic Brain: How the Discovery of Mirror Neurons Changes our Understanding of Human Nature*. Oklahoma, OK: Smashwords, 2011.
Knapp, Ethan. *The Bureaucratic Muse: Thomas Hoccleve and the Literature of Late Medieval England*. University Park, PA: Pennsylvania State University Press, 2001.
Kotsko, Adam. *Awkwardness: An Essay*. Ropley Zero Books, 2010.
La Farge, Catherine. 'Conversation in Malory's "Morte Darthur"'. *Medium Aevum* 56.2 (1987): 225–38.
Lambert, Mark. *Malory: Style and Vision in 'Le Morte Darthur.'* New Haven and London: Yale University Press, 1975.
Langdell, Sebastian. *Thomas Hoccleve: Religious Reform, Transnational Politics, and the Invention of Chaucer*. Exeter Medieval Texts and Studies. Liverpool: Liverpool University Press, 2018.

Lawton, David. 'Dullness and the Fifteenth Century'. *English Literary History* 54.4 (1987): 761–99.
Longsworth, Robert. 'Interpretive Laughter in Sir Gawain and the Green Knight'. *Philological Quarterly* 70.2 (1991): 141–7.
Massumi, Brian. *Parables for the Virtual: Movement, Affect, Sensation*. Durham, NC: Duke University Press, 2002.
McCarthy, Terence. *An Introduction to Malory*. Cambridge: Brewer, 1988.
McGraw, Peter and Joel Warner. *The Humor Code: A Global Search for What Makes Things Funny*. New York: Simon and Schuster, 2014.
McGregor, Hannah. *A Sentimental Education*. Waterloo: Wilfred Laurier Press, 2022.
Metzler, Eric T. '"The Miracle of the Pregnant Abbess": Texts and Contexts of a Medieval Tale of Sexuality, Spirituality, and Authority'. Unpublished doctoral dissertation, Indiana University, 2001.
Meyer-Lee, Robert J. *Poets and Power from Chaucer to Wyatt*. Cambridge: Cambridge University Press, 2009.
Middle English Dictionary. Rev. November 2019. https://quod.lib.umich.edu/m/middle-english-dictionary/dictionary.
Mooney, Linne, et al., ed. The *DIMEV*: An Open-Access, Digital Edition of the *Index of Middle English Verse*, https://www.dimev.net/index.html.
Myklebust, Nicholas. 'Historicizing Hoccleve's Metre'. *Thomas Hoccleve: New Approaches*, edited by Jenni Nuttall and David Watt, 25–46. Cambridge: D.S. Brewer, 2022.
Nuttall, Jenni. *The Creation of Lancastrian Kingship*, Cambridge Studies in Medieval Literature 67. Cambridge: Cambridge University Press, 2007.
Oxford English Dictionary. Rev. 2020. https://www.oed.com/.
'Post-Traumatic Stress Disorder'. *National Institute of Mental Health*. May 2019. https://www.nimh.nih.gov/health/topics/post-traumatic-stress-disorder-ptsd/index.shtml.
Provine, Robert. *Laughter: A Scientific Investigation*. London: Penguin, 2001.
Rosenwein, Barbara. *Emotional Communities in the Early Middle Ages*. Ithaca: Cornell University Press, 2006.
Schieberle, Misty. 'A New Hoccleve Literary Manuscript: The Trilingual Miscellany in London, British Library, MS Harley 219'. *The Review of English Studies* 70.297 (2019): 799–822.
Sennett, Richard. *Together: The Rituals, Pleasures and Politics of Cooperation*. New Haven: Yale University Press, 2012.
Sobecki, Sebastian. '"The writyng of this tretys": Margery Kempe's Son and the Authorship of her Book'. *Studies in the Age of Chaucer* 37 (2015): 257–83.
Sobecki, Sebastian. 'The Series: Thomas Hoccleve's Year of Mourning'. In Last *Words: The Public Self and the Social Author in Late Medieval England*, 65–100. Oxford Textual Perspectives Oxford: Oxford University Press, 2019.
Somerset, Fiona. 'Censorship'. In *The Production of Books in England 1350–1500*, edited by Alexandra Gillespie and Daniel Wakelin, 239–59. Cambridge: Cambridge University Press, 2011).
Spearing, A. C. *Medieval Autographies: The 'I' of the Text*. Notre Dame, IN: Notre Dame University Press, 2012.
Staley, Lynn. *Margery Kempe's Dissenting Fictions*. University Park: Pennsylvania State University Press, 1994.
Strohm, Paul. 'Mellyagant's Primal Scene'. In *Theory and the Premodern Text,* 201–14. Minneapolis: University of Minnesota Press, 2000.

Tashiro, Ty. *Awkward: The Science of Why We're Socially Awkward and Why That's Awesome*. New York: William Morrow, 2017.

Taylor, Andrew. 'The Myth of the Minstrel Manuscript'. *Speculum* 66.1 (1991): 43–73.

Turner, Marion. 'Illness Narratives in the Later Middle Ages: Arderne, Chaucer, and Hoccleve'. *Journal of Medieval and Early Modern Studies* 46.1 (2016): 61–87.

Watson, Nicholas. 'The Composition of Julian of Norwich's Revelation of Love'. *Speculum* 68 (1993): 637–83.

Watson, Nicholas. 'Censorship and Cultural Change in Late Medieval England: Vernacular Theology, the Oxford Translation Debate, and Arundel's Constitutions of 1409'. *Speculum* 70 (1995): 822–64.

Watt, David. *The Making of Thomas Hoccleve's* Series, Exeter Medieval Texts and Studies Liverpool: Liverpool University Press, 2013.

Wilson Tryon, Ruth. 'Miracles of Our Lady in Middle English Verse'. *PMLA* 38.2 (1923): 308–88.

'Zednik's injury brings Malarchuk's own nightmare back to surface.' *ESPN.com news services*. February 12, 2008. https://www.espn.com/nhl/news/story?id=3242226.

Index

The 40-Year-Old Virgin 2, 15–16, 102, 182
'The Abbess Delivered by Our Lady' 32–5, 37, 46, 90, 183
Aberdeen Bestiary 100–1
Affect
   Definition 2–3, 26–7, 30
   Discomfort and Disorientation 2–3, 24–7
   Response to Sensory Input 7, 14, 44–6, 116, 167
   Transmission of 9, 133, 151
After Life 38, 43–6
Ahmed, Sarah
   Feminist Killjoy 5–6, 16–8, 131–3, 141, 179, 183
   Willfulness 55, 165–8
Anger
   And connection 5, 10, 47, 52–3, 133
   As a Response 63–5, 76–7, 123, 186
   As an Emotion 23, 30
Apatow, Judd 1–3, 15, 32, 102, 183–4
Arrested Development 152–3
Assholes
   Am I one? 20, 183–6
   Definition 5–6
   In Practice 33, 50, 119, 153
Atmosphere See also Mood
   Shared 7–8, 30, 52–3, 61–4, 133, 151
   Weather 44, 48, 69, 115–18, 167–8, 174
Attunement
   Lack of 9, 12, 24, 30, 34, 114
   To awkwardness 1–2, 103, 169
   To God 29, 64, 67, 87, 89–90, 128–32, 162–3
   To others 6, 11, 12, 17–18, 19, 21, 34, 73–4, 89–90, 112, 144, 156, 174
Augustine, of Hippo
   Confessions 2, 13–22
      Conversion and Turning 10–1, 81, 92, 134, 146, 171
      Fitting in and Belonging 97, 105, 124, 126, 131, 182

   Grace and Mercy 37, 42, 46, 96, 107
   Human limitations 67, 84, 183
   Shame 110–11, 113
De Trinitate 137
Austen, Jane 184
Autography 114–15
Awkward (Etymology) 28–30, 54

Barr, Jessica 89–90
Beard, Mary 10
Beckwith, Sarah 157
Belonging
   Definition 10
   With others 1–2, 15–16, 38, 40, 85, 105–12, 114–17, 126, 135, 175, 182
   With God 11, 13, 20–2, 46, 87–90, 118, 124, 128, 132, 154–8
   And Laughter 71, 74–5, 84, 95
Bergson, Henry 18
Blushing 14, 72–81, 110–11
Bolens, Guillemette 9, 14, 25, 76
Brennan, Teresa
   Alignment of wills 18, 68, 129, 167
   Emotions 26
   Entrainment 9, 133, 151–2
'Bring us in good ale' 148–152
Brookner, Anita 184
Brown, Bill 2
Brown, Brené
   Fitting in and Belonging 10–11, 15–16, 22, 105, 117, 152–4, 182
   Shame 79, 109, 156
Burrow, John 77, 82, 121
Bury St Edmunds 100–2

Campbell, Joseph 65
Carmina Burana 147
Carroll, Noël 3–4, 49, 103
Cawsey, Kathy 143
Caxton, William 180
Chaucer, Geoffrey 12, 98, 102, 115, 124
Chester *Play of Noah's Flood* 161–8, 184

Christine de Pizan 125
Cleanness 47–58, 107, 133, 164
Clopper, Laurence 144
Coley, David 37n1
Collective speech 53, 132–4, 143, 148–53, 166, 178–9
Communing 10, 46, 85, 109–28, 135–6, 139
Compassion
    As a practice 1, 114, 124, 127, 141, 143–4, 166–8, 180
    Etymology and Definition 89, 134
    Failures of 172, 175, 177
    Others as an impediment 143–4, 147, 157–9
Confession 75–7, 93–5
Consent 49, 136–8, 178
Conversion 11, 13–22, 64, 131, 183
Cooper, Helen 173n5
Curb Your Enthusiasm 3, 12

Dahl, Melissa 7
Dalliance 125, 128, 134
Denny-Brown, Andrea 1
Discomfort
    As an affect 23–30, 41, 47–8, 64, 67, 119, 124–6
    As an effect on audience 77, 105–6, 111–12, 113–15, 121, 127, 131, 163–8, 173–9
    Shared 133–4, 152–53, 158
    Social 1–12, 15–20, 32–4, 55, 59, 102–3, 123, 136, 140–1, 161, 182–6
    Spiritual 20–22, 30, 91–3

Ecclesiastes 4.10 93
Embarrassment 9, 14, 41, 76–7
Emotion
    And Affect 26–27
    Constructed theory of 8–9, 14, 23–4, 119
    Emotional Granularity 27–28
    Experience of 25–27, 30, 34, 44–6, 72–4, 116, 121–3, 174
    And Laughter 95
    Perception of others 34, 72–4, 76–7, 119, 172, 182
    Universal theory of 23, 27
Empathy
    As a skill 11, 112, 126, 182, 186
    Neurological process 11, 119

Response to others 9, 25, 72–3, 97, 108, 124, 171–2
Response to reading 1–2, 114, 127, 141, 181
Entrainment 9–10, 85, 133–4, 151, 182
Evan Almighty 162
Exeter Book Riddles
    Riddle 45 101–2

Feldman Barrett, Lisa
    Construction of Emotion 8–9, 24–7, 34, 119, 182
    Judging Emotions of Others 30
    Simulation 23–4, 25–6, 44–6
Felski, Rita 1
Field, Rosalind 173n4
Fitting In
    Changing the self 15–17
    Distinct from Belonging 10–1, 84–5, 71, 132, 182
    Impediment to Belonging 21–2, 105, 111, 117, 124, 135, 143, 153–8
Flattery 105, 111–12
Fleabag 74–5, 81–4, 105–6, 107–10, 126, 132, 135, 184
Forgetting Sarah Marshall 171
Friends
    Who are attuned 17–19, 118, 126, 145, 156, 166–8
    Who turn away 118, 121, 131, 134
Frozen 26, 169, 173–5, 180

Gadsby, Hannah
    Nannette 4–6, 9, 47, 49, 55, 58, 91–2
    Douglas 4, 88, 96, 115, 181, 182
Genesis 48–53, 133, 164
Genre 4, 88, 113–17, 128–9, 173–4
Geoffrey of Vinsauf 124
Gerhardt, Ernst 161, 166
Gillespie, Vincent 94
Goffman, Erving 9, 120–3
Grace
    Divine 13, 21–2, 37, 50, 63–8, 69, 87, 96, 124, 135–6, 167
    Literary 37, 169
    Reluctance to accept 41–6, 69, 71–6, 83–5
    Social 69, 78–84, 107, 126, 131
    Worthiness 34–5, 47, 51, 146, 157–9, 163

Grief 37–41, 46, 105, 109, 121, 175
Guilt 78, 84–5, 176, 179–80
Gumbrecht, Hans Ulrich 7–8, 44, 116, 118, 167

'Handbags and Gladrags' 116–17
Hoccleve, Thomas 12, 183
   La Male Regle 105–12, 182–3
   The Series 113–26, 127, 183
Homophobia 51–2
Huizinga, Johan 1
Humour
   Benign violation theory 4–5, 19
   Connection to laughter 10, 78–82, 145–6
   Incongruity theory 3–4, 19, 48–9, 103
   Superiority theory 19, 49, 51, 85 146
Humphrey, Duke of Gloucester 124–5

'I have a gentil cock' 97–103, 105, 111, 178
'I syng of a mayden' 99–100
Inside Out 23, 143
'In Tabena Quando Sumus' 147
Intentions
   Alignment with others 11, 16, 20–2, 30, 55, 68, 134, 137–40, 178
   Authorial 32, 101–2, 124, 128–9, 135, 175
   And Impact 12, 97, 102–3
   Individual 4, 9, 55, 76, 89, 120, 167, 170–2, 175–7, 180, 182
Irony 12, 97, 103

James, Aaron 5–6, 33, 50, 183
Jonah, Book of 59–68, 183
Julian of Norwich 3, 10, 35, 87–96, 97, 128, 132, 140, 173, 175, 183

Karras, Ruth Maro 33
Kearney, Richard 48–9, 51, 92
Kempe, Margery
   Comparison to 12, 35, 143, 166, 175, 183, 184–5
   Focus on 127–41
Kendrick, Laura 155
Keysers, Christian
   Bodily state and feelings 72–4, 122
   Empathic response 10–11, 13–14, 24–5, 72–4, 114, 119
   Simulation 8–9, 25, 182
Kinesic Imagery

And Empathic Response 9–10, 119
Blushing or Blanching 13–14, 119
Bowing or Inclining 107
Cringing or Shuddering 25–6, 77, 119, 153
Turning 13, 20, 77, 91–3, 123, 153, 170, 184
Knapp, Ethan 114n2, 116n12, 118n16
Knocked Up 32–4
Kotsko, Adam, *Awkwardness* 1, 3, 64, 181, 183–5
   Cultural Awkwardness 3, 181, 183
   Everyday awkwardness 3, 64, 105
   Radical Awkwardness 3, 50, 64

La Farge, Catherine 176
Lambert, Mark 179
Langdell, Sebastian 116n12
Laughter See also Humour
   Belonging 87, 95–6, 128, 172–5, 182–6
   Discomfort 38
   Idleness 155, 158
   Involuntary 55, 94–6
   Relationship to Awkwardness 1–4, 11–2, 38, 47–50, 69, 85, 97, 103, 114, 124, 132, 181
   Social Function 10, 81–4
      Inclusion 18–21, 70–3, 77–9, 83–4, 145
      Scorn 49–51, 79, 146
Lawton, David 1n2
London, British Library
   MS Additional 39996 32
   MS Additional 42130 See Luttrell Psalter
   Image of leaf 31
   Cotton Nero A.x 12, 37, 47, 59, 67, 69, 87, 97
   Images of leaves 39, 45, 62, 70
   MS Harley 541 148
   MS Sloane 2593 99–100
   Image of leaf 99
Longsworth, Robert 71
Lot's wife 47–8, 51–8
Luttrell Psalter 23, 25–6, 30–5, 37, 90

Malarchuk, Clint 73–4
Malory, Sir Thomas See *Morte Darthur*

Mankind
    Comparison to 12, 35, 93, 100, 161, 183
    Focus on 143–59
Masculinity 143, 184
Massumi, Brian 26–7
Matthew, Gospel of
    Beatitudes 59
    Parable of the Tenants 42–3
    Parable of the Wedding Banquet 47
McCarthy, Terence 172, 175, 178
McGraw, Peter 4
McGregor, Hannah 11n51
Meyer-Lee 1n3
Mimicry 25, 73
Misalignment
    Discomfort 28–30, 34, 110
    Inward and Outward 121–3, 144
    Text and Audience 12, 94, 97
Misogyny 16, 51, 65, 112, 158, 164–8
Mockumentary 114
Monty Python and the Holy Grail 83
Mood See also atmosphere
    As prevailing atmosphere 6–7, 30, 34, 52, 61–4, 72–7, 79–82
    Affected by atmosphere 44, 48, 64–9, 113–19, 174
    Affected by music 131, 151
    Literary effect 8, 49–52, 108, 113–19
Morte Darthur
    Alliterative Morte 28–30, 30, 17
    By Sir Thomas Malory 29, 166, 169–80, 183, 185
    Stanzaic Morte 173, 175
Myklebust, Nicholas 108n8

Ngai, Sianne 2–3, 24
Norms
    As cause of violence 127, 138, 141, 155–6, 180, 183, 185
    Associated with Gender 32, 49, 132, 141, 143, 174, 184
    Associated with Hospitality 53–4, 70, 178
    Associated with Sex 16, 103, 138
    Inapplicable 43, 50, 64, 181
    Social Interactions 9, 19, 59, 105, 107
    Violations of 3–6, 30, 38, 48, 50–2, 55, 69–71, 179, 181
Nuttall, Jenni 112n11

Omnes gentes plaudite 99–100
Oxford, Bodleian Library MS Eng. Poet.E.1 148–9
    Image of leaf 149

Patience 59–68, 69, 90, 92, 183
Pearl
    Comparison to 35, 47, 51, 59, 64, 69, 76, 93, 183
    Focus on 37–46
Personification 23, 109, 143
Perversity 13, 16–18, 22, 146, 156
Pricke of Conscience 29–30, 145, 156, 173
Pronoun
    First person 166, 168
    Masculine 5
    Second person 40, 50, 107
Provine, Robert 10, 18–19, 55, 77–8, 94–6, 145
Psalms
    In General 113, 117
    Psalm 31 117–19, 121, 124, 126
    Psalm 57 33–4

Rhythm 8, 108, 118, 144–5, 148–53, 156, 161, 166
Robbins, Rossell Hope 100
Rosenwein, Barbara 25

Sarah 47–52, 55, 64, 68, 164, 183
Saving face 9, 42, 49–51, 77, 84, 120–5, 132–3, 179
Schieberle, Misty 114–15
Sennett, Richard 11, 126, 182
Shame
    And Anger 71–8, 121
    And Belonging 132–5, 156–9, 182
    And Laughter 69, 143
    And Shamelessness 14–20, 106–7, 137, 177–9
    And Vulnerability 91, 95, 109–11, 127–8
Simulation See Feldman Barratt or Keysers

Sir Gawain and the Green Knight 4, 10, 69–85, 87, 96, 183
Sobecki, Sebastian 115, 130
Somerset, Fiona 185n15
Spearing, A. C. 114–15
Staley, Lynn 130
Stimmung See Atmosphere or Mood
Strohm, Paul 177
Suicidal ideation 38, 46
Sympathy 11–12, 37, 112, 124, 127

Tashiro, Ty 7n23
Taylor, Andrew 99–100
The Office (UK) 3–4
    David Brent 59–61, 113–14, 126–7
    De-skilling 11
    Gender 182–4
    Mood 116–21
    Structure 67, 114–15, 127, 182
The Office (USA) 3–4
    Michael Scott 59, 51, 120
The Taming of the Shrew 165, 184

Trauma 4, 74, 78, 85, 91, 130–1, 135–6, 141
    Post-Traumatic Stress Disorder 74
Turner, Marion 115n1

Ugly feelings 2–3, 24

Vulnerability 46, 51, 84, 90, 110, 112, 135–6, 171, 174

Waller-Bridge, Phoebe 105–9, 112
Warner, Joel 4
Watson, Nicholas 87, 90, 185
Watt, David 115
Wilde, Oscar 109–10
Will
    General Will 133, 140, 154, 158
    God's Will 64–8, 89–90, 128–9, 134–5, 138, 158, 165–8, 175–6
    Individual Will 93, 129, 136–40, 157–8, 165–8
Williams, Serena 30
Wilson Tryon, Ruth 32
Wroth, Lady Mary 184